DIAMONDS
AND BARS

DIE NEUE SAMMLUNG / STAATLICHES MUSEUM FÜR ANGEWANDTE KUNST – DESIGN IN DER PINAKOTHEK DER MODERNE / MÜNCHEN

ZKM / ZENTRUM FÜR KUNST UND MEDIENTECHNOLOGIE KARLSRUHE – MUSEUM FÜR NEUE KUNST

FLORIAN HUFNAGL (ED.)

DIAMONDS AND BARS

DIE KUNST DER AMISCHEN
THE ART OF THE AMISH PEOPLE

QUILTS DER SAMMLUNG SCHLUMBERGER
THE SCHLUMBERGER QUILT-COLLECTION

ARNOLDSCHE ART PUBLISHERS

OBJEKT-PHOTOGRAPHIE
OBJECT PHOTOGRAPHY
RAINER VIERTLBÖCK

INHALTSVERZEICHNIS / **CONTENTS**

010   DIE LEIDENSCHAFT DES SAMMELNS / **THE PASSION OF COLLECTING**
       Ein Interview / **An Interview**

017   DIE KÜNSTLERISCHE REISE AMISCHER QUILTS / **THE ARTISTIC JOURNEY OF AMISH QUILTS**
       Laura Fisher

028   AMISH QUILTS
       SAMMLUNG SCHLUMBERGER / **THE SCHLUMBERGER COLLECTION**
       Wissenschaftliche Bearbeitung / **Scholarly Examination**
       Corinna Rösner

193   DIE RAUTE, DAS QUADRAT UND DER STREIFEN – UND ANDERE FORMEN
       AUS DEM SCHATZ DER GEOMETRIE / **LOZENGE, SQUARE AND STRIPE – AND OTHER FORMS**
       FROM THE GEOMETRIC REPERTOIRE
       Corinna Rösner

208   MONOGRAMME / **MONOGRAMS**

209   BIBLIOGRAPHIE / **BIBLIOGRAPHY**

210   RÜCKSEITEN / **BACKS**

213   REGISTER / **INDEX**

VORWORT / **FOREWORD**

Es ist offensichtlich, dass ich ein Gesetz, einen Plan, ein System proklamiere, welches die Objektivierung aller subjektiven Äußerungen ermöglicht, nämlich des Suprematismus als Formel, nach der die Welt geordnet ist.
KASIMIR MALEWITSCH 1922

It is self-evident that I am proclaiming a law, a plan, a system that makes possible the objectivation of all subjective statements, namely of Suprematism as a formula according to which the world is ordered.
KASIMIR MALEVICH 1922

1910, als in Elkhart County nur aus Quadraten und Rechtecksstreifen der Quilt von Maria Elisabeth Mast entstand (Nr. 20), malte Wassily Kandinsky in München jenes Aquarell, das als erstes abstraktes Bild gilt; und lange vor dem „Schwarzen Quadrat auf weißem Grund" (1913/15) von Kasimir Malewitsch entstanden in Pennsylvania die ältesten „Center Diamond"-Quilts (etwa Nrn. 16, 25) – auch sie radikal abstrakt: ein Quadrat im Quadrat im Quadrat. Und die Protagonisten der Op Art waren noch nicht geboren, als in der zweiten Hälfte des 19. Jahrhunderts in Kanada der Hochzeitsquilt „Tumbling Blocks" mit seiner unwiderstehlichen zentrifugalen Energie (Nr. 46) gestaltet wurde. // Und doch haben abstrakte Malerei, Konstruktivismus, Suprematismus, Colorfield Painting, Hard Edge, Konkrete Kunst oder Op Art einerseits und die mit den Mitteln von Abstraktion und Farbe gestalteten Bettdecken der Amischen auf der anderen Seite nur indirekt miteinander zu tun. // Weder wurden die Protagonisten dieser Kunstrichtungen durch amische Quilts angeregt noch umgekehrt – soweit wir wissen. Die Konzentration der amischen Quiltmacherinnen auf Fläche und Linie, auf pure Form und Farbe – diese vermeintlich so moderne Anmutung entsprang dem Gestaltungswillen einer bewusst altertümlich und isoliert lebenden, fundamentalistischen christlichen Religionsgemeinschaft in Nordamerika, die in ihrem Herkunftsgebiet Europa weitgehend unbekannt

In 1910, while Maria Elisabeth Mast was making a quilt consisting entirely of squares and rectangular stripes (no. 20) in Elkhart County, Indiana, Vassily Kandinsky was painting a watercolor in Munich that is viewed as the first abstract picture. And long before Kasimir Malevich's 'Black Square on a White Ground' was painted (1913/15), the earliest 'Center Diamond' quilts (such as nos. 16, 25) were being made in Lancaster County, Pennsylvania – they, too, are radically abstract: a square in a square in a square. And the exponents of Op art had not been born when the 'Tumbling Blocks' wedding quilt (no. 46) with its irresistible centrifugal force was designed in Canada in the latter half of the 19th century. // Yet abstract painting, Constructivism, Suprematism, Color Field painting, Hard Edge, Concrete art and Op art, on the one hand, and Amish quilts, on the other, which are designed with the devices of abstraction and color, have only indirectly anything to do with one another. // The exponents of those art movements were not inspired by Amish quilts and the converse is equally true – as far as we know. The women who made the Amish quilts concentrated on surface and line, pure form and color – this presumably so modern approach stemmed from the Gestaltungswillen (Alois Riegl: 'will to design') informing an Anabaptist community in North America that chose to live an old-fashioned lifestyle in isolation. This fundamentalist Christian community has remained largely unknown in the Europe from which it came. Its quilts are rooted in an attitude which is perhaps best summed up in the ideas on art expressed as follows by Piet Mondrian, a Calvinist and Theosophist: 'If one does not represent things, scope is left for the divine.' (1922) // The unworldly views espoused by the Amish and their attempt to live lives informed by simplicity and order in harmony with

geblieben ist. Ihre Quilts wurzeln in einer Haltung, die sich auf geistiger Ebene vielleicht am ehesten mit der Kunstauffassung des Calvinisten und Theosophen Piet Mondrian trifft in seinem Postulat: „Wenn man nicht die Dinge darstellt, bleibt Raum für das Göttliche." (1922) // So ließen der weltabgewandte Blick der Amischen und ihr Versuch einer nach Einfachheit und Ordnung strebenden Lebensweise im Einklang mit der umgebenden Natur – aus unserer Sicht fast mönchisch erscheinende Eigenschaften – in der zweiten Hälfte des 19. Jahrhunderts eine sogenannte Volkskunst entstehen, die in diametralem Gegensatz zur europäischen und europäisch geprägten amerikanischen Kunst jener Zeit stand und der Moderne weit vorausgriff. // Mit ihrer klaren Geometrie kommen die Quilts der Amischen – das ist immer wieder bemerkt worden – der modernen amerikanischen Malerei der sechziger und siebziger Jahre des 20. Jahrhunderts nahe, etwa den Streifenbildern von Barnett Newman und Kenneth Noland, den konzentrischen Quadraten von Josef Albers oder dem frühen Frank Stella. Formale Parallelen ergeben sich auch zu Sol Lewitts Gitterbildern, wie überhaupt ein Gestaltungsprinzip der Quilts – die Reihung und Wiederholung – auch ein Kennzeichen der modernen amerikanischen Malerei ist. Die zentrierte Raute oder das Quadrat im Quadrat kehren im Minimalismus eines Ad Reinhardt wieder, die Motive der „Tumbling Blocks" und „Sunshine and Shadow"-Quilts ergeben Parallelen zur Op Art eines Vasarely oder Anuszkiewicz. So verwundert es nicht, dass die Entdeckung der amischen Quilts in den 1960er Jahren einsetzt – parallel zu Konkreter Kunst, Minimal Art oder Op Art. // Einem

the surrounding natural environment – from our standpoint almost monastic qualities – brought forth in the latter half of the 19th century what is called folk art, which is the diametrical opposite of the European and European-shaped art of that time and anticipated Modernism long ahead of its time. // With their stringent geometry, Amish quilts – this has been often noted – have close affinities with modern American painting of the 1960s and 1970s, with the 'zip' pictures of a Barnett Newman and the 'target' pictures of a Kenneth Noland, the concentric squares of a Josef Albers or the 'pinstripe paintings' of the early Frank Stella. There are also formal parallels with Sol Lewitt's grid pictures just as a design principle informing the quilts – parataxis and iteration – is also a distinguishing feature of modern American painting. The centered diamond and the square in the square recur in the Minimalism of an Ad Reinhardt. The 'Tumbling Blocks' and 'Sunshine and Shadow' motifs reveal parallels with the Op art of a Vasarely or an Anuszkiewicz. No wonder then that Europeans discovered Amish quilts in the 1960s – in parallel with Concrete art, Minimal art and Op art. // The 1971 exhibition 'Abstract Design in American Quilts' mounted at the Whitney Museum of American Art in New York to show pieces from the Jonathan Holstein and Gail van der Hoof Collection amassed from the 1960s was like a burst of fanfare – the first major event to set in motion the reception of Amish quilts and give it momentum. // 'Art: Quilts Find a Place at the Whitney' was the headline of an article in the New York Times of 3 July 1971 written by the

Fanal kam 1971 die Ausstellung „Abstract Design in American Quilts" gleich, die mit Stücken aus der seit den Sixties aufgebauten Privatsammlung von Jonathan Holstein und Gail van der Hoof im Whitney Museum of American Art in New York veranstaltet wurde – das erste große, impulsgebende Ereignis in der Rezeptionsgeschichte amischer Quilts. // „Art: Quilts Find a Place at the Whitney" titelte der berühmte Kunstkritiker Hilton Kramer in der New York Times am 3. Juli 1971 und holte diese Kunst gleichsam heim als genuin amerikanische Moderne vor der Moderne: „For a century or more preceding the self-conscious invention of pictorial abstraction in European painting, the anonymous quilt-makers of the American provinces created a remarkable succession of visual masterpieces that anticipated many of the forms that were later prized for their originality and courage."

1991 zeigte Die Neue Sammlung in Anknüpfung an ihre bahnbrechende Ausstellung zur visuellen Kultur der Shaker (1974) Quilts der Privatsammlung Ziegler unter dem Titel „Abstraktion und Farbe. Die Kunst der Amischen" – ganz bewusst mit Blick auf das geplante Museum der Moderne, dessen Architekturwettbewerb damals bereits entschieden war. Im Kontext dieser Pinakothek der Moderne, unter deren Dach seit 2002 vier verschiedene Museen mit freier Kunst und Graphik, Architektur und Design das Spektrum der Bildenden Kunst transdisziplinär darstellen, findet auch die jetzige Ausstellung, die jene damalige fortsetzt und erweitert, ihren richtigen Ort. // Dies scheint umso sinnvoller, als die Sammlung Schlumberger in ständigem engem Wechselbezug mit einer großen und profilierten Sammlung an zeitgenössischer freier Kunst entstand – der Sammlung FER ihres Partners Friedrich E. Rentschler. Vor diesem Hintergrund baute Maria Schlumberger mit Stringenz und Leidenschaft in den letzten 15 Jahren eine der weltweit qualitätvollsten Sammlungen zum Thema Quilts der Amischen auf. Mit heute nahezu 100 Objekten handelt es sich auch um eine der umfangreichsten und – dies kann nicht genug betont werden – vielfältigsten. In Kooperation mit der Sammlerin wurde für die vorliegende Publikation eine Auswahl getroffen. // Es ist besonders folgerichtig, dass Die Neue Sammlung – das Staatliche Museum für angewandte Kunst und Design

distinguished art critic Hilton Kramer and it brought home this art, as it were, as authentic American modernity before Modernism: 'For a century or more preceding the self-conscious invention of pictorial abstraction in European painting, the anonymous quilt-makers of the American provinces created a remarkable succession of visual masterpieces that anticipated many of the forms that were later prized for their originality and courage.'

Linking up in 1991 with a ground-breaking exhibition dealing with Shaker visual culture (1974), the Neue Sammlung showed quilts from the Ziegler Collection in an exhibition entitled 'Abstraktion und Farbe. Die Kunst der Amischen' ['Abstraction and Color. The Art of the Amish'] – intentionally with a view to the planned Museum der Moderne after the competition to design it had already been decided. In the context of this Pinakothek der Moderne, comprising four different museums for fine art and the graphic arts, architecture and design representing the range of the arts in a transdisciplinary approach since 2002, the present exhibition, which is both a sequel to and an enlargement on the earlier one, is in just the right place. // This seems to be a sensible approach, especially since the Schlumberger Collection grew up around a constantly close interrelationship with a large and distinguished collection of contemporary art – the FER Collection owned by Maria Schlumberger's partner, Friedrich E. Rentschler. That is the background against which she has in the past fifteen years built up with consistency and passion one of the finest collections in the world devoted to Amish quilts. Comprising nearly one hundred objects today, this is one of the largest and – this cannot be overemphasized – most diverse of its kind. In collaboration with the collector, a selection has been made for the present publication. // It is more than fitting that the Neue Sammlung – The State Museum of Applied Arts and Design in Munich – should not just realize this project within the Pinakothek der Moderne but that in the ZKM | Center for Art and Media in Karlsruhe, the Neue Sammlung has a partner institution in whose Museum of Contemporary Art the FER Collection figures prominently on a permanent basis. 'In focusing on 1960s Concept art and Minimalism, the FER Collection

in München – dieses Projekt nicht nur innerhalb der Pinakothek der Moderne realisieren kann, sondern dass mit dem ZKM | Zentrum für Kunst und Medientechnologie in Karlsruhe auch jene Institution Partner ist, in deren Museum für Neue Kunst die Sammlung FER ständig präsent ist. „Mit Konzeptkunst und Minimalismus der sechziger Jahre besitzt die Sammlung FER einen Schwerpunkt, der sich als roter Faden durch die Sammlung bis in die Gegenwart zieht. Die Hinterfragung des Kunstbegriffes und der Institution Galerie bzw. Museum, wie sie in den Werken der amerikanischen Minimalisten und Konzeptualisten ihren radikalen Ausdruck gefunden hat, ist ihr Leitmotiv" – so charakterisiert das Karlsruher Museum die Sammlung FER, die den Bezugsrahmen für die amischen Quilts der Sammlung Schlumberger bildet. // So mag als Motto gelten, was Hilton Kramer 1971 formulierte: "Die Ausstellung ist daher nicht nur reich an außergewöhnlichen visuellen Reizen, sondern ist so angelegt, dass sie uns zwingt, das Verhältnis zwischen „hoher" Kunst und jenen Formen visuellen Ausdrucks, die für gewöhnlich als niedriger erachtet werden, zu überdenken."

possesses a red thread that goes through the Collection down to the present. Its guiding principle is critically examining the concept of art as such and the gallery or museum <u>qua</u> institutions as radically expressed in the work of the American Minimalists and Conceptualists'– thus the Karlsruhe museum characterizes the FER Collection which represents the frame of reference for the Amish quilts in the Schlumberger Collection. // The motto of the present exhibition might be formulated as Hilton Kramer expressed it in 1971: 'The exhibition is therefore, not only full of unusual visual pleasures, but it is the kind of exhibition that prompts us to rethink the relation of high art to what are customarily regarded as the lesser forms of visual expressions.'

FLORIAN HUFNAGL
Die Neue Sammlung / Staatliches Museum für angewandte Kunst – Design in der Pinakothek der Moderne/München
Die Neue Sammlung / State Museum of Applied Arts – Design in the Pinakothek der Moderne/Munich

PETER WEIBEL
ZKM / Zentrum für Kunst und Medientechnologie Karlsruhe – Museum für Neue Kunst
ZKM / Center for Art and Media Karlsruhe – Museum of Contemporary Art

DIE LEIDENSCHAFT DES SAMMELNS / **THE PASSION FOR COLLECTING**

// Frau Schlumberger, Ihre Quiltsammlung wurde ja – soweit ich weiß – vor dem Hintergrund einer großen und sehr profilierten Sammlung an zeitgenössischer bildender Kunst angelegt, deshalb meine erste Frage an Sie, Herr Dr. Rentschler: Wie können Sie Ihre Sammlung FER charakterisieren?

Friedrich E. Rentschler (FER): Schon sehr früh habe ich mich für moderne Kunst interessiert. Aber erst Mitte der 60er Jahre begann ich, Originalarbeiten zeitgenössischer Künstler zu sammeln. Es war der leidenschaftliche Ehrgeiz, interessante neue Tendenzen zu entdecken und mit dem Kauf von Kunstwerken, die ich für wichtig hielt, eine Sammlung zu gestalten. Dabei ging es mir immer auch darum, mich mit dem Geist unserer Zeit auseinanderzusetzen. Auch heute sammle ich Kunst junger Künstler, Kunst, die heute entsteht. Insofern spiegelt meine Sammlung einen wesentlichen Teil der Kunstentwicklung während der vergangenen 50 Jahre wider. Ich freue mich, nach 50 Jahren festzustellen, dass Arbeiten, die ich damals sammelte, heute kunstgeschichtlich relevante Bedeutung haben.

// **Ms Schlumberger, your quilt collection was – as far as I know – amassed against a background of a large and very distinguished collection of contemporary art; hence my first question is for you, Dr. Rentschler: How would you characterize your FER Collection?**

Friedrich E. Rentschler (FER): Very early on I was interested in modern art. But I didn't begin to collect original works by contemporary artists until the mid-1960s. It was my ardent ambition to discover interesting new trends and to organize a collection by buying works of art I considered important. What also always mattered to me was studying the spirit of the times. Even today I collect work by young artists, art that is being produced today. In so far my collection reflects an essential part of developments in art during the past fifty years. I am delighted to find that works I collected then now possess art historical relevance.

// Sehen Sie denn einen kategorialen Unterschied zwischen freier und angewandter Kunst?

FER: Für mich existiert nur Kunst als Kunst. Und zwar Kunst als Ausdruck eines Lebensgefühls einer bestimmten Zeit, wie zum Beispiel die Höhlenzeichnungen von Altamira, die religiösen Kunstäußerungen von Romanik, Renaissance und Barock oder die Gestaltungsprinzipien des Bauhauses bis hin zu modernem Design – und Kitsch bleibt Kitsch.

// **Do you see a categorical difference between fine and applied art?**

FER: For my part, art only exists as art. And in fact art as the expression of a feeling for life at a particular time, such as the Altamira cave paintings, the religious statements made in Romanesque, Renaissance and Baroque art or the design principles of the Bauhaus on down to modern design – and kitsch remains kitsch.

// Gibt es Zusammenhänge zwischen Ihren Sammlungsobjekten der zeitgenössischen Kunst und den amischen Quilts? Sehen Sie Verbindungen?

FER: Es ist erstaunlich, dass die Amish People ab der zweiten Hälfte des 19. Jahrhunderts formal viele Strukturen vorweggenommen haben, die in der Mitte des 20. Jahrhunderts in der bildenden Kunst große Bedeutung erlangten. Dabei muss man natürlich feststellen, dass trotz der formalen Ähnlichkeiten der geistige Hintergrund dieser verschiedenen Kunstrichtungen ein vollkommen anderer ist.

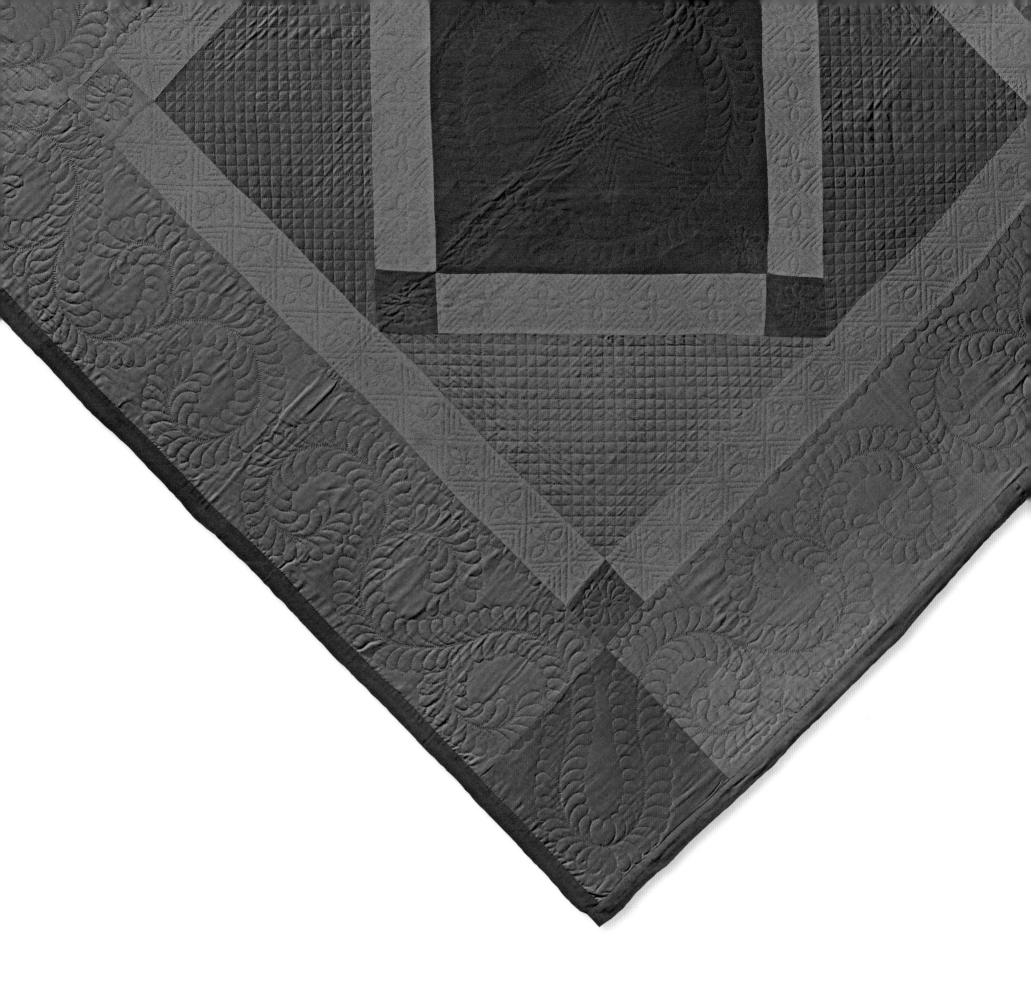

// Are there links between the objects in your collection of contemporary art and Amish quilts? Do you see any links?

FER: It is astonishing that from the latter half of the 19th century the Amish people anticipated formally many structures that would attain enormous significance in fine art in the mid-20th century. One must, however, observe that for all their formal similarities, the intellectual and spiritual backgrounds of these two different currents in art are entirely different.

// Kann man die Sammlung FER besichtigen?

FER: Große Teile meiner Sammlung sind in wechselndem Zusammenhang im Museum für Neue Kunst des ZKM (Zentrum für Kunst und Medientechnologie) in Karlsruhe ausgestellt.

// Is the FER Collection open to the public?

FER: Large parts of my collection are displayed on a rotating basis at the Museum of Contemporary Art run by the ZKM (Center for Art and Media) in Karlsruhe.

// Sind in diese Ausstellung auch einige der amischen Quilts integriert? Sind sie bereits im Zusammenhang mit der zeitgenössischen Kunst gezeigt worden?

FER: Kunstwerke der Amischen und Werke der heutigen zeitgenössischen Kunst wurden, soviel ich weiß, bis jetzt noch nicht „aufeinander losgelassen".

// Are some Amish quilts also integrated in that exhibition? Have they already been shown in connection with contemporary art?

FER: Art works by the Amish and works of current contemporary art have, as far as I know, never been 'set on one another'.

SUNBURST OCTAGON, ca 1920
Amische Quiltmacherin / **Amish Quilt-Maker**, Lancaster County, Pennsylvania / 215 x 190 cm

// Frau Schlumberger, wie sind Sie auf die Quilts der Amischen aufmerksam geworden – und wann war das?

Maria Schlumberger (MS): Das kann ich nicht auf ein Datum festlegen. Die ersten amischen Quilts habe ich vor etwa 20 Jahren in einem Antiquitätengeschäft in New York gesehen und war fasziniert von den Farben und Mustern dieser so genannten „Steppdecken". Mein Mann Friedrich hatte mich darauf aufmerksam gemacht, weil er schon einige Jahre zuvor bei einer Reise in die Vereinigten Staaten auf Long Island einen kleinen amischen Quilt gekauft hatte. Aus Neugier und Staunen wurde Begeisterung.

// Ms Schlumberger, how did you become aware of Amish quilts – and when was that?

Maria Schlumberger (MS): I can't tell you a precise date. I saw Amish quilts for the first time about twenty years ago in a New York antique shop and was fascinated by the colors and designs of those so-called 'quilted bed covers'. Friedrich, my husband, had pointed them out to me because he had bought a small Amish quilt some years before on Long Island while he was on a trip to the United States. What started as curiosity and astonishment grew into enthusiasm.

// Waren es gleich amische Quilts oder zuerst andere?

MS: Quilts der anglo-amerikanischen Folk Art hatten nie mein Interesse, da sie bewusst mit kunstgewerblichem Hintergrund angefertigt wurden und vorwiegend für die Geschichte der USA wichtig sind. Mich interessieren nur amische Quilts, denn nur bei denen geht es um vielfältigste Farbexperimente in wenigen vorgegebenen Formen.

// Was it Amish quilts from the start or at first others?

MS: Anglo-American folk art quilts had never interested me because they were deliberately made in the context of decorative art and are mainly important for US history. I am only interested in Amish quilts because they are the only ones concerned with manifold experiments with color in a few, prescribed forms.

// Wie muss man sich das überhaupt vorstellen: Quilts sammeln? Amische Quilts in Europa sind extrem selten, und Sie haben eine Sammlung aufgebaut, die den Vergleich mit den besten Sammlungen in den USA nicht zu scheuen braucht. Aber es sind ja historische Quilts, die heute nicht mehr hergestellt werden. Kann man einfach zu den Amischen hinfahren, und dann graben die Frauen in einer Kiste ...?

MS: Das weiß ich nicht, aber gute antike Quilts sind auch bei den Amischen selbst selten geworden. Wir sind über Peter und Eva Ziegler – die hohe Fachkenntnis und ästhetisches Einfühlungsvermögen haben – zu den schönsten antiken Quilts gekommen, die auf dem Markt zu haben sind. Dafür umarme ich sie und sage wie die Amischen: „Vergelt's Gott".

// How is one to imagine that in fact: collecting quilts? Amish quilts are extremely rare in Europe and you have amassed a collection which bears comparison with the best US collections. But those are antique quilts, which are no longer made today. Can one simply drive to the Amish and visit families and then the women rummage in a chest ...?

MS: I don't know about that but good antique quilts have become very rare, even among the Amish. We acquired the most beautiful antique quilts available on the market through Peter and Eva Ziegler – who are extremely knowledgeable specialists and have a highly empathetic aesthetic sense. I hug them for that and say, like the Amish: 'God bless you.'

// Frau Schlumberger, was fasziniert Sie am Sammeln?

MS: Anfangs habe ich Quilts gekauft, weil ich von der Schönheit dieser Werke tief beeindruckt war. Mit jedem weiteren Quilt wuchs die Leidenschaft des Sammelns, und es wurde mein Ziel, nicht nur einzelne Stücke zu besitzen, sondern selbst etwas zu gestalten, was die Ausdruckskraft der Amischen in ihrer ganzen Vielfalt zeigt, eine schöpferische Blüte, die – vereinfacht gesagt – etwa von 1850 bis 1950, rund ein Jahrhundert dauerte.

// Ms Schlumberger, what fascinates you about collecting?

MS: Initially I bought quilts because I was profoundly struck by the beauty of these works. With each quilt the passion for collecting grew and it became my aim not just to own individual pieces but to design something myself which would show the expressive powers of the Amish in all their diversity, a creative flowering, which – put simply – lasted from about 1850 to 1950, roughly a century.

// Gibt es einen Zugang für Sie über die Weltsicht oder religiöse Einstellung der Amischen?

MS: Ich interessiere mich vorwiegend für die Kunst, denn nur die Werke werden in der Kunstgeschichte ihre Bedeutung behalten und den Geist einer Zeit festhalten. Durch die Quilts habe ich mich natürlich mit der Geisteshaltung der Amischen beschäftigt und bin fasziniert von ihren in einem festen Glauben begründeten Wertvorstellungen. Nur ein wenig davon täte unserer Gesellschaft gut. Nicht die Geisteshaltung der Amischen erschließt uns die Quilts, sondern die Quilts erschließen uns die Lebenshaltung der Amischen.

// Do you approach them through the world-view or religious attitudes of the Amish?

MS: I'm mainly interested in the art since only the works will retain their significance in art history and capture a particular spirit of the times. Through the quilts I have naturally studied the intellectual and spiritual attitudes of the Amish and am fascinated by their values, which are grounded in a firm faith. Just a bit of that would be good for our society. The quilts don't reveal the Amish mindset to us but the quilts open up the Amish way of life to us.

// Ist es auch ein Gespür für die Macherinnen der Quilts, so eine Art Sicheinfühlen in das Leben und die Lebenshaltung dieser amischen Frauen?

Natürlich führt das Sammeln ganz allgemein dazu, dass man sich mit den Hintergründen der Dinge, die man sammelt, beschäftigt. Dass die Quilts von amischen Frauen gefertigt wurden, spielt für mich keine Rolle. Emanzipatorische Fragen sind ein Phänomen unserer westlichen Industriegesellschaft.

ONE PATCH, PUPPENQUILT /
DOLL QUILT, ca 1935
Amische Quiltmacherin der Familie
Petersheim / **Amish Quilt-Maker**
from the Petersheim Family, Holmes
County, Ohio / 60 x 50 cm

// Is it also a feeling for the women who made the quilts, a sort of empathy with the lives and lifestyle of those Amish women?
Of course collecting generally leads one to a preoccupation with the backgrounds of the things one collects. That the quilts were made by Amish women plays no role for me. Emancipation issues are a phenomenon of our western industrial society.

// Machen Sie selbst Quilts?
MS: Nein.
// Do you make quilts yourself?
MS: No.

// Haben Sie einen Lieblingsquilt? Oder mehrere Lieblingsstücke?
MS: Natürlich gibt es Quilts, die mir ganz besonders ans Herz gewachsen sind. Das große Faszinosum aber, das meinen Mann und mich beschäftigt, sind die Fragen: Was ist Kunst, wie wichtig ist die Kreativität für unser Leben und wie können wir diese Fragen noch anderen interessierten Menschen vermitteln.
// Do you have a favorite quilt? Or several favorite pieces?
MS: Naturally there are quilts that I've grown particularly fond of. The most fascinating thing, however, with which my husband and I are preoccupied, is questions such as what is art, how important is creativity for our lives and how can we involve other interested people with these questions.

// Welche Rolle hat der Galerist dabei gespielt?
MS: Galeristen spielen immer eine ganz große Rolle. Galeristen helfen, dass die Zwiesprache mit den Objekten, mit der Kunst und mit interessierten Freunden nicht ins Stocken gerät. Peter Ziegler war und ist in unserer Auseinandersetzung mit der Kunst der Amischen ein wichtiger, lebendiger, erfahrener und in der Sache absolut kompetenter Gesprächspartner. Er hat uns als führender Händler auf diesem Gebiet ein sehr breit gefächertes Hintergrundwissen vermittelt.
Das gemeinsame Gefühl für Qualität hat uns von Anfang an verbunden und basierte von Anfang an auf gegenseitigem Vertrauen. Und nachdem Zieglers zu den ganz wenigen Galeristen für antike amische Quilts gehören, war diese Verbindung, man kann fast sagen: alternativlos. In allem, was antike amische Quilts betrifft, haben uns die Gespräche mit Peter Ziegler in hohem Maße bereichert.
// What role has the gallerist played?
MS: Gallerists always play a very big role. Dealers help to ensure that the dialogue with the objects, with art and with interested friends, doesn't falter. Peter Ziegler has always been an important, invigorating, experienced and in the field utterly competent dialogue partner in our study of Amish art. As the leading dealer in this field he has conveyed to us a very broad-based background knowledge. A mutual feeling for quality has linked us from the outset and has been based from the beginning on mutual trust. And since the Zieglers are among the very few gallerists in antique Amish quilts, this connection, one might even say: was without an alternative. In everything relating to antique Amish quilts, our talks with Peter Ziegler have been enormously enriching.

// Gibt es eine Art Sammlerszene in Europa? In den USA?
MS: Kontakt zu anderen Quiltsammlern habe ich nicht. Natürlich weiß man von einigen anderen Sammlern in Europa; in den Vereinigten Staaten von Amerika gibt es allerdings bedeutende private und museale Sammlungen von amischen Quilts.

// Is there some kind of collector scene in Europe? In the US?

MS: I have no contact to other quilt collectors. Naturally one knows of a few other collectors in Europe; in the United States of America, on the other hand, there are important private and museum collections of Amish quilts.

// Haben Sie Pläne, offene Wünsche, Sehnsüchte, Begehrlichkeiten im Hinblick auf Ihre Quiltsammlung?

MS: Natürlich ist es ein großer Wunsch, dass sich möglichst viele, neugierige und aufgeschlossene Menschen auf dieses – ja – „Seherlebnis" einlassen. Wir sind uns bewusst, dass die Qualität unserer Sammlung ein hohes Niveau erreicht hat und die Vielfalt amischer Quiltkunst in ihrer ganzen Fülle repräsentiert. Mein Mann Friedrich Rentschler und ich sind uns heute sicher, amische Quilts, die zwischen 1850 und 1950 entstanden sind, sind großartige Werke, die durch ihren Einfallsreichtum, ihre Originalität, ihre Farben und auch ihre handwerkliche Perfektion zu großer Kunst gerechnet werden können.

// **Have you any plans, outstanding wishes, yearnings, burning desires with respect to your quilt collection?**

MS: Of course it is a major wish that as many curious and receptive people as possible give themselves up to this – well – 'visual impact'. We are well aware that the quality of our collection has attained a high standard and represents the diversity of the art of Amish quilt-making in all its richness. My husband, Friedrich Rentschler, and I are today sure that Amish quilts made between 1850 and 1950 are splendid works, which, due to the imagination and originality that went into making them, their colors and the consummate craftsmanship, will be regarded as great art.

Das Gespräch führten Florian Hufnagl und Corinna Rösner im Januar 2007.

The interview was conducted by Florian Hufnagl and Corinna Rösner in January 2007.

**LOG CABIN – STRAIGHT FURROW,
CRIB QUILT**, ca 1950
Amische Quiltmacherin Celina Beiler /
Amish Quilt-Maker Celina Beiler, Lancaster
County, Pennsylvania / 100 x 100 cm

DIE KÜNSTLERISCHE REISE AMISCHER QUILTS / **THE ARTISTIC JOURNEY OF AMISH QUILTS**

Laura Fisher

UNSERE AUGEN SCHAUEN, UNSER GEIST SIEHT // Einfachheit ist voller Kraft, vor allem bei den Quilts der Amischen von Lancaster County, Pennsylvania. Farbe ist bezwingend, vor allem wenn sie in unerwarteten Zusammenstellungen auftritt, in dichten, satten, monochromen Farbflächen, die den reizvollen bedruckten Stoffen, die man gemeinhin mit dem amerikanischen Patchwork-Quilt assoziiert, so gar nicht ähneln. Beides trifft auf die Quilts der Amischen zu, einer Gruppe von Amerikanern, die in isolierten Gemeinschaften leben und eine streng traditionelle Lebensweise pflegen, wobei Ordnung, Disziplin, das Festhalten an religiösen Glaubensgrundsätzen, die Einheit der Familie und gemeinsame Werte wesentliche Bestandteile sind. // Auch wenn die Amischen in ihren Quilts Motive verwenden, die von ihrer Umgebung und ihrem Glauben angeregt wurden – wie Barn Raising (Scheunenbau), Courthouse Steps (Stufen zum Gerichtsgebäude), Sunshine and Shadow (Sonne und Schatten), Crown of Thorns (Dornenkrone), Stairway to Heaven (Himmelsleiter) oder Shoofly (ein Melassekuchen) –, so ist doch keines von ihnen bildhaft oder narrativ; das nämlich ist untersagt. // Die Quilts der Amischen sind in ihrem Erscheinungsbild durch spezifische Vorschriften der jeweiligen Gemeinde bestimmt und basieren alle auf dem Block: den – meist quadratischen – Einzelfeldern. Sie sind fast ohne Ausnahme geometrisch gestaltet, ob sie nun aus einem großen zentralen Quadrat oder einem auf die Spitze gestellten Quadrat – dem Diamond – bestehen oder aus einer Kombination von vier oder neun kleineren Quadraten, die zu einer Einheit zusammengefügt und über die gesamte Oberseite des Quilts wiederholt werden, oder diagonal durchschnittenen Quadraten, deren Zusammenstellung und Farbigkeit die Quilts – aus welcher Gemeinschaft auch immer sie stammen – wiedererkennbar machen. // Zwar verändert sich die äußere Welt, doch die Amischen folgen keinem Trend und lösen auch keinen aus. Jahrzehntelang behielten sie dieselben Muster bei, jedenfalls in der so genannten „klassischen" Zeit vom späteren 19. Jahrhundert bis zu den 1950er Jahren, als Quilts noch einzig und allein für den persönlichen Gebrauch hergestellt wurden. Man könnte das als stilistische Nichtentwicklung bezeichnen – zu beobachten vor allem bei den am weitesten östlich in Pennsylvania lebenden Amischen. Doch ist es gerade diese immer gleich gebliebene Herangehensweise an die Gestaltung von Quilts, die uns ein kostbares Vermächtnis kraftvoller „Ikonen" überantwortet hat, die heute geschätzt und auch materiell gewürdigt werden. // Auf ihrem Zug nach Westen durch die Vereinigten

OUR EYES LOOK, OUR MINDS SEE // Simplicity is powerful, especially in the quilts of the Lancaster County, Pennsylvania Amish. Color is compelling, especially in unexpected combination, in dense rich solid planes of color, so unlike the charming prints most associated with the term 'patchwork' quilt from America. Both of these truths apply to the quilts of the Amish, a sub-group of Americans who live separately in communities that observe a strict cultural upbringing stressing order, discipline, adherence to religious beliefs, family unity, and shared values. // Though they used patterns in their quilts inspired by their surroundings and beliefs, such as Barn Raising, Courthouse Steps, Sunshine and Shadow, Crown of Thorns, Stairway to Heaven, or Shoofly, none is pictorial or narrative, because that is forbidden. // Amish quilt formats are regulated by community standards, and all are based on the block form. Nearly all are geometric, whether a large center square or diamond set on point, or a combination of four or nine small squares joined together and repeated on the quilt surface, or squares bisected on the diagonal and joined in combination and in colors that make them recognizable no matter which community they come from. // Despite changes in the world outside,

Staaten entliehen die Amischen, die sich in Ohio, Indiana, Illinois, Iowa und Kansas niederließen, Gestaltungsideen von ihren nichtamischen Nachbarn, mit denen sie mehr und mehr in Kontakt traten. Aus diesem Grund – so vermuten einige – zeigen die Quilts der Amischen in Illinois die größte Eigenständigkeit, wenn auch innerhalb bestimmter amischer Regeln. Hierzu im Gegensatz stehen die Arbeiten aus den ersten amischen Siedlungen in Lancaster County und anderen Bezirken Pennsylvanias. // In ihrem Aussehen unterscheiden sich die Quilts der Amischen deutlich von jenen, die von Nichtamischen – die sie als ihre „englischen" Nachbarn bezeichnen – hergestellt wurden. Anhand von Farbgebung und Format ist es möglich, einen Quilt als amisch zu identifizieren und einer speziellen Gemeinschaft zuzuordnen, ohne den Namen der Gestalterin oder der Gemeinde zu kennen, aus der sie stammt (wobei man sich der Geschichte und der Unterschiede zwischen den Gemeinschaften bewusst sein muss). Die Amischen sind so traditionell und so wenig modebewusst, dass zuweilen in ein und demselben Haushalt mehrere Quilts mit identischem Muster hergestellt wurden, als Geschenke für die flügge gewordenen Kinder (siehe Nrn. 5 und 47, aber auch Nrn. 66 und 72 oder 51 und 52). // Die Bevölkerungszahl der in den USA lebenden Amischen wuchs von etwa 1.200 im Jahr 1800 auf heute etwa 200.000 an. So ist das Angebot an authentischen, alten, sammlungswürdigen amischen Quilts aus den Jahren vor 1950 im Vergleich zu den Millionen erhaltener Stücke, die von Nichtamischen überall in den Vereinigten Staaten hergestellt wurden, sehr begrenzt. Amische Quilts sind selten, schwer zu finden, und sie tauchen kaum noch aus dem Haushalt der ursprünglichen Gestalterin oder ihrer Familie auf. Sie wechseln unter Sammlern und Händlern ihre Besitzer, und da die Nachfrage über das Angebot hinausgeht, steigt ihr Wert.

the Amish do not follow or initiate trends. Quilts from the 'classical' period of the late 19th century through the 1950s, made for their personal use, contained the same designs for decades. One might call this the non-evolution of style, especially among the eastern-most Pennsylvania Amish. Yet it is precisely this unchanging approach to quilt design that has given us an important legacy of powerful iconic images that are valued – and valuable – today. // As they moved westward across the United States, the Amish who settled in Ohio, Indiana, Illinois, Iowa and Kansas borrowed design ideas as they interacted increasingly with non-Amish neighbors. That is why some think the quilts of the Illinois Amish show greater originality, albeit within an orderly Amish format, than do those works from the first Amish settlements in Lancaster and other Pennsylvania counties. // The appearance of Amish quilts is distinct from non-Amish quilts made by those they call their 'English' neighbors. In palette and format, one can recognize a quilt as Amish and locate it within a community (having awareness of the communities' socio-cultural history and differences) without knowing the maker's name or town. So traditional and untrendy were the Amish that sometimes one can find the identical pattern in multiples from one household, made as gifts for various grown children leaving home to start their own families (see nos. 5 and 47, but also nos. 66 and 72 or 51 and 52). // The actual numbers of Amish in America grew from around 1,200 people in 1800, to about 200,000 nationwide today. So the supply of authentic, old, collectible Amish quilts before 1950 is so limited compared to the millions extant made by non-Amish across the U.S. Amish quilts are scarce, hard to find, and rarely emerge from the households of the original maker or family anymore. Trading hands among dealers and collectors, their value increases as demand exceeds supply.

WHICH CAME FIRST – THE PAINTING OF ALBERS OR THE QUILT OF BEILER? // Amish quilts are usually compared with 20th century art such as modernism, minimalism, and color field painting, as if those movements came first. In fact, it is the Amish female quilt maker who created such powerful forms on a flat plane, beginning in the late 19th and extending into the mid-20th century. These quilts are often likened to the oeuvre of artists like Josef Albers, Frank Stella, Bridget Riley, Ellsworth Kelly, Victor Vasarely, Sean Scully, and Richard Anuszkiewicz with whom the art world is more familiar … // While it might be charming to think of some mid-20th century Greenwich Village painters traveling

WAS WAR ZUERST DA – DAS BILD VON ALBERS ODER DER QUILT VON BEILER? // Die Quilts der Amischen werden häufig bestimmten Kunstrichtungen des 20. Jahrhunderts gegenübergestellt – etwa der Klassischen Moderne, dem Minimalismus und der Farbfeldmalerei –, als seien diese zuerst da gewesen. Tatsächlich war es aber die amische Quiltmacherin, die seit dem späten 19. Jahrhundert – und ungefähr bis Mitte des 20. Jahrhunderts – solch kraftvolle Formen auf einer planen Fläche entwarf. Sie werden häufig mit Werken von Künstlern wie Josef Albers, Frank Stella, Bridget Riley, Ellsworth Kelly, Victor Vasarely, Sean Scully und Richard Anuszkiewicz verglichen, die freilich in der Kunstwelt bekannter sind als die Gestalterinnen von Quilts. // Obwohl es durchaus seinen Reiz hat, sich irgendeinen der Greenwich-Village-Maler vorzustellen, wie er Mitte des 20. Jahrhunderts durch das ländliche Pennsylvania wandert und durch die Farbe und visuelle Schockwirkung amischer Quilts inspiriert wird, gibt es doch keinen Nachweis für solche Geschichten. Viel eher war es eine an der Moderne geschulte Art des Sehens, die damals in Design, Architektur und Kunst international um sich griff und die uns wahrscheinlich hoch empfänglich machte für die Ästhetik amischer Quilts als verwandte Ausdrucksform. // Ein amischer Quilt fordert unsere Wahrnehmung heraus. Sehen wir Farbe auf Leinwand? Oder Stoff, der zerschnitten und zusammengesetzt wurde? Wir sind so sehr daran gewöhnt, die abstrakte Kunst berühmter Größen aus den sechziger bis neunziger Jahren des 20. Jahrhunderts zu sehen, dass wir meinen, ihre Gemälde anzuschauen, und nicht Bettdecken von Elisabeth Yoder, Susan Beiler, Mary Glick, Mary Stoltzfus und Amanda Schlabach. // Die Farbe ist der Schlüssel. Die Farbwahl der Amischen stellt unser räumliches Empfinden auf die Probe. Träger der Farben sind einfarbige Stoffe, sie sind strahlend, intensiv und lebendig, insbesondere im Kontrast zu Hintergründen oder Umrahmungen in dunklen Tönen. Auch wenn die Amischen als „plain people"

the rural Pennsylvania countryside, getting inspired by the color and visual impact of Amish quilts, there are no such anecdotal reports. Instead, the 'modern' way of seeing that was taking place then in design, architecture and art internationally likely spurred our response to Amish quilts as parallel forms of expression. // We look at an Amish quilt and our perception is challenged – are we looking at paint on canvas, or cut and pieced fabric? So accustomed are we to seeing modern art by big names of the 1960s–1990s that one might think we are looking at <u>their</u> paintings, not bedding made by Elisabeth Yoder, Susan Beiler, Mary Glick, Mary Stoltzfus, or Amanda Schlabach. // Color is key. Our experience of space is challenged as a consequence of Amish color choices. The colors are brilliant, solid fabrics, intense, vivid, especially in contrast to the dark grounds or borders framing them. Though called the 'plain people' because of their preference for living simply without embellishment in clothing or home furnishings, their quilts are anything but plain. // Some Lancaster quilts (see. Diamond in the Square nos. 32 and 33, or Bars nos. 10 and 14) seem to vibrate as we view them because of the color contrast, especially in the case of adjacent red and green. In others, such as the Midwestern Bow Ties (no. 56) or Log Cabin (no. 39), the identical pieced blocks can seem to advance or recede, dissolve or clearly look pieced depending on color juxtapositions, even though everything within was cut to the same size and shapes. // Rules within the various Amish communities about quilt making extended to such issues as the appropriate colors to use, even the color of the quilting thread in relation to the background. For example, in Holmes County, Ohio, white quilting contrasts with the black sateen background (their regional hallmark), while in Illinois quilting thread colors might echo the color of each piece and ground fabric (cf. Fans no. 38, Ocean Waves no. 65, Ohio Stars no. 42, Lone Star no. 34). As the Amish moved west, rigid adherence loosened and pattern variety increased, perhaps a sign of also increasing personal expression and individuality the further away the migrants traveled from their Lancaster County roots. // The Amish brought no quilt making tradition from Europe to the United States, as did the English, Scandinavians, Dutch, French and others. Rather the Amish learned quilt making from those Europeans, and created here a distinctive aesthetic that we value – even romanticize – highly today. No remnants of Amish life in Europe remain.

Bau einer Scheune – alle helfen mit. /
Barn raising – a communal event.

(schlichte Menschen) bezeichnet werden, weil sie einem einfachen Leben ohne verzierende Elemente an Kleidung und Einrichtungsgegenständen den Vorzug geben, sind ihre Quilts alles andere als schlicht. // Einige Quilts aus Lancaster County (siehe Diamond in the Square Nr. 32 und 33 oder Bars Nr. 10 und 14) scheinen zu vibrieren, wenn wir sie ansehen. Grund hierfür ist der Farbkontrast, vor allem wenn Rot und Grün benachbart sind. Bei anderen, wie Bow Ties (Nr. 56) und Log Cabin (Nr. 39) aus dem Mittleren Westen, scheinen die gleich großen Blöcke – auch wenn alle Teilstücke der Blöcke gleichen Zuschnitt besitzen – sich mal nach vorne zu schieben, mal zurückzuweichen, sich aufzulösen oder zu verselbständigen, je nachdem, welche Farben nebeneinanderliegen. // Innerhalb der einzelnen Amischen-Gemeinden gingen die Regeln der Quiltherstellung bis hin zur Festlegung der erlaubten Farben, oder es wurde sogar die Farbe des Quiltingfadens für einen bestimmten Hintergrund vorgeschrieben. In Holmes County, Ohio, hebt sich beispielsweise weißes Quilting von dem für diese Gegend charakteristischen schwarzen Satin-Hintergrund ab; in Illinois können die Farben der Quiltingfäden die Farbe eines jeden einzelnen darunterliegenden Stoffstückes wiederholen (vgl. etwa Fans Nr. 38, Oceean Waves Nr. 65, Ohio Stars Nr. 42, Lone Star Nr. 34). Als die Amischen nach Westen zogen, lockerte sich das strenge Festhalten an Regeln und die Mustervielfalt nahm zu. Vielleicht ist das ein Zeichen dafür, dass auch der persönliche Ausdruck und die Individualität zunahmen, je weiter sich die Wegziehenden von ihren Wurzeln in Lancaster County entfernten. // Im Gegensatz zu Engländern, Skandinaviern, Niederländern, Franzosen und anderen brachten die Amischen <u>keine</u> eigene Tradition der Quiltherstellung aus Europa in die Vereinigten Staaten mit. Vielmehr erlernten sie das Quilten von den anderen europäischen Einwanderern und schufen jene ganz eigene Ästhetik, die wir heute so hoch schätzen – und sogar verklären. In Europa selbst hat sich vom Leben der Amischen nichts erhalten.

WHAT WOULD FREUD SAY? SEPARATIST PSYCHOLOGY AND CREATIVITY // What does the term Amish mean? Does it refer to a people, a religion, a cult, a sociological phenomenon, a place? Historically, the Amish began as a group of religious followers of Jacob Amman, a Swiss Mennonite bishop who broke with that church in 1693. Conservative Amman believed in the literal interpretation of the Bible, preferred adult baptism, disdained fancy, embellished dress, disdained ornate churches, opposed what he felt was the increasing decadence of the Catholic and Protestant Churches, and chose to live as simply as did the earliest Christians. // Deviants would be shunned (denied interaction with their families) and even banned forever (excommunicated, not just forgiven) for violating the <u>Ordnung</u> (rules of behavior). Persecuted, Amman and followers moved from the Swiss Palatinate along the Rhine valley to the Netherlands and to the Alsace region (at times German, at times French), settling in Sainte-Marie-aux-Mines. In the early 1700s they migrated to America for its promise of religious freedom, at the invitation of William Penn. // The Amish separate themselves from the communities around them. They choose not to participate in the American way of life or to change. They do not vote or participate in politics. They send children only up to the eighth grade in their own school system. At home, the children learn a High German dialect, Pennsylvanian Dutch. The Amish do not pay taxes, do not join the military, do not use technology or electricity (though they do use some labor saving, human-powered devices). They live as they did in earlier centuries in mostly agrarian communities in several states across America. This has had a profound effect on their handiwork. // They adhere to strict rules of conduct called the 'Ordnung' that in written and unwritten terms defines acceptable personal behavior, community interaction, everyday activity, and religious beliefs and practice, in varying degree of orthodoxy depending on each community's choices. // So well understood are the relationships to family, to work, to their belief system, and are the roles of women and men, that the pressure and stress from unlimited choice we of the outside world experience is less or even absent for the Amish. One might argue that as a consequence creativity gets restricted among Amish women. Or, conversely, that the inevitable, unconscious, instinctual (creative) life finds expression in the sublimation of passion and self in quilt making.

WAS WÜRDE FREUD SAGEN? PSYCHOLOGIE UND KREATIVITÄT IN SEPARATISTISCHEN GEMEINSCHAFTEN // Was bedeutet der Begriff Amische? Bezieht er sich auf ein Volk, eine Religion, einen Kult, ein soziales Phänomen, einen Ort? Historisch gesehen waren die Amischen zunächst eine Gruppe von religiösen Anhängern des Schweizer Mennonitenbischofs Jakob Ammann, der im Jahr 1693 mit seiner Kirche brach. Der konservative Ammann glaubte an die wortgetreue Auslegung der Bibel, befürwortete die Erwachsenentaufe, ächtete modische, gemusterte Kleidung und reich geschmückte Kirchen, wandte sich gegen das, was er als die zunehmende Dekadenz der katholischen und protestantischen Kirchen empfand, und entschloss sich, so einfach wie die ersten Christen zu leben. // Abtrünnige wurden mit Meidung belegt (der Kontakt zu ihrer Familie wurde ihnen verwehrt) und sogar für immer verbannt (exkommuniziert und aus der Gemeinschaft ausgestoßen – Vergebung ausgeschlossen), weil sie die Ordnung (die Verhaltensregeln) verletzt hatten. Da sie in der Schweiz verfolgt wurden, zogen Ammann und seine Anhänger das Rheintal entlang bis ins Elsass, wo sie sich in Sainte-Marie-aux-Mines niederließen, nach Lothringen etc. Im frühen 18. Jahrhundert wanderten sie auf Einladung von William Penn nach Amerika aus, das ihnen religiöse Freiheit verhieß. // Die Amischen isolieren sich von der andersgläubigen Gesellschaft, innerhalb derer sie leben. Sie haben sich entschieden, nicht am amerikanischen Lebensstil teilzuhaben und die eigene Lebensweise nicht zu verändern. Sie wählen nicht und nehmen nicht am politischen Leben teil. Sie schicken ihre Kinder auf ihre eigenen Schulen, die nur bis zur achten Klasse gehen. Zu Hause lernen sie einen deutschen Dialekt, Pennsylvania Dutch (verballhornt von „Pennsylvania Deutsch"). Sie zahlen keine Steuern, gehen nicht zur Armee, verwenden keine moderne Technologie oder Fernstrom, jedoch nutzen sie einige die Arbeit erleichternde, von Mensch oder Tier angetriebene Geräte, wie etwa Mähdrescher mit Zugpferden oder pedalbetriebene Nähmaschinen. Sie leben wie in vergangenen Jahrhunderten in großenteils agrarischen Gemeinden. Auf ihre handwerklichen Erzeugnisse hat dies starken Einfluss ausgeübt. // Die Amischen folgen äußerst strengen Verhaltensregeln, die sie als Ordnung bezeichnen und die in geschriebenen und ungeschriebenen Geboten das zulässige Benehmen des Einzelnen, die Beziehungen innerhalb der Gemeinschaft, die alltäglichen Tätigkeiten und auch die Glaubensgrundsätze und religiösen Gepflogenheiten definieren, wobei der Grad der Strenggläubigkeit je nach Gemeinde variiert. // Die Beziehungen des Individuums zur Familie, zur Arbeit und zu den Glaubensgrundsätzen wie auch die Rolle von Mann und Frau sind in solch hohem Maße akzeptiert, dass der Druck und Stress, den wir in unserer modernen Welt infolge unbegrenzter Wahlmöglichkeiten erleben, für die Amischen mehr oder weniger nicht vorhanden ist. Man könnte behaupten, dass mithin auch die Kreativität der amischen Frauen eingeschränkt sei. Oder umgekehrt, dass der unabweisbare, unterbewusste (kreative) Trieb sich in einem Vorgang der Sublimierung durch Selbstverwirklichung im Quilten ausdrückt.

DIAMONDS ARE FOREVER // For Swiss Germans in Europe, utilitarian bedding was featherbeds, blankets, homespun linens. In fact, it is in the United States that the Amish learned to quilt from neighboring European settlers during the 19th century, adopting their centuries-old formats such as the English center medallion (think Lancaster County 'Diamond in the Square'), and the Welsh 'strippy' (think Lancaster County 'Bars'), transforming these bold geometric designs with their own aesthetic. The colors in these iconic early Lancaster quilts were saturated and brave, thanks to their use of thinner, finer imported English woolens, available up until World War II. // No traces of Amish existence remained in Europe after emigration. So it is fascinating that the Germans, Swiss, and French – each group that lays claim to originating the Amish – sought out Amish quilts to bring 'back home' to enhance interiors both private and public. Perhaps it is the design DNA from centuries of their own history that draws them all to Amish quilts. // Collecting interest in Amish quilts has flourished worldwide, especially during the last quarter of the 20th century, and again now. A whole industry has developed. Dealers specialize in Amish quilts on both sides of the Atlantic. Design magazines feature brilliantly colored Amish quilts on the wall as art. Inch for inch, their bold graphics look like contemporary paintings,

DIAMONDS ARE FOREVER // Bei den in Europa lebenden Vorfahren waren Federbetten, Wolldecken und handgewebtes Leinzeug als Bettwäsche üblich. Tatsächlich lernten die Amischen erst im Laufe des 19. Jahrhunderts von den in ihrer Nachbarschaft lebenden anderen europäischen Siedlern zu quilten, wobei sie jahrhundertealte Motive wie das aus England stammende zentrale Medaillon – man denke an „Diamond in the Square" in Lancaster County – und das walisische „strippy" – man denke an das Streifenmuster der „Bars" – übernahmen und diese beiden auffälligen geometrischen Motive in ihre eigene Formensprache abwandelten. Die Farben der frühen Quilt-„Ikonen" aus Lancaster County waren kühn und satt; ihre Farbtiefe verdanken sie der Verwendung von relativ dünnen, feinen englischen Wollstoffen, die bis zum Zweiten Weltkrieg erhältlich waren. // Nach Auswanderung der Amischen blieben in Europa keine Zeugnisse ihrer Existenz zurück. So ist es faszinierend, dass gerade die Deutschen, Schweizer und Franzosen – all jene, die Anspruch darauf erheben könnten, die Amischen hervorgebracht zu haben – nach amischen Quilts gesucht haben, um diese gleichsam „nach Hause" zurückzubringen und dort mit ihnen sowohl private als auch öffentliche Interieurs zu schmücken. Vielleicht fühlen sie sich aufgrund ihrer schöpferischen Erbmasse aus Jahrhunderten eigener Geschichte so von den Quilts der Amischen angezogen. // Weltweit ist das Sammlerinteresse an amischen Quilts sehr gewachsen, insbesondere im letzten Viertel des 20. Jahrhunderts und heute erneut. Auf beiden Seiten des Atlantiks spezialisieren sich Händler auf amische Quilts; Designzeitschriften präsentieren diese farbenprächtigen Quilts, die nun an der Wand hängen, als Kunstwerke. Jeder Zentimeter ihrer kühnen grafischen Gestaltung ähnelt zeitgenössischen Gemälden, doch sind Quilts für einen Bruchteil des Preises zu erwerben. Andere amerikanische Quilts sind für ein paar Hundert Dollar erhältlich, für Quilts der Amischen hingegen zahlt man, seit sie in die öffentliche Wahrnehmung gerückt sind, Tausende – ein Zeugnis ihrer künstlerischen Wirkungskraft. // In den 1960er und 1970er Jahren durchkämmten clevere junge Männer von den Colleges, darunter viele Kunststudenten, die ländlichen Gemeinden der Amischen und füllten ihre VW-Busse mit Quilts, die sie von den Wäscheleinen und aus den Eingangsveranden für manchmal nur elf Dollar geholt hatten. Jahrzehnte später, als der Markt für diese kraftvollen Quilts boomte, wurden auf Auktionen Rekordpreise mit dem Vieltausendfachen erzielt. Vorsteher amischer Gemeinden aus Lancaster County fuhren nach New York, um das Erbe ihrer Vorfahren zurückzuerwerben und in Pennsylvania wieder zu verkaufen!

yet are available at a fraction of the cost. While other American quilts sell in the hundreds of dollars, since the beginning of public notice Amish quilts have sold in the thousands of dollars, a testament to their artistic impact. // And what of their cost? In the 1960s and 1970s, savvy young college men, art students many of them, scoured rural Amish settlements to fill their Volkswagen buses with quilts grabbed from clotheslines and porches for as little as $11 (as one early 'picker' likes to boast). Decades later at the height of the market for these powerful quilts they were fetching record prices that were thousands of times higher than they had been in the past. Lancaster County Amish leaders even rode with non-Amish friends to New York City to buy back their patrimony to sell in Pennsylvania!

ESPRIT DE CORP(ORATE) // A California women's clothing company called Esprit seems to have been first to focus their art collection on hanging Amish quilts in their new headquarters in 1976, so enamored were the owners and workers of their color, their graphics, their soulfulness. Esprit published a catalog (expanded to the book on early Amish quilts); allowed the public in to view them on guided tours; and were written about widely for this innovative approach to art. Companies with diverse corporate collections followed suit and added quilts to their paintings and sculpture because they were the art most favored by employees. Esprit acquired its first five Amish quilts for $500. By the time they made their last purchase, the price had soared out of sight. When buying the 82 Amish quilts featured in the Robert Hughes book on the Esprit Collection (1990), the Heritage Center of Lancaster County, Pennsylvania, paid a great deal more than Esprit when they first purchased them.

ESPRIT DE CORP(ORATE): GEMEINSCHAFTSGEIST – FIRMENGEIST // Ein kalifornischer Hersteller von Frauenbeklei-dung namens Esprit scheint das erste Unternehmen gewesen zu sein, das sich mit seiner Kunstsammlung auf amische Quilts konzentrierte: 1976 wurden sie im neuen Hauptsitz der Firma aufgehängt, so hingerissen waren Eigentümer und Arbeitnehmer von ihren Farben, ihrer grafischen Erscheinung, ihrer Seele. Esprit veröffentlichte einen Katalog (der zu dem Buch über frühe amische Quilts erweitert wurde) und machte die Stücke im Rahmen von Führungen der Öffentlichkeit zugänglich – insgesamt ein neuartiger Zugang zu Kunst, über den viel berichtet wurde. Unternehmen mit ganz unterschied-lichen Sammlungen folgten diesem Vorbild und fügten ihren Gemälden und Skulpturen Quilts hinzu, da diese Kunst von ihren Angestellten am meisten geschätzt wurde. Esprit erwarb die ersten fünf Quilts der Amischen für insgesamt 500 Dollar, für seinen letzten Ankauf zahlte das Unternehmen mehrere hundert Mal soviel. Und entsprechend hoch war auch der Preis, als das Heritage Center of Lancaster County, Pennsylvania die 82 Quilts aus der Esprit-Sammlung, die im Standardwerk von Robert Hughes (1990) publiziert worden waren, im Jahr 2002 erwarb.

ZEIG MIR, WELCHE FARBE DEIN PFERDEWAGEN HAT: EINE KURZE GESCHICHTE DER AMISCHEN IN DEN VEREI-NIGTEN STAATEN // Nach ihrer Einwanderung in die USA Ende des 18. Jahrhunderts ließen sich die Amischen zunächst in Lancaster County in Pennsylvania nieder und gründeten weitere Gemeinden in den Countys Berks, Somerset, Lebanon, Chester und Mifflin. Einige zogen sofort weiter nach Westen, ins heutige Illinois. // Als die Familien größer wurden und weiteres fruchtbares Farmland benötigten, setzte sich der Zug nach Westen von den ersten Siedlungen in Pennsylvania weiter fort, in einem breiten Streifen durch Ohio, Illinois, Indiana, Kansas und Iowa. Bis zur Mitte des 19. Jahrhunderts trafen weiterhin auch Amische aus Europa ein. // Die Amischen errichteten keine Kirchengebäude, sondern schufen stattdessen aus zwanzig bis dreißig Familien bestehende Kirchenbezirke. Ihre Gottesdienste finden sonntags in Häusern ihrer Mitglieder statt, in einigen Gemeinden auf Englisch, in anderen auf Pennsylvania Dutch, also Deutsch. Diese Veranstaltungen werden seit eh und je von einem Bischof abgehalten, der die Befugnis hat, alle Vorgänge der Gemeinschaft zu regeln. Dies trug zu

SHOW ME THE COLOR OF YOUR BUGGY: A BRIEF HISTORY OF THE AMISH IN AMERICA // After emigrating to the U.S. in the late 1700s, the Amish settled first in Lancaster County, Pennsylvania and established other communities in Berks, Somerset, Lebanon, Chester and Mifflin Counties. Some immediately traveled as far west as what is now Illinois. // As families grew in size and needed fertile farmland, emigration proceeded from the original Pennsylvania settlements in a swath westward through Ohio, Illinois, Indiana, Kansas, and Iowa. Until the mid-19th century some Amish also continued to come from Europe. // They built no churches, but instead created church districts of 20 to 30 families, and conducted worship services in members' homes on Sundays, in High German, led by a male bishop with authority to regulate all community practices. This contributed to differences among Amish communities across the country. // The universal Amish quilt icons are from Lancaster County, Pennsylvania – four monumental, square quilt designs: the Center Square, Diamond in the Square, Bars, and Sunshine and Shadow (examples nos. 9, 12, 22, 25). The earlier examples are made of fine wools, solid, not patterned, in rich deep colors, with wide borders and superb hand quilting, though pieced by treadle foot-powered machines. As few were signed or dated, age can typically be determined by the fabrics used on the back and the quilting motifs that changed over the years. // In other Pennsylvania counties, the level of orthodoxy varied as seen in buggy styles, clothing, household decorations, and to us most visibly in the quilts. In Mifflin County, for example, also known as the Big Valley or Kish Valley (from Kishacoquillas), five distinct groups made quilts using only square patches assembled in groups of four or nine, sometimes square and sometimes more rectangular, of cotton or combination fabrics like cotton/rayon. Most conservative among the Amish nationwide was

den Unterschieden zwischen den amischen Gemeinden überall im Land bei. // Die „Ikonen" amischer Quilts stammen aus Lancaster County, Pennsylvania – vier imposante, quadratische Quiltmotive: Center Square, Diamond in the Square, Bars und Sunshine and Shadow (siehe die Nrn. 9, 12, 22 und 25). Frühe Quilts wurden aus feinen Wollstoffen hergestellt, die einfarbig und nicht gemustert waren, in tiefen, prächtigen Farben. Sie haben breite Ränder und sind vorzüglich von Hand gequiltet, wobei die einzelnen Stoffstücke mit Hilfe von pedalbetriebenen Nähmaschinen zusammengenäht wurden. Einige wenige sind signiert oder datiert, und ihr Alter kann normalerweise anhand der für die Unterseite verwendeten Stoffe und der sich im Laufe der Jahre ändernden Quiltingmuster ermittelt werden. // In anderen Counties von Pennsylvania variierte der Grad der Orthodoxie, wie man an den Formen der Pferdewagen, der Kleidung, des Zierrats in Häusern und, für uns am besten zu sehen, an den Quilts erkennen kann. In Mifflin County – auch als Big Valley oder Kish Valley (von Kishacoquillas) bekannt – beispielsweise lassen sich fünf Gruppen unterscheiden, die für ihre Quilts – die manchmal quadratische, manchmal eher rechteckige Form haben – ausschließlich quadratische Stoffstückchen verwendeten, und zwar angeordnet zu Vierer- oder Neunerfeldern. Diese Quilts wurden aus Baumwolle oder Mischgeweben, etwa Baumwolle-Viskose, hergestellt. Am konservativsten von allen Amischen im ganzen Land war der Kirchenbezirk der so genannten Nebraska Amish in Mifflin County – nach ihren Pferdewagen mit weißem Verdeck auch als White Topper bezeichnet. Am wenigsten konservativ waren die Byler- oder Yellow-Topper-Amischen, die leuchtendere Farben verwendeten, und in der liberaleren Mitte gab es die Peachey Amish oder Black Topper, die auch Muster von außerhalb aufnahmen. // Die größte Gruppe von Amischen lebt heute in Holmes County, Ohio. Sie ist vor allem aufgrund ihrer rechteckigen Baumwollquilts bekannt, in denen sich Edelstein-farben in quadratischen Blocks von einem dunklen Hintergrund abheben und die einen schmaleren Innenrahmen und einen breiteren Außenrahmen besitzen. Schwarzer Baumwollsatin und manchmal ein tiefdunkles Blau sind typisch für diese Quilts. // Quilts aus Illinois sind am vielfältigsten, sie weisen künstlerische Neuerungen und sogar Asymmetrien auf, wobei die ältesten Quilts kräftige Farben haben und aus selbstgewebten Stoffen bestehen. Aus der Gemeinde Arthur stammt ein zum Erkennungszeichen gewordenes Motiv – ein zentraler Stern in Form eines Quadrates mit acht dreieckigen Strahlen. Ihre Quilts sind charakterisiert durch verschieden breite oder mehrfache Rahmungen und eine große Bandbreite an Mustern. // Andere, in nicht so starkem Maße selbstreglementierte Amischen-Gemeinden im Mittleren Westen entliehen Muster

Mifflin's church district known as the Nebraska Amish (White Topper buggy). Least conservative were the Byler or Yellow Topper, who used brighter colors, and somewhere more liberal in between were the Peachey Amish or Black Topper, who even adopted outside patterns. // The largest Amish population today is in Holmes County, Ohio, known best for their rectangular cotton quilts, with dark grounds contrasted with jewel tone colors set in square blocks, in a format of a narrow inside and wider outside border. Black sateen cotton and sometimes deep blue are characteristic there. // Illinois quilts show the most variety, painterly innovation and even asymmetry, with strong colors and home-spun fabrics in their earliest quilts. From the Arthur community came a hallmark design – a center Star made from a square with eight triangle arms. Their quilts are distinguished by unequal or several borders, and a wide pattern variety. // Other less self-regulated Midwestern Amish settlements borrowed patterns from outside, using even published designs from the Ladies' Art Company – a mail-order firm selling quilt patterns from the 1890s onwards – but in their own distinctive colorations. The Midwest Amish are also known for an in-between size called 'lounge' quilt of long narrow dimension for use on daybeds in the living room. // After 1950 Amish quilts included brighter, lighter synthetic poly fabrics for the pieced tops and interior batting. When their quilts became of interest and marketable as artworks to outsiders (though not considered such to themselves), the Amish began copying old quilts to order. These may look Amish, but are felt to lack the spiritual beliefs and lifestyle that infused their predecessors. Today, the Amish in Lancaster and elsewhere make quilts for tourists for money in conventional non-Amish patterns that may be called Amish-made

von außen und verwendeten sogar Entwürfe, die von der Ladies' Art Company – einer Mail-Order-Firma, die ab den 1890er Jahren Quiltmuster verkaufte – publiziert worden waren, allerdings in der ihnen eigenen unverwechselbaren Farbgebung. Die Amischen des Mittleren Westens sind auch für den so genannten Lounge Quilt bekannt geworden, einen länglichen Quilt mittlerer Größe, der auf Tagesbetten im Wohnzimmer verwendet wird. // Nach 1950 tauchen auch hellere, leichtere synthetische Stoffe in den Schauseiten und Füllungen amischer Quilts auf. Als ihre Quilts das Interesse von Außenstehenden erregten und als Kunstwerke (obwohl von ihnen selbst nicht als solche angesehen) Marktwert erlangten, begannen die Amischen, alte Quilts auf Bestellung zu kopieren. Diese mögen zwar amisch aussehen, doch fühlt man, dass ihnen der geistige Hintergrund und die Lebenshaltung fehlen, von denen ihre Vorläufer durchdrungen waren. Heute stellen die Amischen in Lancaster County und anderswo Quilts mit den üblichen nichtamischen Mustern her, um sie an Touristen zu verkaufen. Man mag das zwar als amische Arbeiten bezeichnen, doch sind sie nicht höher zu schätzen als andere hübsche handgenähte Quilts. // Die Ästhetik der Amischen hat sich auf der ganzen Welt verbreitet, wie sich an solch eigentümlichen Stiladaptionen wie den Bodenbelägen des Unternehmens Armstrong zeigt – hier soll sich der Käufer der PVC-Platten auf dem Boden seinen eigenen amischen Quilt kreieren – und bei Modeschöpfern wie Jean Paul Gaultier oder Christian Francis Roth, die in den 1990er Jahren „amische" Kleiderkollektionen schufen. // Es entbehrt nicht einer gewissen Ironie, dass diese einzigartige Gruppe von Menschen – die über Jahrhunderte an ihren Werten und Traditionen festzuhalten vermochte und stets so darauf bedacht war, sich von der Außenwelt und Äußerlichkeiten fernzuhalten – ausgerechnet bei einem äußerlichen, dekorativen Aspekt ihrer Lebensführung nachgeahmt wird, den sie nicht einmal als Kunst einschätzen. Und dabei sind es doch zweifellos ihr Pazifismus und die Einheit von Familie und Gemeinschaft, mit denen die Amischen andere zu beeinflussen hoffen.

but are not valued as anything more than pretty hand sewn quilts. // The Amish aesthetic has pervaded life all over the world, as seen in such curious co-opting of the look as the floor coverings from the Armstrong Company with which vinyl tile buyers could create their own Amish quilt on the floor, and by couturiers like Jean Paul Gaultier and Christian Francis Roth who created 'Amish'-derived clothing collections in the 1990s. // How ironic for this unique group of people – able to hold on to their values and traditions over centuries, and so intent upon distancing itself from the outside world – to be emulated for the visual decorative aspect of their lifestyle, which they don't even value as art, when surely it is their pacifism and unity of family and community they hope might influence others.

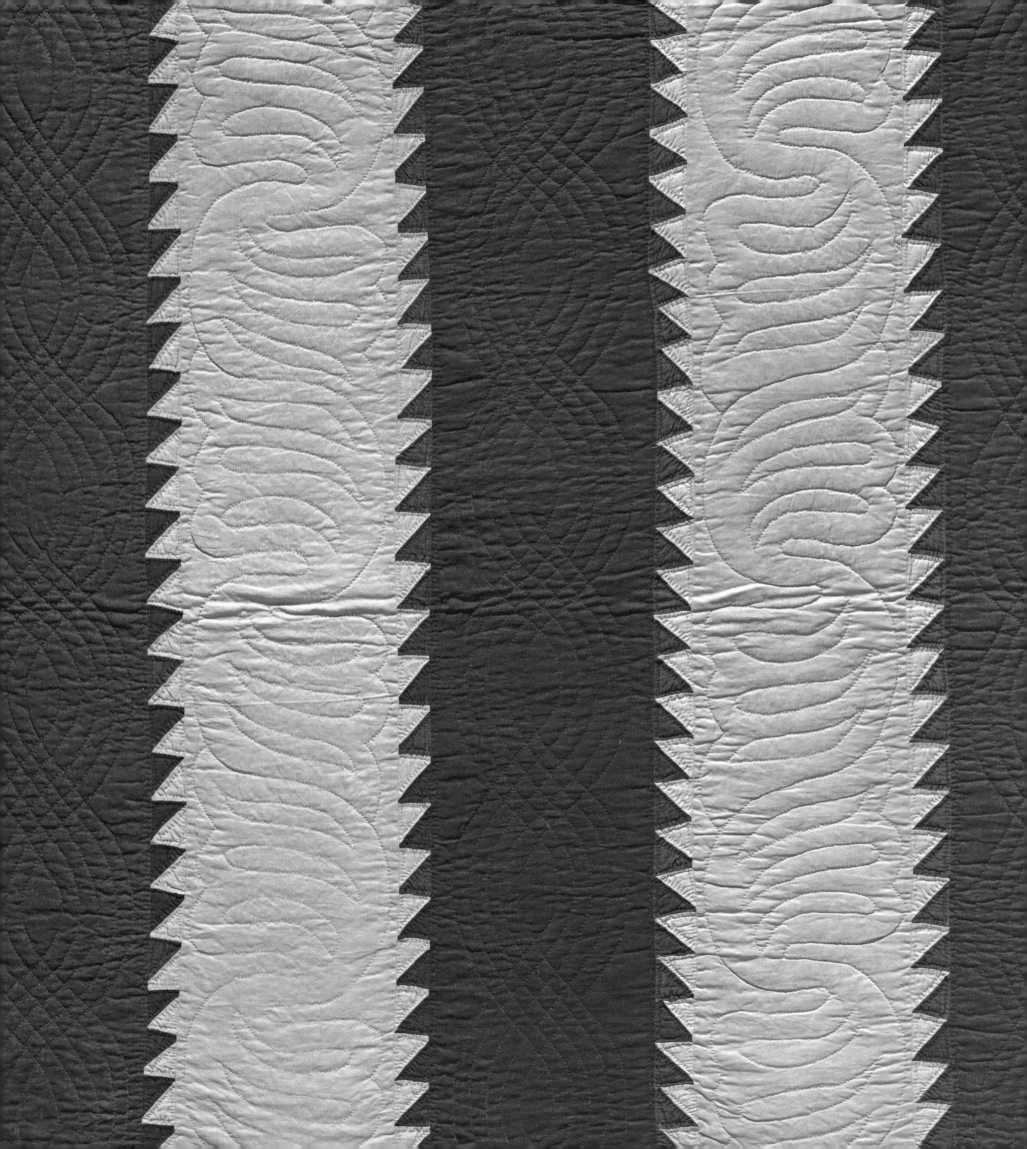

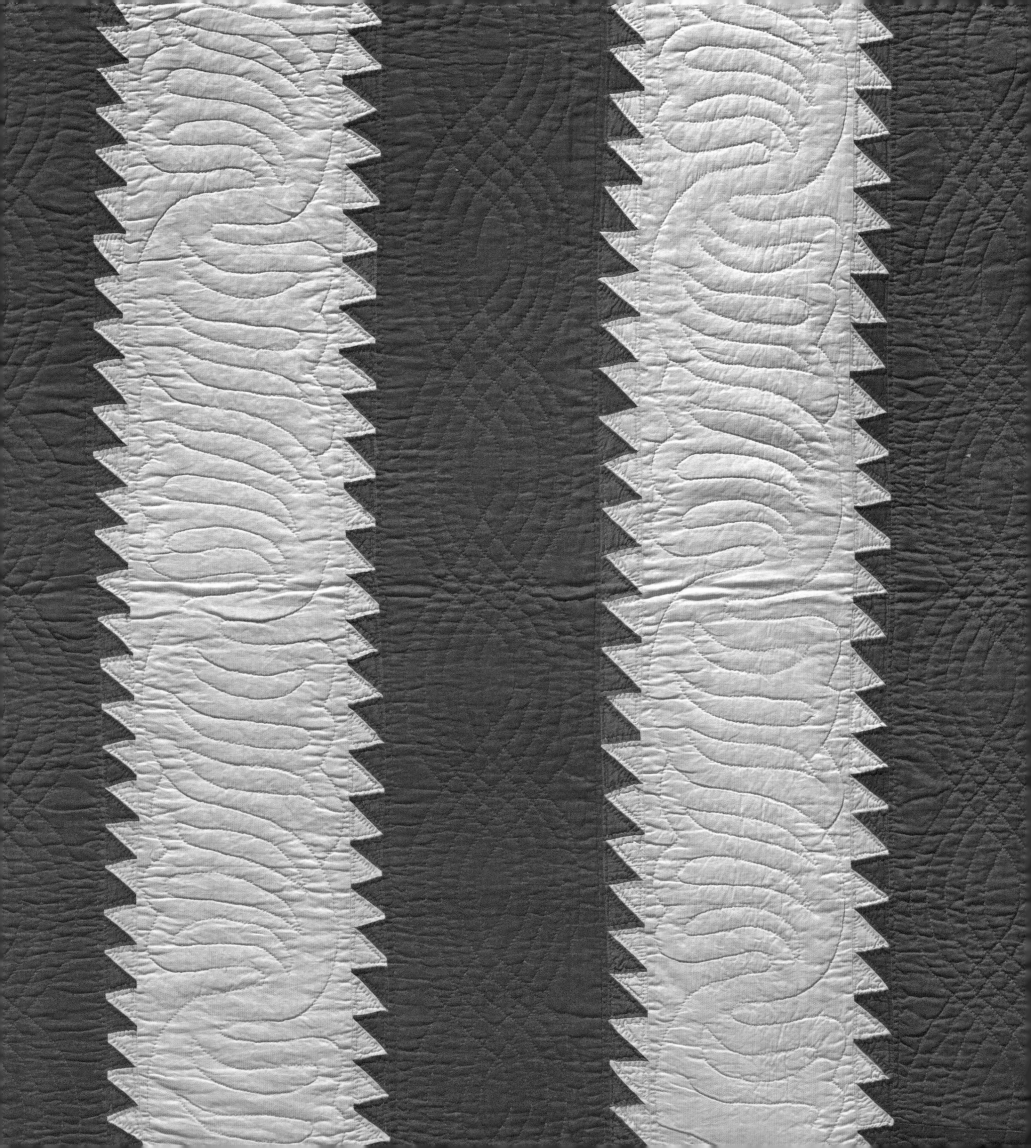

001

SAWTOOTH BARS

CA 1895
AMISCH-MENNONITISCHE QUILTMACHERIN LEAH LANDIS / **AMISH MENNONITE QUILT-MAKER LEAH LANDIS**,
READING, LANCASTER COUNTY, PENNSYLVANIA
BAUMWOLLE / **COTTON** / RÜCKSEITE: BAUMWOLLSTOFF MIT ARABESKENMUSTER /
BACKING: COTTON CLOTH WITH ARABESQUE DESIGN / 206 x 205 CM

Der im 19. Jahrhundert zu datierende Quilt ist zwar in Lancaster County entstanden, aber genau wie der Bars Nr. 3 nicht bei Old Order
Amish, sondern im weniger konservativen amisch-mennonitischen Umfeld. Bisher ist kein zweites Stück dieser Art bekannt. Wo hier Muster
und wo Grund ist, lässt sich nicht entscheiden. Die Fläche setzt sich aus farblich scharf kontrastierenden Bars zusammen, deren Längsränder
dicht an dicht mit kleinen Dreiecken besetzt sind. Da diese „Sägezähne" auf der einen Seite nach oben, auf der anderen nach unten gerichtet
sind, entsteht ein fast flimmernder, sehr lebhafter Effekt. Eine alles umrandende Einfassung gibt es nicht; oben und unten ist der Stoff einfach
auf die Rückseite umgenäht – auch das trägt zum Eindruck von Unkompliziertheit bei. // QUILTING: Flechtbänder, Ranken aus krautigen, an
Akanthus erinnernden Blättern.

Lit. u. a.: Holstein Jonathan, Abstract Design in American Quilts. Louisville/Ken. 1991, 142, Taf. 42 [ähnlicher Sawtooth Bars, „Tree Everlasting" benannt und ca. 1890 datiert]

This quilt, which dates back to the 19th century, was made in Lancaster County, but, as is the case with Bars no. 3, not by Old Order
Amish but was instead created in a less conservative Amish Mennonite environment. To date no second exemplar of this kind is known.
Here there is no distinction between pattern and ground. The field consists of Bars in sharply contrasting color, whose edges are
closely set with small triangles. Since these 'saw teeth' are directed upwards on one side and downwards on the other, the effect
created is almost pulsing, in any case, it is a very lively one. There is no edging enclosing the field; at top and bottom the cloth is simply
sewn to the backing – this feature, too, contributes to creating an impression of simplicity. // QUILTING: cable, foliate sprays reminiscent of Acanthus.

References include: Holstein, Jonathan, Abstract Design in American Quilts. Louisville/Ken. 1991, 142, pl. 42 [similar Sawtooth Bars, called 'Tree Everlasting' and dated
to ca 1890]

002

ZIG ZAG BARS, CRIB QUILT

CA 1900
AMISCH-MENNONITISCHE QUILTMACHERIN DER FAMILIE HAFNER / **AMISH MENNONITE QUILT-MAKER**
FROM THE HAFNER FAMILY, LANCASTER COUNTY, PENNSYLVANIA
BAUMWOLLE / **COTTON** / RÜCKSEITE: VERSCHIEDENE BAUMWOLL-KALIKOS (KATTUN) /
BACKING: VARIOUS CALICOES / 114 x 108 CM

Dieser kleine Quilt für ein Kinderbett stammt wie der Sawtooth Bars Nr. 1 aus einer amisch-mennonitischen Familie in Lancaster County, und auch er ist sehr kühn. Leuchtendes Rot und Grün bilden den expressiven Zickzack – auch Streak of Lightning genannt – im quadratischen Innenfeld. Ein hellgrüner Rahmen fasst es ein; er ist an zwei gegenüberliegenden Seiten bis zum Rand der Fläche verlängert, so dass es keinen durchgängigen Außenrahmen gibt, sondern zwei längere und zwei kürzere Balken – eine ganz ungewöhnliche Variante. Die fast quadratische Decke bekommt damit eine Längsausrichtung. Aber vielleicht lief der Zickzack ja auch quer über das Bettchen. // Die Rückseite besteht aus zwei verschiedenen Stoffen mit kleinem Blüten- bzw. Sternchendekor, die zu Bars verarbeitet sind. // QUILTING: Flechtbänder, Fächer, parallele Zickzacklinien, Dreiecke.

This little quilt for a child's crib came, like the Sawtooth Bars quilt no. 1, from an Amish Mennonite family in Lancaster County, and it, too, is very bold. Glowing red and green form the expressive zigzag pattern – also called Streak of Lightning – in the square inner field. A light green border encloses it; it extends on the two opposite sides to the edge of the field so that there is no continuous outer border but rather two longer and two shorter strips – a highly unusual Bars variant. Although the quilt is virtually square, the decoration makes it look elongated. However, the zigzag may also have run across the crib. // The backing consists of two different types of cloth, printed with small flowers and stars, worked into Bars. // QUILTING: cable, Fans, parallel zigzag lines, triangles.

003

BARS

1910
AMISCH-MENNONITISCHE QUILTMACHERIN DER FAMILIE CHRISTIAN RHIEL / **AMISH MENNONITE QUILT-MAKER**
FROM THE FAMILY OF CHRISTIAN RHIEL, LANCASTER COUNTY, PENNSYLVANIA
BAUMWOLLE / **COTTON** / RÜCKSEITE: GEBLÜMTER BAUMWOLLSTOFF / **BACKING: FLOWER-PRINTED COTTON CLOTH** /
189 x 177 CM

Bei einer Versteigerung 1992 in Lancaster kam dieser eindrucksvolle Bars in neuen Besitz. Quilts der Old Order Amish sehen trotz ähnlicher Elemente ganz anders aus als diejenigen von amisch-mennonitischen Quiltmacherinnen. Bei diesen gibt es nicht das Beharren auf dem Thema Quadrat im Quadrat; die Außenrahmen sind, wenn überhaupt vorhanden, schmaler; häufig wird auf eine farblich abgesetzte Umrandung verzichtet (siehe etwa Nr. 1), und anstelle von feiner Wolle wird Baumwolle bevorzugt – um nur einige Unterschiede zu nennen. // Man kann dieses Beispiel entweder als rote Bars auf grünem Grund sehen oder als rot-grün gestreift. Jedenfalls handelt es sich um ein auffälliges, ungewöhnliches Muster mit seinen vielen schmalen Balken (es sind 25!) und dem flirrenden, springenden Effekt der Komplementärfarben – eine freudige, energiegeladene Ausstrahlung. // QUILTING MIT HELLEM GARN: Flechtbänder, Diagonalgitter.

This impressive Bars quilt changed hands at a Lancaster County auction in 1992. Quilts made by Old Order Amish differ entirely from those made by Amish Mennonite quilt-makers. The latter do not persist in sticking to the square in the square theme. Outer borders are, if present at all, narrower; often a border in a contrasting color is eschewed (see for instance no. 1) and cotton is preferred to fine woolen cloth, just to list a few differences. // This exemplar can be viewed either as red Bars on a green ground or as red and green striped. In any case, this is a stunningly unusual design with all the many narrow bars (twenty-five in all!) and the pulsing, throbbing effect created by the juxtaposition of complementary colors – an aura charged with joyous energy. // QUILTING IN LIGHT-COLORED YARN: cable, diagonal grid.

004

SUNSHINE AND SHADOW

CA 1925
AMISCHE QUILTMACHERIN / **AMISH QUILT-MAKER**, WATERLOO COUNTY, ONTARIO, KANADA
WOLLE, BAUMWOLLE / **WOOL, COTTON** / RÜCKSEITE: WOLLFLANELL MIT GROSSEM
GRÜNSCHWARZEN KARO / **BACKING: WOOL FLANNEL WITH A LARGE, GREENISH BLACK CHECK** /
221 x 217 CM

Auch bei diesem großen farbenprächtigen Quilt ist noch die Ableitung des kleinteiligen Musters aus dem Kompositionsschema der Center Diamonds spürbar. // Der sehr schmale Rahmen des Stückes ist typisch für Quilts aus Mid West und Kanada, und auch das einfache Quilting zeigt, dass die Randzone für wenig bedeutend gehalten wurde. Es wurde sogar auf eine besondere Umrandung verzichtet und stattdessen der Flanell der Rückseite nach vorne umgenäht. // Obwohl das Sunshine and Shadow-Feld aus ziemlich vielen – 33 mal 33 – einzelnen kleinen Stoffquadraten besteht, ist der amische Quilt schlicht (plain), verglichen mit den Stücken der angelsächsischen Nachbarinnen, bei denen es zeitweise fast zum Sport wurde, immer mehr und mehr, ja bis zu Tausende an Stoffstückchen zu verarbeiten. // QUILTING: Diagonalgitter, Diagonalkreuze.

This large, magnificently colored quilt still reveals the derivation of the intricate pattern from the Center Diamonds composition scheme. // The very narrow outer border of this quilt is typical of Midwestern and Canadian quilts; even the simple quilting shows that the border zone was not considered important. In fact, a border as such was eschewed entirely. Instead, the flannel of the backing was turned round the front to form edging. // Although the 'Sunshine and Shadow' field consists of a great many individual small squares of cloth, thirty-three by thirty-three of them, the Amish quilt is plain in comparison to quilts made by the neighboring 'English', who often made a game of working more and more patches, indeed thousands of them, into their quilts. // QUILTING: diagonal diamond grids, diagonal crosses.

005

DOUBLE NINE PATCH

CA 1930
AMISCHE QUILTMACHERIN KATIE FISHER, GEB. STOLTZFUS / **AMISH QUILT-MAKER KATIE FISHER, NÉE STOLTZFUS,**
LANCASTER COUNTY, PENNSYLVANIA
SIGNIERT AUF DER RÜCKSEITE DER EINFASSUNG: KF / **SIGNED ON THE BACK OF THE EDGING: KF**
FEINE WOLLE, BAUMWOLLE / **FINE WOOL, COTTON** / RÜCKSEITE: DUNKELGRAUER BAUMWOLLSTOFF /
BACKING: DARK GRAY COTTON CLOTH / 216 x 213 CM
PROVENIENZ / **PROVENANCE**: DAVID WHEATCROFT, WESTBOROUGH, MASSACHUSETTS

Ein von seiner Macherin signierter Quilt, was bei den Amischen selten vorkommt – und tatsächlich handelt es sich auch in gestalterischer Hinsicht um ein Ausnahmestück. // Die innersten Neuner-Quadrate enthalten allesamt ein Pink, das mit unterschiedlichen Farben – mal mit Rot, mal mit Violett, mal mit Grün usw. – das kleine Schachbrett bildet. Innerhalb der großen Regelmäßigkeit des Musters gibt es eine freie und sehr gekonnte Farbverteilung. Gegenüber den anderen Double Nine Patches der Sammlung Schlumberger besitzt dieser noch eine zusätzliche Komplikation: Katie Fisher hat die Rahmenleiste, die das große Innenfeld umschließt, aus kleinen Diamonds und Dreiecken konstruiert. // In den großen einfarbigen Flächen dominieren Blau und Violett. Dabei sollte man genau hinschauen: Im Außenrahmen besitzt einer der Balken ein etwas helleres Violett als die anderen – möglicherweise sollte er markieren, in welcher Position die Decke auf dem Bett liegen sollte. // Ein bis auf das Quilting identisch gestalteter Quilt, der jedoch offenbar nicht monogrammiert ist, befand sich in der Esprit Collection. Zweifellos war es ein und dieselbe Frau, die beide Quilts fertigte – vermutlich für zwei ihrer Kinder. Anlass für solch prächtige Geschenke waren meist die Hochzeiten der Kinder. // QUILTING: Fruchtkörbe, Kreuzblüten, Dreiecke, Margeriten, Rosetten, Gitterwerk, Diagonalkreuze.

Lit. u. a.: Hughes Robert u. Julie Silber, Quilts. Die Kunst der Amischen. Schaffhausen u. a. 1990, Taf. 68 [Vergleichsstück der Esprit Collection]

A quilt signed by its maker is a rarity among the Amish – and indeed even the design of this quilt is exceptional. // The inmost Nine Patch squares all contain a pink that, combined with various other colors, such as red, purple, green, etc., forms the little chessboard. Within the overall regularity of the pattern, there is a free, highly effective distribution of color. Compared to the other Double Nine Patches in the Schlumberger Collection, this one boasts an additional distinctive touch: Katie Fisher constructed the border enclosing the large inner field of small Diamonds and triangles. // Blue and purple are the dominant colors in the large monochrome fields. However, look closely: one of the strips of the outer frame is of a somewhat lighter purple than the others – it may have been intended to mark the position in which the bedcover was to lie on a bed. // There was a quilt of identical design, except for the quilting, in the Esprit Collection. It was, however, apparently not monogrammed. The same woman undoubtedly made both quilts – presumably for two of her children. Such magnificent quilts were usually made as wedding gifts when sons and daughters married. // QUILTING: fruit baskets, Starflowers, triangles, daisies, rosettes, waffle grids, diagonal crosses.

References include: Hughes, Robert and Silber, Julie, Amish. The Art of the Quilt. New York 1990, no. 68 with illustration [piece for comparison from the Esprit Collection]

006

LOG CABIN – STRAIGHT FURROW

CA 1920
AMISCHE QUILTMACHERIN KATHY LAPP / **AMISH QUILT-MAKER KATHY LAPP**, LANCASTER COUNTY, PENNSYLVANIA
WOLLE / **WOOL** / RÜCKSEITE: KARIERTE BAUMWOLLE / **BACKING: CHECKED COTTON** / 199 x 178 CM

Bei Kelims und Orientteppichen spricht man von Abrasch, wenn innerhalb einer Farbe Abweichungen durch die Verwendung von Wolle aus verschiedenen Farbbädern auftreten. Einen Abrasch haben auch die „geraden Ackerfurchen" dieses Quilts, der dadurch große Lebendigkeit gewinnt. // Es heißt, dass beim Typus Log Cabin die Blockhütte – jene amerikanische „Urhütte" in der Wildnis – in stilisierter Weise dargestellt sei und dass das kleine rote Quadrat die Feuerstelle als Zentrum des Hauses symbolisiere. Hier sind jedoch die schmalen länglichen Stoffstreifen, die das – auf die Spitze gestellte – Quadrat der Blockhütte bilden, farblich so geordnet, dass eine Hälfte schwarz, die andere farbig ist und breite, gerade Streifen entstehen. // Sehr ungewöhnlich ist es, diese rahmenlose Variante des Musters bei Amischen in Lancaster County zu finden, die sonst Quilts mit großem zentralem Motiv (medallion-style quilts) bevorzugen. Dennoch: Gemusterte Stoffe als Rückseite, so wie hier, tauchen fast nur bei Lancaster-Quilts auf. Zum Vergleich etwa Seite 15: ein Kinderquilt, bei dem das Log Cabin-Feld zentralisiert, in die Mitte eines breiten Rahmens gesetzt wurde.

Applied to kelims and Oriental carpets, the term 'abrash' signifies aberrations in color occurring when wool has been used from different dye lots. The 'Straight Furrows' of this quilt also reveal abrash, which is what makes it so vivid. // As the story goes, the Log Cabin type is a stylized representation of that very structure – the American 'primal dwelling' in the wilderness – and the little red square symbolized the hearth as the center of the house. Here, however, the narrow elongated strips of cloth, which form – placed on end – the square ground-plan of the Log Cabin, have been arranged by color so that one half is black, the other in color and broad, straight stripes have been thus created. // It is highly unusual to find this unedged variant of the pattern among Lancaster County Amish, who otherwise prefer quilts with a large central motif (medallion-style quilts). Still, patterned materials as backing, as on this quilt, appear almost exclusively on Lancaster quilts. Compare, for instance, page 15: a Crib quilt on which the Log Cabin field is centralized and set in the center of a broad frame.

007

CENTER DIAMOND / DIAMOND IN THE SQUARE

CA 1925
AMISCHE QUILTMACHERIN BARBARA EBERSOL / **AMISH QUILT-MAKER BARBARA EBERSOL**, GORDONVILLE,
LANCASTER COUNTY, PENNSYLVANIA
WOLLE / **WOOL** / RÜCKSEITE: BAUMWOLLE / **BACKING: COTTON** / 196 x 193 CM

Bei angelsächsischen Quilterinnen waren Dekore mit großem zentralem Motiv (central medallion) bereits in Mode gewesen und schon längst wieder „out", als amische Frauen den Typus aufgriffen – eine charakteristische Verzögerung, ein absichtliches Sichunterscheidenwollen von den „Englischen" und ihren weltlichen Gepflogenheiten. In der Folge wurde Diamond in the Square mit seinen zahllosen Varianten zum bedeutendsten gestalterischen Thema der Amischen in Lancaster County. // Das lässt sich gut nachvollziehen, wenn man die Beispiele in der Sammlung Schlumberger nach steigender Komplexität ordnet und etwa die einfachere Nr. 11 dem hier abgebildeten Stück gegenüberstellt. Die nächste Stufe wären die Quilts 28, 32 oder 62: immer mehr Rahmen und Eckquadrate. Das bedeutet aber nicht unbedingt eine chronologische Abfolge – bei den genannten Arbeiten handelt es sich durchweg nicht um sehr frühe Quilts; auch Nr. 9 – ohne Eckquadrate – gehört zeitlich in diese Gruppe. // Bei den Quilts 7, 11 und 32 zeigen sich aber auch sehr reizvolle verschiedene Lösungen der Komposition mit einem roten Diamond. Barbara Ebersol ordnet farblich die kleinen und großen Eckquadrate dem zentralen Motiv zu, das allerdings ein etwas anderes Rot besitzt. // QUILTING: Federranken, umrankte Herzen, kleine Herzen, Kreuzblüten-Rauten-Leiste, Rosetten; innen: dreifacher Federkranz, geometrische Blüten aus einander überschneidenden Kreisen, Gitterwerk.

Among 'English' American quilt-makers, decorations featuring a large central motif (central medallion) had already come into fashion and were long since 'out' again by the time Amish women adopted the type – a characteristic time lapse, a deliberate act of distinguishing themselves from the 'English' and their worldly habits. The upshot was that the 'Diamond in the Square' and countless variants of it became the most important design theme used by the Amish in Lancaster County. // This can be easily traced if the examples in the Schlumberger Collection are arranged in order of growing complexity and the somewhat simpler no. 11 is compared to the piece shown here. The next step would be represented by nos. 28, 32 and 62: increasingly more borders and square corner fields. Order of complexity, however, does not necessarily imply chronological order – none of the works mentioned in this connection are very early quilts; even no. 9 – without corner blocks – belongs chronologically to this group. // Quilts 7, 11 and 32, however, reveal various very attractive solutions to the composition with a red Diamond. Barbara Ebersol has assigned the same color to the small and large corner blocks and the central motif, which, however, is of a somewhat different red. // QUILTING: feather scrolls, hearts in scrolls, small hearts, Starflower-lozenge strip, rosettes; inner field: triple feather wreath, geometric flowers of intersecting circles, waffle grid.

008

SUNSHINE AND SHADOW – FLOATING

CA 1920
AMISCHE QUILTMACHERIN DER FAMILIE LAPP / **AMISH QUILT-MAKER FROM THE LAPP FAMILY**,
LANCASTER COUNTY, PENNSYLVANIA
WOLLE, BAUMWOLLE / **WOOL, COTTON** / RÜCKSEITE: GEBLÜMTER BAUMWOLLSTOFF /
BACKING: FLOWER-PRINTED COTTON CLOTH / 198 x 196 CM

Die sehr konservativen Lancaster-Amischen konzentrierten sich beim Muster-Repertoire ihrer Quilts auf relativ wenige Motive, darunter Sunshine and Shadow als eines der beliebtesten. Innerhalb des strengen Kanons waren jedoch zahlreiche Variationen möglich. Hier ein „Floating Sunshine and Shadow" (vgl. den Floating Diamond Nr. 9). Der sehr breit dimensionierte Außenrahmen besitzt keine Eckquadrate, und so hat das Quadratfeld gleichsam Raum zum Atmen. Frei und ruhig schwebt es mit seinem dunkelblauen Rahmen auf der intensiv leuchtenden roten Fläche. // Die Quilterin hat sich bei ihrem Farbkonzept für das Innenfeld noch etwas Besonders überlegt. Die schrägen Reihen sind nicht immer durchgängig in einer Farbe (im Unterschied etwa zu Nrn. 60 oder 63); so markieren zum Beispiel hellere Stückchen die Spitzen des gedachten Rhombus. Auch sonst gibt es hier und da leichte Abweichungen – ein graues Quadrat in einer blauen Reihe usw. Kein Zweifel: Hier wurden – dafür bietet sich das Muster ja an – Stoffreste verwendet, aber mit welcher Raffinesse wurden sie komponiert. Ganz sicher verstärkt dies die besonders lebendige Ausstrahlung dieses Stückes. // QUILTING: Rosenranken, zwei verschiedene Blattranken mit Blüten, Diagonalkreuze.

In the design repertory they used for their quilts, very conservative Lancaster Amish concentrated on relatively few motifs, including Sunshine and Shadow, which was one of the most popular. Within this stringent canon, however, numerous variants were possible. Here we have a 'Floating Sunshine and Shadow' (cf. the Floating Diamond no. 9). The very broad outer border boasts no corner blocks so the square field has, as it were, enough space to breathe. Free and calm, it floats with its dark blue border on the intensely glowing red field. // The quilt-maker thought up something special indeed for her color concept in the inner field. The diagonal rows are not all in a single color throughout (in this unlike nos. 60 and 63, for example); lighter-colored patches mark the corners of the rhombus as planned. Here and there other slight aberrations occur – a gray square in a blue row, etc. No doubt about it: here – the design is made for it – scraps of material were used but combined with stunning sophistication. This feature definitely enhances the particularly lively aura of this piece. // QUILTING: rose scrolls, two different foliate scrolls with flowers; diagonal crosses.

009

FLOATING DIAMOND

CA 1920
AMISCHE QUILTMACHERIN / **AMISH QUILT-MAKER**, LANCASTER COUNTY, PENNSYLVANIA
WOLLE / **WOOL** / RÜCKSEITE: KLEIN GEMUSTERTER BAUMWOLLSTOFF / **BACKING: COTTON CLOTH**
WITH SMALL PATTERNS / 200 x 200 CM

Viele der Center Diamond-Quilts aus Lancaster County beschränken sich auf nur drei Farben, aber welche Fülle an Kompositionsmöglichkeiten die amischen Quiltmacherinnen dieser vermeintlichen Einengung abgewannen, zeigen die Beispiele dieses Typus in der Sammlung Schlumberger, unter anderem Nrn. 11, 17, 25, 59. // Keineswegs immer besitzen Außenrahmen und der Diamond im Zentrum dieselbe Farbe – hier (wie bei Nrn. 32 und 33) ist es so. Floating Diamond bedeutet, dass keine Eckquadrate das zentrale Motiv auf der großen Fläche verankern. Ganz vorne und ganz präsent wirken die tiefroten Innenrahmen und die dunkelblauen Dreieckflächen zwischen ihnen. Der Effekt ist, als ginge der Blick durch ein blau-rot gerahmtes, rautenförmiges Fenster in malvenfarbene Weiten. // Wie meist bei Lancaster-Quilts ist die Einfassung relativ breit und besitzt eine andere Farbe als der Außenrahmen, so dass der Rand betont wird. Ist die eine Ausbesserung Zufall? Oder ein absichtlicher „Fehler", um die Perfektion dieses Stückes zu mildern? // AUFWÄNDIGES QUILTING: Federranken, Rosetten, Weinranken, Tulpen-Rosen-Zweige; innen: Federkranz, Palmetten; großer achtzackiger Stern, kleine sechszackige Sterne, Palmetten.

Many Center Diamond quilts from Lancaster County are limited to only three colors but the wealth of composition possibilities available to Amish women who made quilts despite this supposed constraint is shown by examples of this type in the Schlumberger Collection, inter alia nos. 11, 17, 25, 59. // The outer border and the Diamond at the center are certainly not always the same color – here (as in nos. 32 and 33), however, it happens to be the case. Floating Diamond means that there are no corner squares to anchor the central motif on the large field. The deep red inner border and the dark blue triangular fields between them appear right at the front and are vibrant indeed. The effect achieved is as if one's glance were going through a lozenge-shaped window framed in blue and red into a mauve vastness of space. // As in most Lancaster quilts, the border is relatively broad and is of color different to that of the outer border, one that emphasizes the border. Is the repair accidental? Or was it an intentional 'mistake' to alleviate the perfection of this piece? // ELABORATE QUILTING: feather scrolls, vines, roses and tulips; inner field: feather wreath, palmettes; large Eight-Pointed Star, small Six-Pointed Star, palmettes.

010

BARS

CA 1939/40
AMISCHE QUILTMACHERIN CELINA BEILER / **AMISH QUILT-MAKER CELINA BEILER**, LANCASTER COUNTY, PENNSYLVANIA
WOLLE / **WOOL** / RÜCKSEITE: BLAUER BAUMWOLLSTOFF / **BACKING: BLUE COTTON CLOTH** / 204 x 200 CM

Dieser edle, strenge Quilt, den eine Frau namens Celina Beiler gemacht haben soll, ist zwar nicht komplizierter aufgebaut als das sicher viel
frühere Stück Nr. 44 – im Gegenteil –, besitzt aber völlig andere Proportionen zwischen Außenrahmen, Innenfeld und den Balken. Auch hier
dominiert wie bei dem schlichteren, frühen Floating Bars Nr. 12 ein Farbakkord aus Rot- und Brauntönen. Jedoch ist das Rot intensiver, und
es tritt eine weitere Farbe hinzu, ein Beigeton. Dass er abwechselnd mit dem Rot für die Bars verwendet wurde, verleiht dem Zentrum star-
ke Leuchtkraft. // Wie bei allen Bars kommt das Quilting hier besonders gut zur Geltung: Federranken, Herzen, Bogenborten, Gitterwerk.

Lit. u. a.: [Kat. Ausst.] Abstraktion und Farbe. Die Kunst der Amischen: Quilts der Sammlung Ziegler. Die Neue Sammlung. München 1991, 48–49 (m. Abb.)

This nobly austere quilt, said to have been made by a woman named Celina Beiler, may not be more complex in composition than no. 44,
which is surely a much earlier piece – quite the contrary, in fact – but boasts entirely different proportions between outer border, inner
field and bars. Here, too, as in the simpler, early Floating Bars, no. 12, a color accord of reds and browns is dominant. However, the
red is more intense and another color has been added, a shade of beige. Used alternately with red for the bars, it lends the center a
vibrant glow. // As is the case with all Bar-patterned quilts, the quilting shows up especially well here: feather scrolls, hearts, scallop,
waffle grid.

References include: [Exhib. cat.] Abstraktion und Farbe. Die Kunst der Amischen: Quilts der Sammlung Ziegler. Die Neue Sammlung. Munich 1991, 48–49 (with illus.)

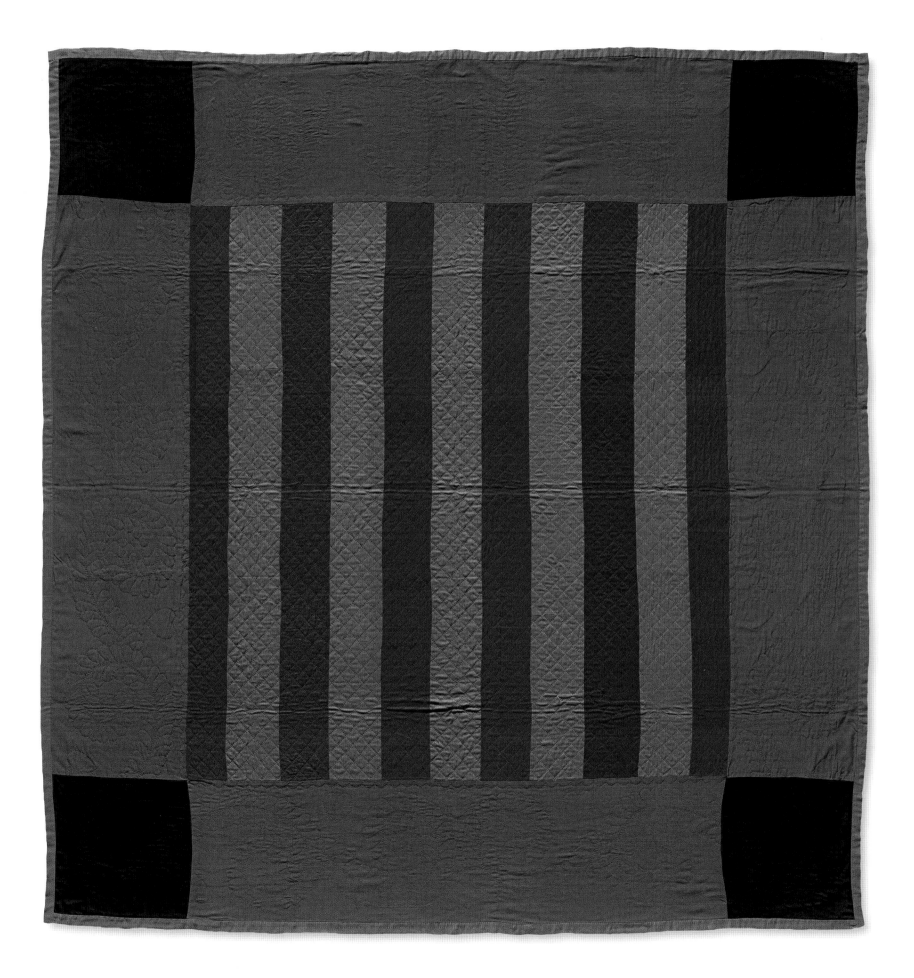

011

CENTER DIAMOND / DIAMOND IN THE SQUARE

CA 1930
AMISCHE QUILTMACHERIN DER FAMILIE LAPP / **AMISH QUILT-MAKER FROM THE LAPP FAMILY**, LANCASTER COUNTY, PENNSYLVANIA
WOLLE / **WOOL** / RÜCKSEITE: BLAUWEISS MELIERTE BAUMWOLLE / **BACKING: BLUE-AND-WHITE MOTTLED COTTON** / 200 x 195 CM

Satte Farben sind charakteristisch für klassische Quilts aus Lancaster County. Der prächtige Zusammenklang von Dunkelrot und Violett dominiert dieses Stück; eher selten ist der Olivton der Balken im Außenrahmen. So entsteht der Eindruck einer doch ungewöhnlichen, sehr strengen Farbkomposition. Im Zentrum steht in leuchtendem Rot der Diamond, der ja stets ein auf die Spitze gestelltes Quadrat ist; der Innenrahmen und die Ecken des Außenrahmens zeigen dieselbe Farbe: Variationen zum Thema Rotes Quadrat. Die Einfassung greift das Violett des Innenfeldes auf und gibt der Komposition noch einmal zusätzlichen Halt. // REICHES QUILTING: Federranken, Fruchtkörbe, Rosen-Tulpen-Zweige, Kreuzblüten-Rauten-Leiste; innen: Federkranz, sechszackiger Stern, Rosenzweige.

Saturated colors are characteristic of classical Lancaster County quilts. The magnificent accord of dark red and purple dominates this piece; the olive shade of the strips forming the outer borders is quite rare. Thus the impression of an unusual, startlingly stringent color composition is created. At the center stands the Diamond, which is always a square standing on one corner, in glowing red; the inner border and the corners of the outer border boast the same color: variations on the red square theme. The border takes up the purple of the inner field, thus additionally anchoring the composition. // RICH QUILTING: **feather scrolls, baskets, roses and tulips, Starflower-lozenge strip; inner field: feather wreath, Six-Pointed Star, rose sprays.**

012

BARS

CA 1910
AMISCHE QUILTMACHERIN DER FAMILIE LAPP / **AMISH QUILT-MAKER FROM THE LAPP FAMILY**,
LANCASTER COUNTY, PENNSYLVANIA
WOLLE / **WOOL** / RÜCKSEITE: GRAU KARIERTER BAUMWOLLSTOFF /
BACKING: GREEN CHECKED COTTON CLOTH / 185 x 177 CM
PROVENIENZ / **PROVENANCE**: DAVID WHEATCROFT, WESTBOROUGH, MASSACHUSETTS

Lancaster-County-Quilts sind meist quadratisch oder annähernd quadratisch und besitzen durchweg den gleichen Aufbau: Um ein quadratisches Innenfeld legt sich ein sehr breiter Rahmen, der von einer fast immer andersfarbigen Einfassung umrandet wird. Während das Innenfeld bei den Center Diamonds ein auf die Spitze gestelltes Quadrat aufnimmt, gliedert es sich bei den Bars in breite, parallele Balken von ungerader Zahl (meist sieben), die sich farblich abwechseln. Großflächigkeit herrscht vor, und es sind große geometrische Stücke Stoff, die dies ermöglichen – mit Resteverwertung oder Recycling gebrauchter Textilien wie bei Fleckerlteppichen hat das nichts zu tun. // Dieses Objekt ist ein Floating Bars, denn das Innenquadrat sitzt ohne Eckstücke in dem braunen Rahmen, den eine schwarze Einfassung umrandet. Die wenigen, gedeckten Farben, die Proportionen und die Schlichtheit weisen auf eine frühe Entstehung hin. Ein Quilt von verhaltener Kraft, perfekter Ausgewogenheit und großem Ernst. Mit dem Ausdruck „schlicht" ist ein zentraler Wert der Amischen überhaupt angesprochen. // Zur Herkunft der Quiltmacherin aus einer Familie Lapp sollte bedacht werden, dass es unter den Amischen allein rund 2000 Personen mit dem Namen Lapp gibt, wie übrigens auch Tausende von Riehls oder sogar etwa 4000 namens Stolzfuß in den verschiedensten Schreibweisen. // QUILTING: Federranken, Diagonalgitter.

Lancaster County quilts are usually square, or almost square, and always feature the same composition: a very broad border, which is almost invariably framed by a border in a different color, surrounds a square inner field. Whereas the inner field of Center Diamond quilts is occupied by a square tilted to stand on a corner, the inner field of Bars quilts is articulated by an uneven number (usually seven) of broad, parallel strips in alternating colors. Spaciousness predominates and large, geometric blocks of material are what make this possible – unlike the technique used for patchwork quilts, this has nothing to do with using up or recycling scraps. // This object is a Floating Bars since the inner square sits without corner blocks in the brown frame with a black border. The limited use of subdued colors, the proportions and the plainness of this quilt suggest an early date. A quilt of restrained power, perfect harmony and great seriousness. The word 'plain' designates a value that is pivotal to the Amish. // As to the origin of the maker from a family surnamed Lapp, it should be borne in mind that there are some two thousand people among the Amish bearing the name Lapp just as there are thousands of Riehls, by the way, or even four thousand Amish surnamed Stolzfuß, spelt in many different ways. // QUILTING: feather scrolls, diagonal grid.

013

SUNSHINE DIAMOND

CA 1935
AMISCHE QUILTMACHERIN / **AMISH QUILT-MAKER**, LANCASTER COUNTY, PENNSYLVANIA
VERSCHIEDENE WOLLSTOFFE / **VARIOUS WOOL FABRICS** / RÜCKSEITE: VERSCHIEDENE SCHWARZE STOFFE /
BACKING: VARIOUS BLACK FABRICS / 220 x 222 CM

Verboten sind bei den Amischen zwar gemusterte Stoffe, nicht aber kräftige oder leuchtende Farben, und so tauchen diese nicht nur in den Kleidern der Frauen auf, sondern auch in den Quilts, die aus den gleichen Stoffen gemacht werden. // Mit ihrer Komposition würde diese Variante eines Diamond in the Square am Ende einer Reihe ansteigender Komplexität stehen, die mit einem Floating Diamond (Nr. 9) beginnt oder gar mit einem ganz einfachen Center Square, bei dem in der Mitte des großen Quadrats der ganzen Bettdecke ein quadratisches Innenfeld sitzt, das ein schmaler Rahmen umfasst. Im nächsten Schritt kommen Eckquadrate dazu, dann im Zentrum ein auf die Spitze gestelltes Quadrat (der Diamond), ein weiterer Rahmen etc. Hier ist der zentrale Diamond darüber hinaus mit dem Sunshine and Shadow-Motiv gefüllt – eine Kombination, die bei Lancaster-Amischen nicht allzu oft vorkommt. Genauer gesagt handelt es sich um eine Variante mit den Namen Trip around the world (oder: Grandmother's Dream, siehe auch Nrn. 22, 24), bei der die kleinen Quadrate nicht auf der Seite stehen, sondern auf der Spitze. Umschlossen ist dieses farblich geradezu pulsierende Zentrum von Felderungen und Rahmungen in ungewöhnlich vielen Farben, nämlich acht. // QUILTING: einander überkreuzende Federranken, Blattstab, Kreuzblüten, Diagonalkreuze, Diagonalgitter.

Patterned fabrics are forbidden to the Amish but not powerful or glowing colors; consequently they appear not just in women's clothing but also in quilts made from the same materials. // The composition of this variant of the Diamond in the Square would rank at the end of a series arranged in order of complexity, one that began with a Floating Diamond (no. 9) or even with a very simple Center Square: at the center of the large square field that comprises the entire quilt is a square inner field, framed by a narrow border. In the next step, corner squares were added, then, at the center, a square set on one corner (the Diamond), another border, etc. Moreover, here the central Diamond is filled with the 'Sunshine and Shadow' motif – a combination not all that frequently encountered in Lancaster County Amish quilts. More precisely, this is a variant, called 'Trip around the World' (or: 'Grandmother's Dream'; see also nos. 22, 24) among non-Amish, in which the small squares rest on a corner rather than on a side. Apart from the throbbing color of the core, this design allows for the unusual quantity of eight colors on the outside as well. // QUILTING: intersecting feather scrolls, Aron's rod, Star-flowers, diagonal crosses, diagonal grid.

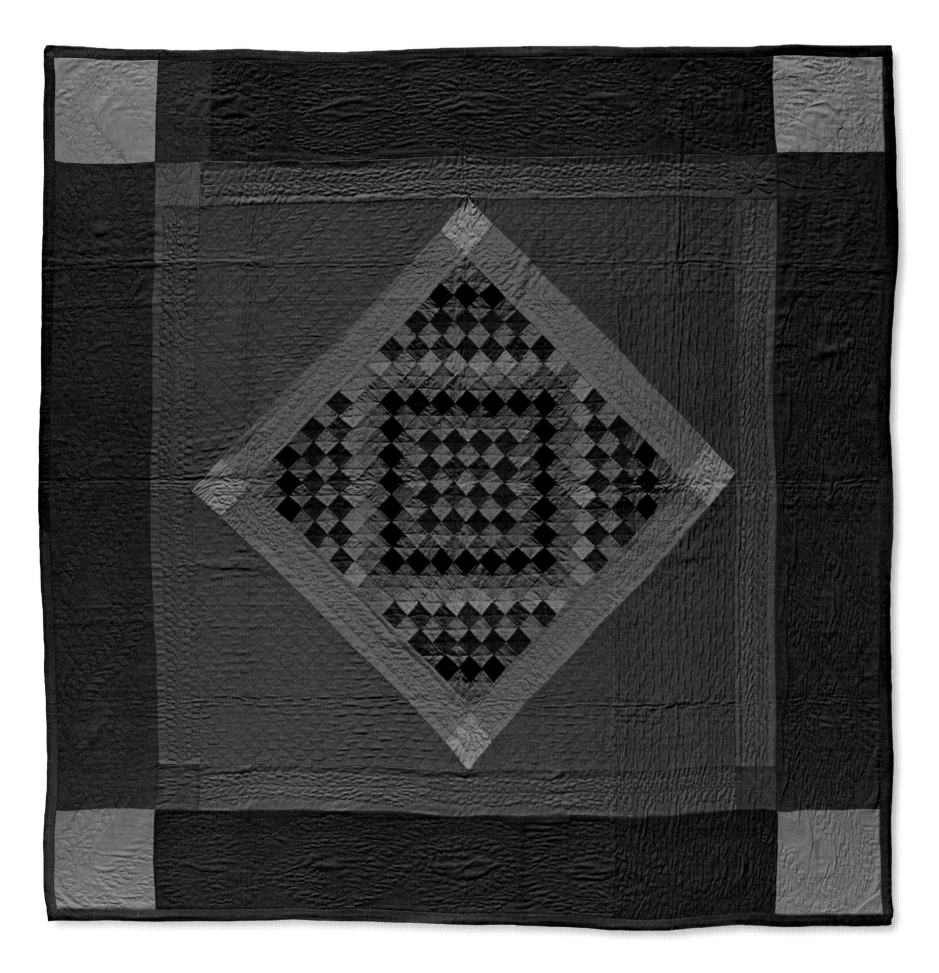

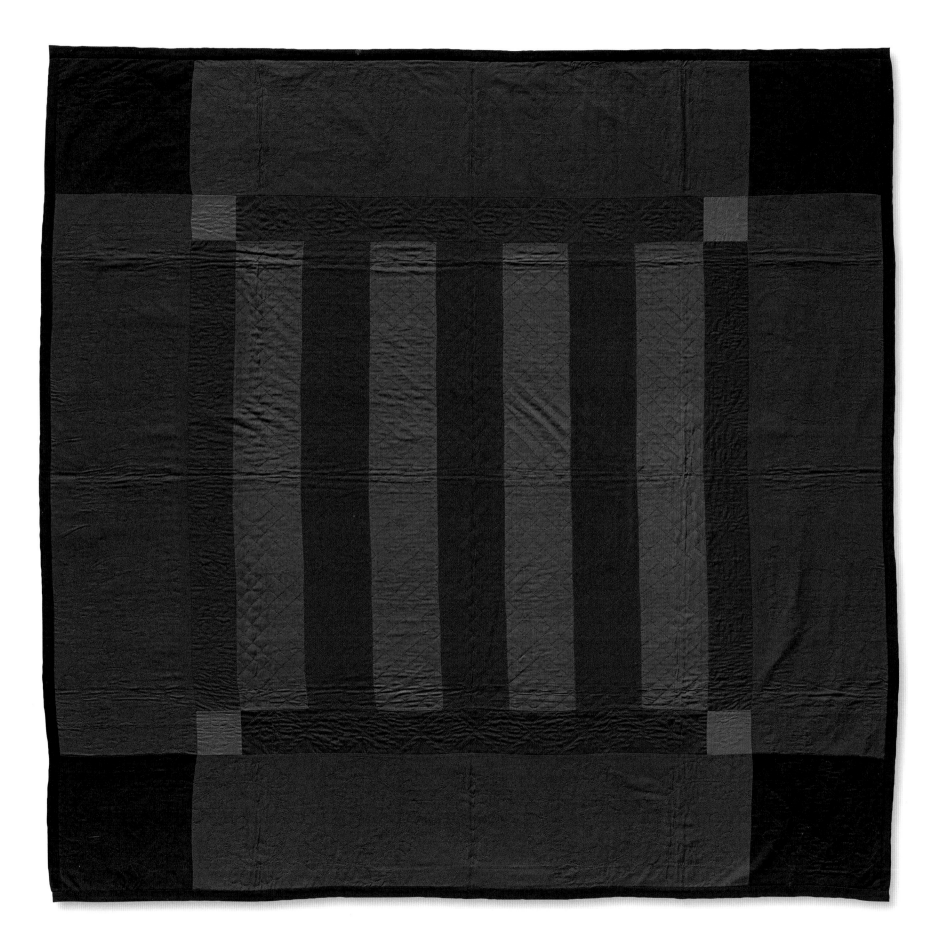

014

BARS

CA 1930
AMISCHE QUILTMACHERIN DER FAMILIE ENOS BEILER / **AMISH QUILT-MAKER FROM THE FAMILY OF ENOS BEILER**, BIRD IN HAND, LANCASTER COUNTY, PENNSYLVANIA
WOLLE / **WOOL** / RÜCKSEITE: BLAUER BAUMWOLLSTOFF / **BACKING: BLUE COTTON CLOTH** / 192 x 192 CM

Aus derselben Ortschaft, Bird in Hand, kommt auch der Center Diamond Nr. 59 – ein reizvoller Vergleich, zumal wohl beide Stücke etwa zur selben Zeit entstanden sein dürften. Ungewöhnlich viele, nämlich sieben Farben verwendete die Gestalterin des Bars: vom Schwarz für die Einfassung bis zu Rosarot. Die raffinierte Abstufung der Farben mit Mut zum grellen Akzent – die kleinen Eckquadrate, die wie Edelsteine herausblitzen – unterscheidet die Wirkung dieses gut proportionierten Quilts allerdings grundlegend von Nr. 59. // QUILTING: Federranken, federumrankte Herzen, Kreuzblüten-Rauten-Leiste, Rosetten, Diagonalgitter.

The Center Diamond no. 59 came from the same hamlet as this quilt: Bird in Hand – an apt comparison since the two pieces are probably of the same date. The artist used an unusual number of colors, seven in all: ranging from black for the border to pink. However, the sophisticated gradation of the colors, enhanced by boldly shrill touches – the little corner blocks that dazzle like gems – make in this beautifully proportioned quilt an impact that differs radically from the effect created by no. 59. // QUILTING: feather scrolls, hearts surrounded by feathers, Starflower-lozenge strip, rosettes, diagonal grid.

015

NINE PATCH

CA 1920
AMISCHE QUILTMACHERIN DER FAMILIE STOLTZFUS / **AMISH QUILT-MAKER FROM THE STOLTZFUS FAMILY**,
LANCASTER COUNTY, PENNSYLVANIA
WOLLE, BAUMWOLLE / **WOOL, COTTON** / RÜCKSEITE: BAUMWOLLE / **BACKING: COTTON** / 190 x 195 CM

Während Sunshine and Shadow wie Center Square und Center Diamond zentriert ist, handelt es sich bei Nine Patch um ein Reihenmuster, genauer: um eine Art Schachbrett. Allerdings ist es der Quiltmacherin bei diesem Objekt gelungen, durch die Farbkomposition die Mitte hervorzuheben, denn hier besitzen die Stoffstückchen ein anderes Rot und ein helles Grün, und auch die leeren Diamonds haben einen anderen Farbton. Ansonsten wechseln sich wie in Nr. 23 einfarbige Quadrate mit solchen ab, die aus neun kleinen Quadraten in zwei Farben bestehen, nur dass sie hier auf die Spitze gestellt sind – eine sehr beliebte Variante. // Frei, ohne Rahmen und ohne Eckquadrate schwebt die Innenfläche auf dem Blau, das eine ziemlich breite Einfassung besitzt. Ihr Rot antwortet dem Rot der Nine Patches – zusammen mit Grün- und Violettönen ein freudiger Farbklang. // Üblicherweise bestehen Pennsylvania-Quilts immer aus Wolle, meist sogar einer sehr feinen Qualität; dass hier Baumwolle verwendet wird, ist eine Ausnahme. // QUILTING: breites Flechtband, Blumenkörbe, achtzackige Sterne, Diagonalkreuze.

Whereas Sunshine and Shadow, Center Square and Center Diamond are centered, Nine Patch is a row pattern, more precisely: a sort of checkerboard. However, the maker of this object has succeeded in emphasizing the center by means of the color composition. Here the little blocks are in a different red and light green and the empty Diamonds are of a different tone. Otherwise, monochrome squares alternate with squares made up of nine small squares in two colors, as in no. 23, except that they rest on their corners – a very popular variant. // Without a border and devoid of corner blocks, the inner field floats free on the blue, which boasts quite a broad border. Its red corresponds to the red of the Nine Patches – together with greens and purples a joyous color note. // Pennsylvania quilts are almost always made of woolen cloth, usually of very fine quality; that cotton cloth was used here is the exception, not the rule. // QUILTING: broad cable, flower baskets, Eight-Pointed Stars, diagonal crosses.

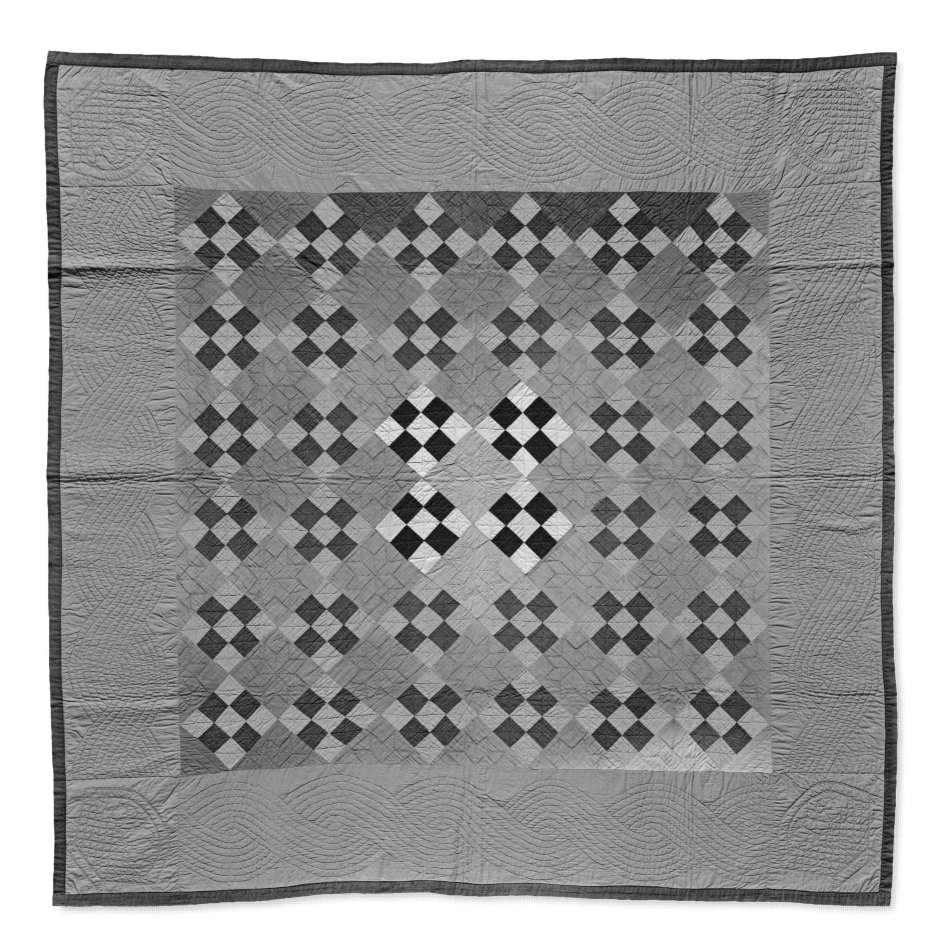

016

CENTER DIAMOND / DIAMOND IN THE SQUARE

CA 1895
AMISCHE QUILTMACHERIN / **AMISH QUILT-MAKER**, LANCASTER COUNTY, PENNSYLVANIA
WOLLE „HENRIETTA" / **WOOL 'HENRIETTA'** / RÜCKSEITE: KLEIN GEMUSTERTER BAUMWOLLSTOFF /
BACKING: COTTON CLOTH WITH A SMALL PRINT / 191 x 193 CM

Noch im 19. Jahrhundert könnte dieser Quilt entstanden sein. Sein perfekter Erhaltungszustand beweist, in welch hohem Maße seinen früheren Besitzern die herausragende Qualität bewusst war. Sicher wurde der Quilt im Dunkeln aufbewahrt und nur zu seltenen, festlichen
Anlässen ans Licht geholt – etwa zum Gottesdienst, der ja reihum in den Häusern einer Gemeinde abgehalten wurde. An die Öffentlichkeit
kam er, als er bei einer Benefizveranstaltung zugunsten bedürftiger amischer Familien versteigert wurde. // Die Farben wie auch die Komposition erinnern an den ebenfalls sehr frühen Center Diamond Nr. 25: ein lichtes Blau, das wie bei jenem das Innenfeld über die Diagonalen
mit dem Außenrahmen verbindet; Grün, hier nicht außen, sondern im Innenrahmen; und Rot. Raffinierterweise sind es zwei leicht differieren-
de Rottöne. Der dunklere nimmt das Zentrum ein, der leuchtendere bildet die Balken des Außenrahmens. Eine äußerst intensive, festliche
Ausstrahlung. // SEHR AUFWÄNDIGES QUILTING: Federranken, Bogenborten, Kreuzblüten-Rauten-Leiste, sechszackige Sterne, Diagonalgitter;
innen: Federkranz, achtzackiger Stern, geometrisches Blütenmuster aus einander überschneidenden Kreisen.
Die feine Wollqualität, die die Lancaster-Amischen für Sonntagsquilts wie diesen bevorzugten, wurde von ihnen als „Henrietta" bezeichnet (auch Nr. 31)

This quilt may have been made as far back as the 19th century. Its perfect condition proves how well aware its earlier owners were
of its outstanding quality. The quilt must have been kept in the dark and only rarely taken out into the light of day on festive occasions
– for instance, for divine service, which was held at a different house of a congregation each Sunday. This quilt first attracted public
notice when it was sold off at a benefit auction held in aid of needy Amish families. // The colors and the composition are reminiscent
of those of Center Diamond no. 25, another very early quilt: light blue that, as in no. 25, links the inner field via the diagonals with the
outer border; green, in the present instance in the inner frame rather than outside, and red. There are two slightly different shades
of red, a sophisticated touch. The darker red occupies the center; the more glowing red forms the strips of the outer border. Overall
an extremely vibrant, festive quality. // VERY ORNATE QUILTING: feather scrolls, scallop, Starflower-lozenge strip, Six-Pointed Stars,
diagonal grids; inner field: feather wreath, Eight-Pointed Star, geometric floral pattern formed of intersecting circles.
The Lancaster Amish called this fine quality woolen cloth, their material of choice for Sunday quilts, 'Henrietta' (also no. 31).

017

CENTER DIAMOND / DIAMOND IN THE SQUARE

CA 1925
AMISCHE QUILTMACHERIN / **AMISH QUILT-MAKER**, LANCASTER COUNTY, PENNSYLVANIA
WOLLE / **WOOL** / RÜCKSEITE: BLAU-WEISS GESTREIFTER BAUMWOLLSTOFF /
BACKING: BLUE-AND-WHITE STRIPED COTTON CLOTH / 203 x 203 CM

Sehr helle Farben kommen bei klassischen Quilts aus Lancaster County nicht häufig vor. Dieses relativ große Stück, das in die zwanziger Jahre datiert wird, zeigt jedoch neben changierendem Blau und Rot auch ein Beige. Die helle Farbe folgt der Diagonalen von den Dreiecken im Innenfeld zu den Eckquadraten von Innen- und Außenrahmen. Das Blau bleibt auf die äußeren Balken beschränkt. Eingefasst ist die Decke mit roter Umsäumung – ein kräftiger Akzent als Echo auf das Rot des zentralen Diamond und des Innenrahmens. // Die für Diamond in the Square-Quilts typische Farbordnung über die Diagonalen findet sich bei mehreren Beispielen in der Sammlung Schlumberger: Nrn. 16, 25, 28, 32, 33, 59. Dennoch entstehen, je nach Wahl der Farben, ganz unterschiedliche Stimmungen – hier der Eindruck von Eindeutigkeit, Frische und Klarheit. // QUILTING: Federranken, Kreuzblüten-Rauten-Leiste, Andreaskreuze; Rosenzweige, Federkranz, achtzackiger Stern, geometrisches Blütenmuster aus einander überschneidenden Kreisen.

Very light colors do not occur very frequently on classic Lancaster County quilts. This relatively large quilt, which is dated to the 1920s, boasts, alongside pulsing blue and red, a beige tone. The light color follows the diagonals of the triangles in the inner field to the corner blocks of the inner and outer borders. Blue is restricted to the outer borders. The quilt is edged with a red seam – a forceful touch echoing the red of the central Diamond and the inner border. // The color arrangement via diagonals typical of 'Diamond in the Square' quilts occurs on other quilts in the Schlumberger Collections: nos. 16, 25, 28, 32, 33, 59. However, depending on the color combinations chosen, entirely different moods may be created – here the impression made is unequivocally fresh and clear. // QUILTING: feather scrolls, Starflower-lozenge strip, crosses of St Andrew, rose sprays, feather wreath, Eight-Pointed Star, geometric floral patterns formed of intersecting circles.

018

MINIATURE NINE PATCH

CA 1930
AMISCHE QUILTMACHERIN / **AMISH QUILT-MAKER**, LAWRENCE COUNTY, PENNSYLVANIA
BAUMWOLLE / **COTTON** / RÜCKSEITE: KHAKIFARBENE BAUMWOLLE / **BACKING: KHAKI COTTON** / 196 x 168 CM
PROVENIENZ / **PROVENANCE**: DAVID WHEATCROFT, WESTBOROUGH, MASSACHUSETTS

Nach Lancaster County in Südost-Pennsylvania und Holmes County in Ohio ist Lawrence County in West-Pennsylvania das drittgrößte Siedlungsgebiet der Amischen in den USA. Es liegt an der Grenze zu Ohio, und tatsächlich erinnert das abgebildete Stück mit seiner schmalen Rahmenzone, dem länglichen Format und Baumwolle als Material an Midwest-Quilts. // Das große Innenfeld ist gefüllt mit einem Nine-Patch-Muster „en miniature", bei dem die Quadrate nicht auf der Spitze stehen (wie Nrn. 5, 15, 19, 20, 26 und 31), sondern auf der Seite (wie Nr. 23) und sich für das Auge des Betrachters zu Diagonalreihen ordnen. Die Farbstimmung mit Schwarz als Fond, einem kühlen Braun für Einfassung und Innenrahmen und vorwiegend Blau-, Violett- und Brauntönen bei den kleinen Quadraten lässt vermuten, dass der Quilt in einem recht orthodoxen Umfeld entstand. Und doch ist innerhalb des strengen Schemas ein freier und sicherer Umgang mit den Farben festzustellen. // QUILTING: Parallellinien, geometrisches Muster aus einander überschneidenden Halbkreisen (an einen Astragal erinnernd), Diagonalgitter.

After Lancaster County in south-east Pennsylvania and Holmes County in Ohio, Lawrence County in western Pennsylvania is the third biggest Amish settlement area in the US. It borders on Ohio and the quilt shown here with its small framing zone, elongated format and cotton cloth is indeed reminiscent of Midwestern quilts. // The large inner field is filled with a 'miniaturized' version of the Nine Patch design, in which the squares are not standing on their corners (as in nos. 5, 15, 19, 20, 26 and 31) but instead rest on their sides (as in no. 23) and are arranged for the viewer's eye in diagonal rows. The mood created by the color scheme, with a black ground, a cool brown for both the outer border and the inner frame and primarily blues, purples and browns for the little squares, suggests that this quilt was made in a pretty orthodox environment. Yet within the astringent scheme, color has been handled freely and with assurance. // QUILTING: parallel lines, geometric patterns formed of intersecting semicircles (reminiscent of a bead and reel molding), diagonal grid.

019

DOUBLE NINE PATCH

CA 1880
AMISCHE QUILTMACHERIN / **AMISH QUILT-MAKER**, LANCASTER COUNTY, PENNSYLVANIA
WOLLE, BAUMWOLLE / **WOOL, COTTON** / RÜCKSEITE: BAUMWOLLE / **BACKING: COTTON** / 180 x 102 CM

Dieser frühe Quilt wurde nicht für ein Ehebett, sondern für das Bett eines Jugendlichen oder Farmarbeiters gefertigt – daher das Abweichen von dem sonst in Lancaster County so typischen Quadratformat. Das Stück zeigt sehr deutlich, in welch entscheidendem Maße auch einfache Steppornamentik die ästhetische Wirkung eines Quilts prägen kann – und tatsächlich entsteht der Eindruck einer „Prägung". Die parallelen Linien, die in gleichmäßigen Abständen schräg über Außen- und Innenrahmen laufen, das Gitterwerk auf den großen Diamonds und Dreiecken des Innenfeldes und die parallelen Doppellinien auf den Neunerquadraten strukturieren als wohl-organisiertes Muster die gesamte Decke – eine „zweite Ebene" zusätzlich zur Komposition der farbigen Flächen. // QUILTING: parallele Linien, Gitterwerk.

This early quilt was made for the bed of an adolescent or hired hand rather than for a marriage bed – hence the deviation from the square format otherwise so typical of Lancaster County. This piece clearly reveals the crucial extent to which even simple quilting decoration can mould the aesthetic impact made by a quilt – and indeed an impression of 'molding' has been created. The parallel lines running in equidistant diagonals across the outer and inner borders, the waffle grid on the big Diamonds and Triangles of the inner field and the parallel double lines on the Nine Patch squares structure the entire quilt in a skillfully organized design – a 'second plane' in addition to the color-field composition. // QUILTING: parallel lines, waffle grid.

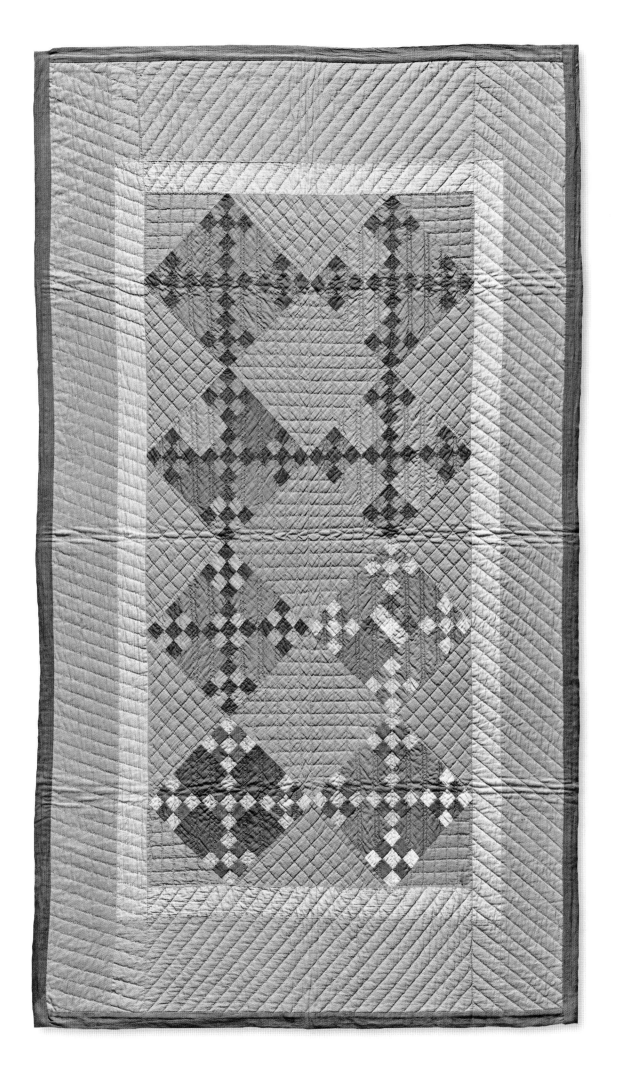

020

NINE PATCH

1910
AMISCHE QUILTMACHERIN MARIA ELISABETH MAST / **AMISH QUILT-MAKER MARIA ELISABETH MAST,**
ELKHART COUNTY, INDIANA
SIGNIERT UND DATIERT IN DEN ECKEN DES INNENFELDES, OBEN: 1910; UNTEN: MEM /
SIGNED AND DATED IN THE CORNERS OF THE INNER FIELD, TOP: 1910; BOTTOM: MEM
WOLLE / **WOOL** / RÜCKSEITE: DUNKELBLAUER BAUMWOLLSTOFF /
BACKING: DARK BLUE COTTON CLOTH / 208 x 166 CM

Elkhart County liegt etwa 100 Meilen östlich von Chicago im höchsten Norden von Indiana an der Grenze zu Kanada. Hier und vor allem im benachbarten LaGrange County leben ebenfalls zahlreiche Amische – ihre Vorfahren kamen ursprünglich, im 18. Jahrhundert, aus Lancaster County, Pennsylvania. // In den Proportionen unterscheiden sich die Mid West-Quilts meist deutlich von denen aus Lancaster County; so ist etwa der Außenrahmen schmaler, und längliche Formate kommen häufiger vor, wie bei dem hier gezeigten Stück. Auf dem dunkelgrünen Grund sind, scheinbar ganz einfach und unkompliziert, die zweifarbigen Nine Patches aneinandergereiht, wie es dem Schema entspricht. Maria Elisabeth Mast, die den ursprünglichen Besitzern zufolge den Quilt gemacht hat, gelang jedoch eine Variation, die trotz des strengen Regelwerks, dem die Amischen zu gehorchen haben, erlaubt war. Sehr lebendig und unkonventionell wirkt das Farbspiel der kleinen bunten Würfelchen. Noch „ordentlich" die grüne und die violette Reihe, aber dann die Reihen mit verschiedenen Rottönen in freier Verteilung. // QUILTING: Fächer, einander überschneidende Halbkreise, Tulpen, parallele Doppellinien.

Elkhart County is about 100 miles east of Chicago in the northernmost part of Indiana bordering on Canada. Numerous Amish settled here and in neighboring LaGrange County especially – their 18th-century ancestors came originally from Lancaster County, Pennsylvania. // Midwestern quilts usually differ considerably in their proportions from Lancaster County quilts; the outer border is narrower and elongated formats, such as the quilt shown here, occur more frequently. The bicolored Nine Patches are arrayed, seemingly in a very simple, uncomplicated manner, on the dark green ground corresponding to the design scheme. However, Maria Elisabeth Mast, who, according to the original owners, made this quilt, succeeded in creating a variation that was permitted despite the strict rules the Amish had to obey. The play of color in these small, bright cubes looks very lively and unconventional. The green and purple row is still 'tidy' but is followed by rows featuring various reds that are freely distributed. // QUILTING: Fans, intersecting semicircles, tulips, parallel double lines.

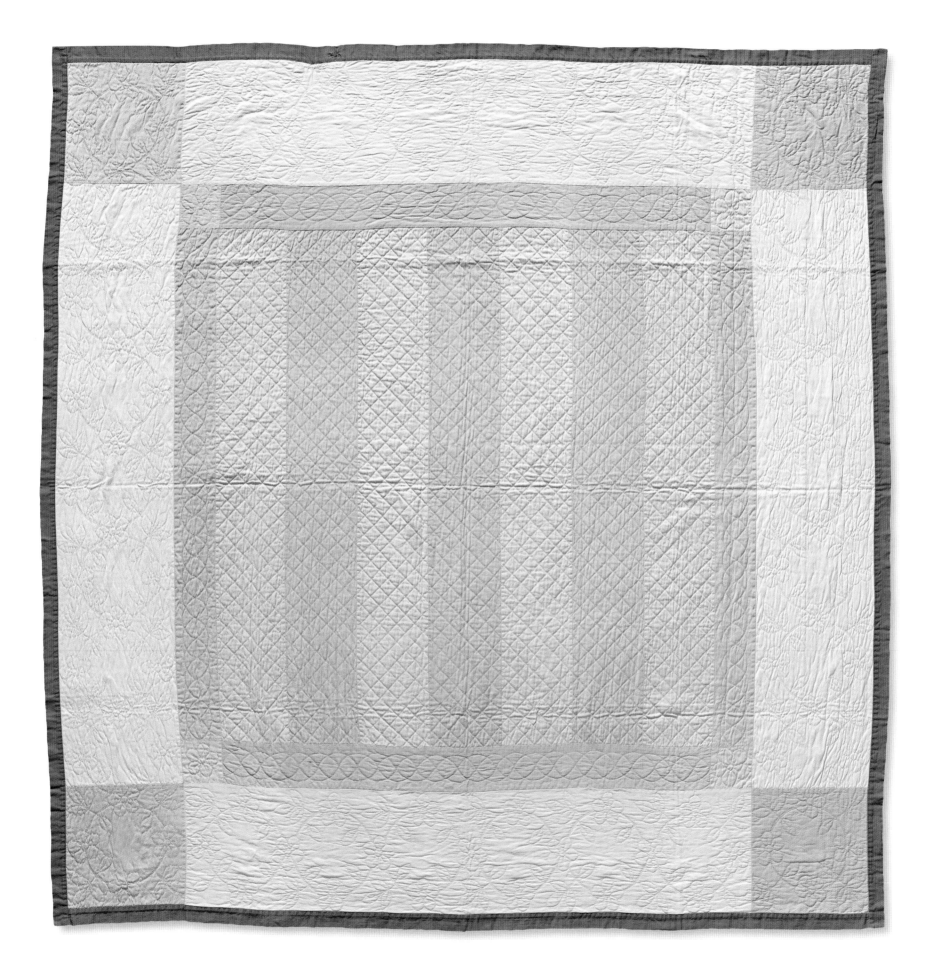

021

BARS

CA 1935
AMISCHE QUILTMACHERIN DER FAMILIE STOLTZFUS / **AMISH QUILT-MAKER FROM
THE STOLTZFUS FAMILY**, LANCASTER COUNTY, PENNSYLVANIA
BAUMWOLLE / **COTTON** / RÜCKSEITE: BAUMWOLLE / **BACKING: COTTON** / 199 x 192 CM

Aus einer der zahlreichen Stoltzfus-Familien kommt dieser Quilt, dessen lichte Farbigkeit für Lancaster County-Amische ungewöhnlich ist. Ein dunkelgrüner Rand umgrenzt die Fläche mit Entschlossenheit. Das Innenquadrat ist – wie bei Quilts Nrn. 14 und 44 – von einem Rahmen eingefasst, der allerdings kaum in Erscheinung tritt, da seine schmalen Balken aus demselben Grau bestehen wie die inneren Bars und die Ecken des Außenrahmens. So dient alles dem Auftritt des aparten Zitronengelbs. // Gemusterte Stoffe – seien die Muster gedruckt oder gewebt – und erst recht gegenständliche Darstellungen sind bei den Amischen untersagt, gelten sie doch als „weltlich". Etwa seit der 2. Hälfte des 19. Jahrhunderts gibt es nichtsdestoweniger die amischen Quilts mit ihren abstrakten Mustern, die aus geometrisch zugeschnittenen, verschiedenfarbigen Stoffstücken zusammengenäht sind. Dazu kommt die Steppornamentik – das Quilting, das weit über das rein Funktionale hinausgeht. So viele Stiche wären für das Zusammennähen jener zwei Lagen Stoff mit der Füllung dazwischen, aus denen die Decken bestehen, nicht notwendig, und hier sind sogar figürliche Motive gestattet. // QUILTING: wellenförmig verschlungene Blütenranken, die in den großen Ecken sorgfältig platzierte Kränze bilden; Wellenmuster aus drei Linien, Rosetten, Diagonalgitter.

This quilt came from one of the many Stoltzfus families and its light color scheme is unusual for the Lancaster County Amish. A dark green border definitively encloses the field. The inner square is – as in quilts nos. 14 and 44 – surrounded by a border, which, however, hardly shows up at all since its narrow strips are of the same gray as the inner Bars and the corners of the outer field. Everything goes to showcase the delightful lemon yellow. // Patterned materials – with either printed or woven designs – and representational figurations especially are forbidden to the Amish since they are regarded as 'worldly'. Nevertheless, there have been Amish quilts with abstract patterns sewn from geometrically cut scraps of material in various colors since the latter half of the 19th century. Then there is the decorative quilting – it goes far beyond the bounds of the purely functional. So many stitches were unnecessary to sew together the two layers of material with padding in between which make up the quilts and here even figurative motifs are permitted. // QUILTING: wavy, intertwined floral scrolls that form carefully placed wreaths in the large corners; scallop patterns consisting of three lines, rosettes, diagonal grid.

022

SUNSHINE AND SHADOW – GRANDMOTHER'S DREAM

1924
AMISCHE QUILTMACHERIN MARY STOLTZFUS / **AMISH QUILT-MAKER MARY STOLTZFUS**, LANCASTER COUNTY, PENNSYLVANIA
SIGNIERT UND DATIERT AUF DER RÜCKSEITE: MS 1924 / **SIGNED AND DATED ON THE BACK: MS 1924**
WOLLE / **WOOL** / RÜCKSEITE: BAUMWOLLSTOFF MIT PAISLEYMUSTER / **BACKING: PAISLEY-PATTERNED COTTON CLOTH** / 197 x 201 CM

Eine Signatur auf amischen Quilts ist selten, käme sie doch verwerflichem „Hochmut" gefährlich nahe. Vor allem bei den Amischen des mittleren Westens bezieht sie sich dann auch eher auf die Person, für die das Stück gemacht wurde. Bei Lancaster-County-Quilts sind jedoch hin und wieder die Initialen der Macherin zu finden; so bei diesem exzellent erhaltenen Stück. Wohl ein sogenannter Sonntagsquilt, den man nur zum Gottesdienst, der reihum in den Farmhäusern einer Gemeinde abgehalten wurde, hervorholte und über die Bänke oder Betten breitete. // Bei „Traum der Großmutter" – einer Variante von Sunshine and Shadow – stehen die kleinen Stoffquadrate nicht auf der Seite, sondern auf ihrer Spitze – ein völlig anderer Eindruck verglichen etwa mit Quilt Nr. 8. Ähnlich wie dieses Motiv einem zentralen Diamond eingefügt sein kann (Nr. 13), so ist es hier in einen Center Square integriert. // Die Liebe der Lancaster-Amischen zum Quadrat wird bei diesem Stück besonders augenfällig. In ausgewogenen Proportionen entwickelt sich das Motiv Rahmen um Rahmen um Rahmen um Rahmen – wie ein Mandala. // FEINES QUILTING: zwei kreisförmig ineinander laufende Federranken, Kreuzblüten-Rauten-Leiste, Diagonalkreuze.

A signature is rarely encountered on Amish quilts because signing one's work comes perilously close to 'pride', a reprehensible character trait. Among the Midwest Amish in particular, a signature tends to refer to the person for whom the quilt was made. The maker's initials are nonetheless occasionally encountered on Lancaster County quilts as well, as for instance, on this superbly preserved example. It was probably what is known as a Sunday quilt, brought out to be spread over benches or beds for divine service, which was held at the various farms of a community by turn. // In 'Grandmother's Dream' – a non-Amish name for a variant of Sunshine and Shadow – the little squares of cloth have been stood on their corners to form diamonds rather than on their sides – an entirely different impression is created compared to quilt no. 8, for instance. Just as this motif can be added to a Central Diamond (no. 13), here it has been integrated in a Center Square. // The fondness shown by the Lancaster Amish for the square is particularly apparent in this piece. The motif is developed in harmonious proportions frame by frame by frame – like a mandala. // FINE QUILTING: double concentric feather scrolls, Starflower-lozenge strip, diagonal crosses.

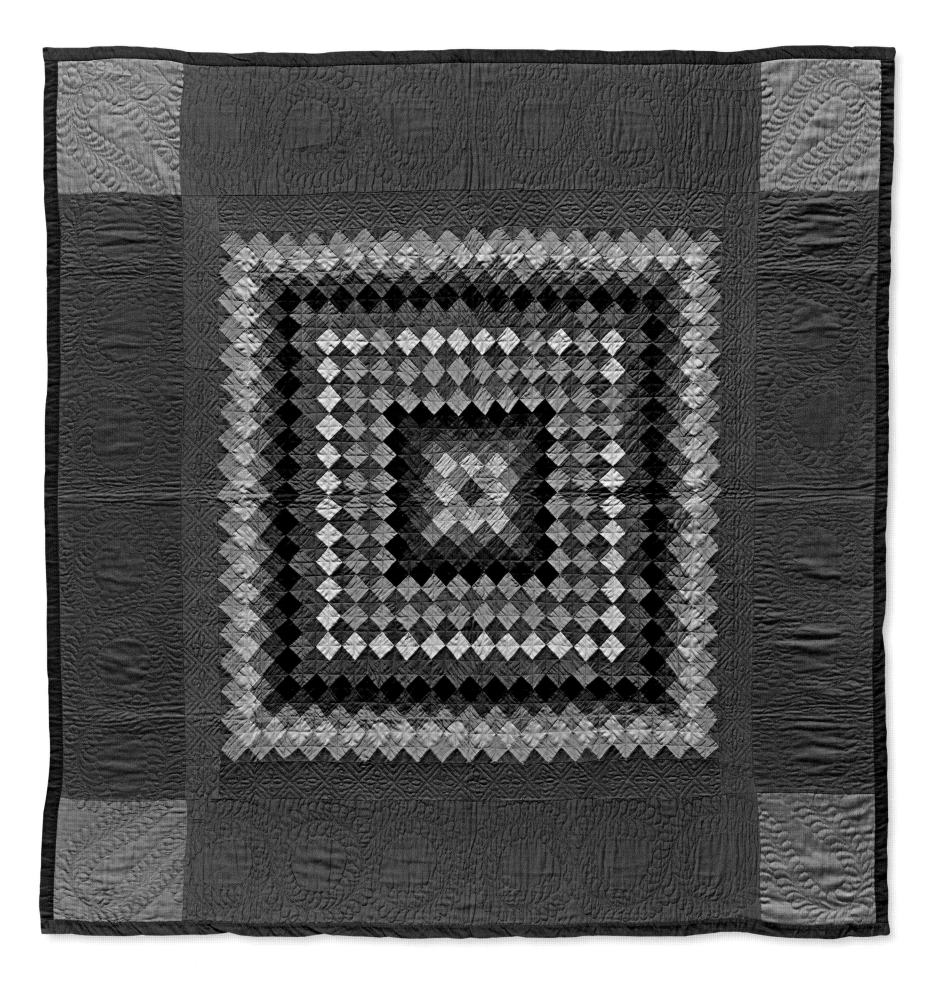

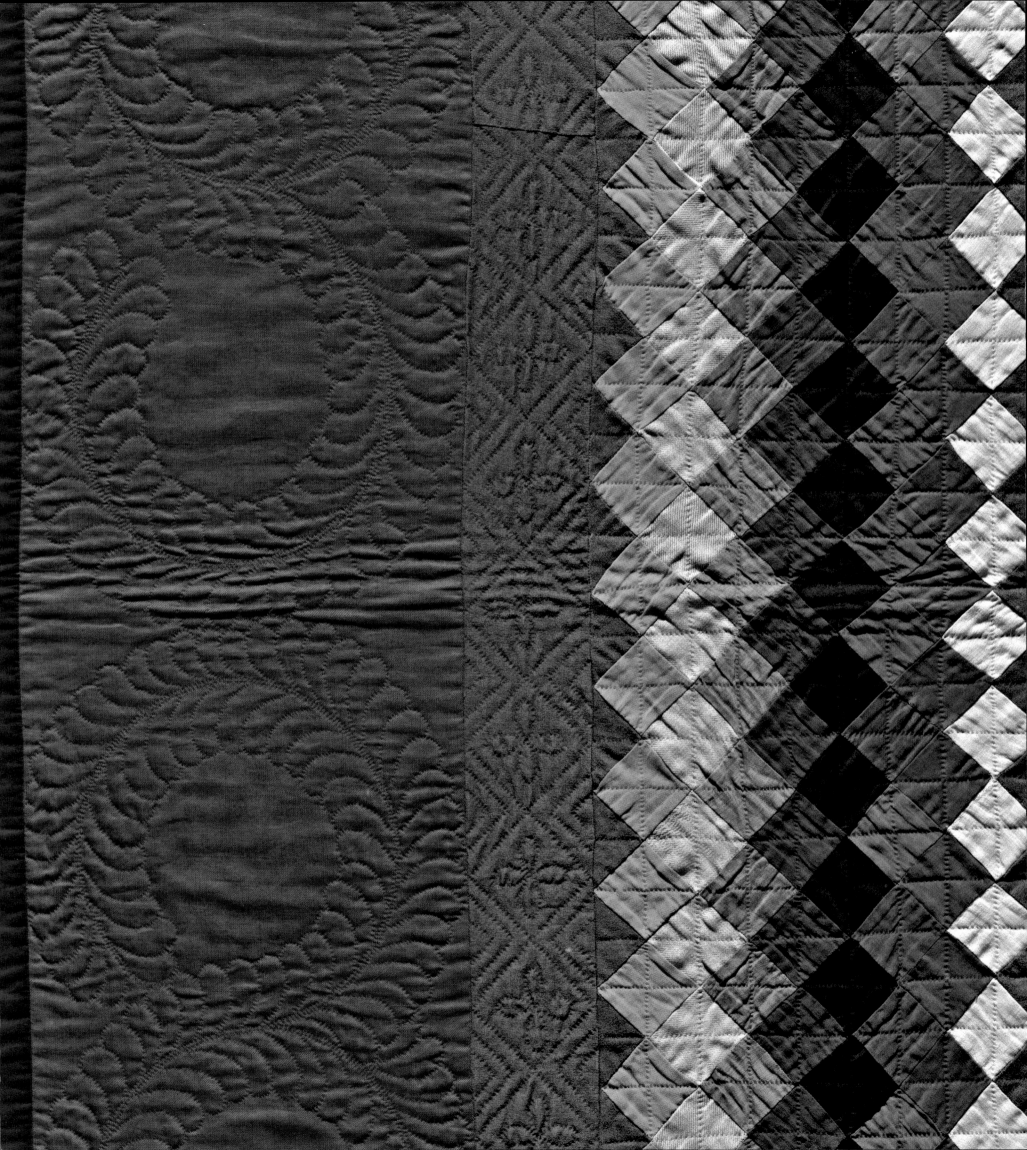

023

NINE PATCH

CA 1900
AMISCHE QUILTMACHERIN DER FAMILIE JAKOB LAPP / **AMISH QUILT-MAKER FROM THE**
FAMILY OF JAKOB LAPP, BIRD IN HAND, LANCASTER COUNTY, PENNSYLVANIA
BAUMWOLLE / **COTTON** / RÜCKSEITE: GEMUSTERTER BAUMWOLLSTOFF / **BACKING: PRINTED COTTON CLOTH** /
186 x 188 CM

Ein frühes Beispiel für das Kompositionsprinzip eines Nine Patch, den nach Auskunft der ursprünglichen Besitzer eine Frau aus der Familie Jakob Lapp gefertigt haben soll. Einfarbige Quadrate wechseln sich ab mit solchen, die aus neun kleinen Quadraten in zwei Farben zusammengesetzt sind. Die Anzahl der Reihen ist gerade – eigentlich unerwartet, wenn man an die Bars denkt, bei denen die Balkenanzahl immer ungerade ist. Auf diese Weise wird jedoch das gleichmäßige Fortlaufen der Reihen stärker unterstrichen. Umschlossen wird die Schachbrettfläche von einem inneren Rahmen, den Eckquadrate im Außenrahmen mit der Gesamtfläche verankern. So entsteht aus einem Reihenmuster, das eigentlich nicht zentralisiert ist, dennoch wieder eine Variante des bei den Lancaster-Amischen so beliebten Kompositionsprinzips „Center Medallion". // Die einfache Komposition, die lichten Farben, eine merkliche Nonchalance beim Zuschneiden und Zusammennähen der Stücke und das unbekümmerte Ersetzen einiger hellgrauer Quadrate durch hellblaue verleihen dem Stück etwas angenehm Selbstverständliches. Dieser Quilt wurde wirklich im Alltag benutzt – seine Farben sind ausgewaschen, und er gewinnt gerade durch die Spuren des Gebrauchs hohe Authentizität und besondere Ausstrahlung. // QUILTING: Wellenband, Flechtband, achtzackige Sterne, Diagonalkreuze.

An early example of the **Nine Patch** composition principle, which, according to the former owners, was made by a woman from the family of Jakob Lapp. Monochrome squares alternate with squares composed of nine small squares in two colors. There is an even number of rows – actually surprising, when one thinks of 'Bars', in which there is always an uneven number of stripes. However, the uniform continuity of the rows is more strongly underscored in this way. The checkerboard field is enclosed by an inner border, which corner blocks in the outer border anchor to the field as a whole. Thus once again a variant of the 'Center Medallion' composition principle so beloved of the Lancaster Amish is created from a row design, which is in itself not centralized. // The simple composition, the light colors, a noticeable insouciance in the cutting out and piecing together of the patches and the casual replacement of some light gray squares by light blue ones lend this piece a pleasantly matter-of-fact quality. This quilt was really used in everyday life – the colors are washed-out and it is the traces of use that make it so convincingly authentic and so compelling. // QUILTING: scallop, cable, Eight-Pointed Stars, diagonal crosses.

024

SUNSHINE AND SHADOW – GRANDMOTHER'S DREAM

CA 1935
AMISCHE QUILTMACHERIN / **AMISH QUILT-MAKER**, HOLMES COUNTY, OHIO
BAUMWOLLE / **COTTON** / RÜCKSEITE: HELLBLAUER BAUMWOLLSTOFF / **BACKING: LIGHT BLUE COTTON CLOTH** / 190 x 164 CM

Die Quilts der Amischen aus dem Mittleren Westen der USA, also aus Ohio und Indiana, unterscheiden sich ebenso wie jene aus Kanada (siehe Nr. 4) in ihren Proportionen von den Pennsylvania-Quilts – vor allem von denjenigen aus Lancaster County. Meist sind bei den nicht aus Lancaster County stammenden Stücken die Rahmen schmaler, und häufiger kommen längliche Formate vor. // „Der Traum der Großmutter" ist eine Variante des Typus Sunshine and Shadow, die auch Trip around the world heißt – „Reise um die Welt" (siehe auch Nrn. 13 und 22). Man versteht den Namen besser beim Betrachten dieses Quilts mit seinen extrem gleichmäßigen Reihen kleiner Quadrate, die ohne Anfang und Ende das längliche Zentrum umziehen. // QUILTING: Flechtband mit Herzen und Blüten, Flechtband, Parallellinien.

Quilts made by Amish from the Midwest, that is, Ohio and Indiana, like those from Canada (see no. 4), differ in proportions from Pennsylvania quilts, especially from those made in Lancaster County. Most quilts that have not come from Lancaster County have narrower borders and elongated formats occur more frequently. // 'Grandmother's Dream' is a non-Amish name for a variant of the Sunshine and Shadow type, which is also known among non-Amish as 'Trip around the World' (also see nos. 13 and 22). The alternative names are easier to understand when one gazes at this quilt with its utterly uniform rows of little squares arranged about the elongated center without beginning or end. // QUILTING: cable with hearts and flowers, cable, parallel lines.

025

CENTER DIAMOND / DIAMOND IN THE SQUARE

CA 1905
AMISCHE QUILTMACHERIN J. K. LAPP / **AMISH QUILT-MAKER J. K. LAPP**, NEW HOLLAND, NORTH GROFFDALE, LANCASTER COUNTY, PENNSYLVANIA
WOLLE / **WOOL** / RÜCKSEITE: GEBLÜMTER BAUMWOLLSTOFF / **BACKING: FLOWER-PRINTED COTTON CLOTH** / 210 x 202 CM

Nicht zuletzt das schöne, sehr aufwändige Quilting, aber vor allem die Farbigkeit und die ausgewogenen Proportionen erlauben die frühe Datierung dieses Center Diamond. // Dasselbe diagonale Prinzip der Farbordnung wie bei den Quilts Nrn. 17, 28, 32, 33, 59 und vor allem 16, der sogar sehr ähnliche Farben besitzt – und doch eine ganz eigene Stimmung von Ruhe, Gelassenheit und großer Kraft. Bewirkt wird sie durch das satte Dunkelrot im Zentrum, das bei den Amischen vor allem im 19. Jahrhundert beliebte matte helle Blau in den Dreiecken und Eckquadraten und das Grün des Außenrahmens. Aus Resten entstand solch ein Quilt natürlich nie; es handelt sich um ungebrauchte Stoffe, die vermutlich speziell für diesen Zweck gekauft wurden. // Der Familienüberlieferung nach soll eine Frau namens J. K. Lapp diesen Quilt gemacht haben. Bei dem Ort New Holland handelt es sich um einen kleinen Weiler mit fünf bis sechs Höfen, typisch für die Siedlungsform der Amischen in Lancaster County. // SEHR AUFWÄNDIGES QUILTING: Federranken, gegenständige geschuppte Pyramiden, Bogenborten, Kreuzblüten-Rauten-Leiste, Rosen-Tulpen-Zweige; innen: sechszackiger Stern, Rosetten, Blätter.

The early dating of this Center Diamond quilt rests not least on the beautiful, very elaborate quilting and especially on the colors and harmonious proportions of the fields. // The same diagonal principle of arranging the colors as in quilts nos. 17, 28, 32, 33, 59 and especially 16, which even boasts a very similar color scheme – yet a mood all its own of peace, calm and great latent power. It is evoked by the saturated dark red at the center, the matt light blue, so popular with the Amish in the 19th century especially, in the triangular fields and corner blocks and the green of the outer border. A quilt of this kind was, of course, never made of left-over scraps of material; these are pieces of unused material, which was presumably bought expressly for the purpose. // According to family tradition, this quilt was made by a woman named J. K. Lapp. New Holland is a small hamlet comprising five or six farmsteads, a form of settlement typical of the Lancaster County Amish. // VERY ORNATE QUILTING: feather scrolls, opposing scaled pyramids, scallop, Starflower-lozenge strip, roses and tulips; inner field: Six-Pointed Star, rosettes, foliage.

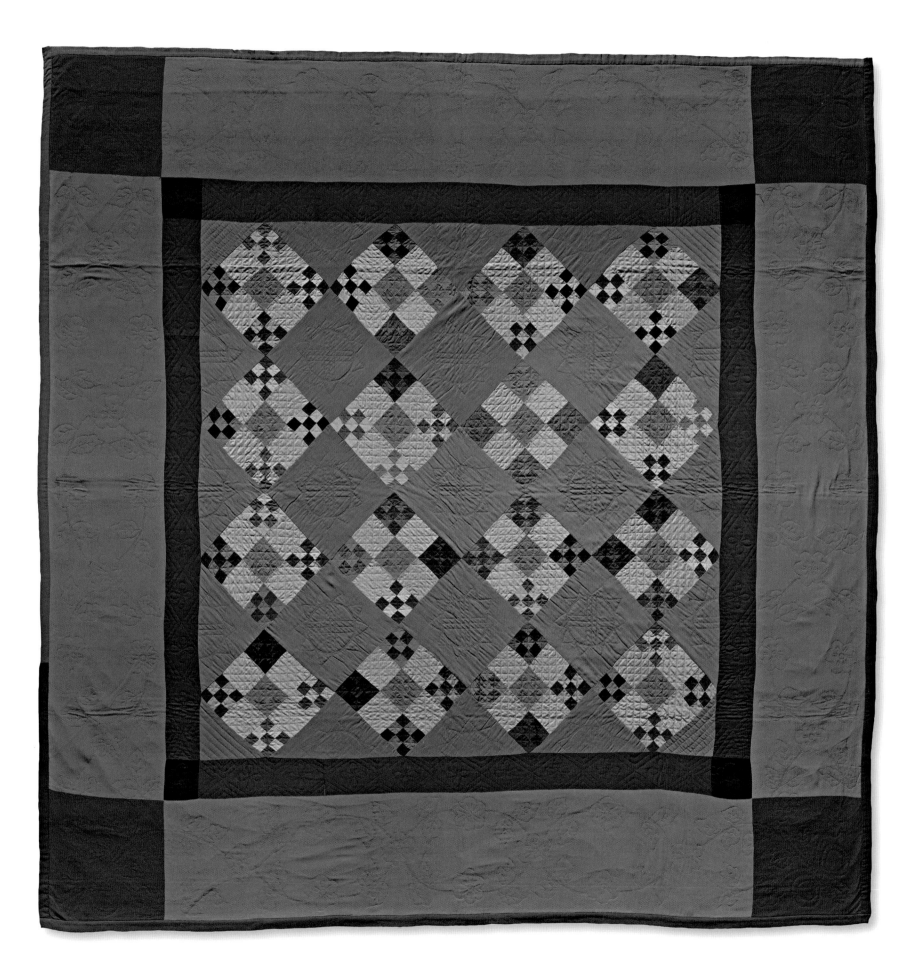

026

DOUBLE NINE PATCH

CA 1940
AMISCHE QUILTMACHERIN / **AMISH QUILT-MAKER**, LANCASTER COUNTY, PENNSYLVANIA
WOLLE, WOLLKREPP / **WOOL, WOOL CREPE** / RÜCKSEITE: FEIN GEMUSTERTER BAUMWOLLSTOFF /
BACKING: COTTON CLOTH WITH A FINE PRINT / 218 X 215 CM

Im Unterschied zu den Quilts Nrn. 5 und 31 ist bei diesem Double Nine Patch das Innenfeld nicht durch die Farbe der Eckquadrate mit der Rahmenzone verbunden – so zieht es bei sonst vergleichbarer Komposition den Blick viel stärker auf sich. Zudem wirken die großen Neunerquadrate mit ihren relativ hellen leeren Diamonds und die mitunter krasse Farbigkeit der kleinen Neunerquadrate dominanter. Anders als die Gestalterin von Nr. 31 hat diese Quilterin Wert auf Farbgleichheit der kleinen, innersten Nine Patches gelegt: Blau im Wechsel mit Pink – eigentlich ein recht gewagtes Stück. // Sehr bald nach ihrer Markteinführung 1856 wurden (pedalbetriebene) Nähmaschinen auch bei den Amischen gebräuchlich und für die Herstellung der Quilts verwendet. Das Zusammennähen der Stoffstücke zu Blocks war dadurch wesentlich einfacher. Allerdings blieb das Quilting Handarbeit, und auch die Umsäumungen sind sehr oft von Hand ausgeführt. // QUILTING: Blütenranken, Kreuzblüten-Rauten-Leiste, Rosetten, Gitterwerk, Diagonalkreuze, Sonnen mit einbeschriebenem Kreuz in den leeren großen Diamonds.

Lit. u. a.: [Kat. Ausst.] Abstraktion und Farbe. Die Kunst der Amischen: Quilts der Sammlung Ziegler. Die Neue Sammlung. München 1991, 44–45 [m. Abb.]

Unlike quilts nos. 5 and 31, this Double Nine Patch features an inner field that is not linked with the border zone through the color of the corner blocks – although the composition is otherwise similar, it is far more compelling. Moreover, the large squares of Nine Patches with their relatively light, empty Diamonds and the occasionally lurid colors of the small squares of Nine Patches are also more dominant. Unlike the maker of no. 31, the quilt-maker here has attached importance to the inner Nine Patches being of the same color: blue alternating with pink – actually quite a daring piece. // Very soon after they were launched on the market in 1856, (foot-driven) sewing machines also became widespread among the Amish and were used for quilt making. This made sewing patches into blocks far easier. However, quilting was still done by hand and so was edging in many cases. // QUILTING: floral scrolls, Starflower-lozenge strips, rosettes, waffle grid, diagonal crosses, Suns with an inset cross in the empty larger Diamonds.

References include: [Exhib. cat.] Abstraktion und Farbe. Die Kunst der Amischen: Quilts der Sammlung Ziegler. Die Neue Sammlung. Munich 1991, 44–45 [with illus.]

027

TRIPLE IRISH CHAIN – VARIATION

1944
AMISCHE QUILTMACHERIN / **AMISH QUILT-MAKER**, TUSCARAWAS COUNTY, OHIO
MONOGRAMMIERT UND DATIERT IN DEN BEIDEN KLEINEN ECKDREIECKEN DES INNENFELDES: KR 1944 /
MONOGRAMMED IN THE TWO SMALL CORNER TRIANGLES OF THE INNER FIELD: KR 1944
BAUMWOLLE / **COTTON** / RÜCKSEITE: BAUMWOLLE / **BACKING: COTTON** / 198 x 198 CM
PROVENIENZ / **PROVENANCE**: DAVID WHEATCROFT, WESTBOROUGH, MASSACHUSETTS / JUDI BOISSON, NEW YORK, NEW YORK

Tuscarawas County liegt im Osten von Ohio und grenzt an Holmes County an. Auch dieser Landstrich wurde ursprünglich – um die Mitte des 18. Jahrhunderts – von Lancaster County, Pennsylvania, aus besiedelt. // Im letzten Jahr des Zweiten Weltkrieges entstand dieser Mid West-Quilt mit seiner freien, undogmatischen Farbverteilung. Im Unterschied zu Nr. 29 ist hier die Dreifachkette durch ergänzende kleine Dreiecke begradigt worden. Und so lässt nicht nur die bunte Farbigkeit, sondern auch die Organisation der kleinen Elemente eine gänzlich andere, sehr lebhafte Wirkung entstehen. Nicht durchgängige Ketten werden wahrgenommen, sondern eher Anordnungen winziger One Patches, die manchmal Schachbrettmotive, manchmal Four Patches bilden. Manchmal springen die kleinen roten Dreiecke ins Auge, mit denen einige der leeren Diamonds eingefasst sind. // Auch bei diesem Quilt ist eine Seite des Rahmens mit Stoff von anderer Farbe ausgeführt, vielleicht um so das Kopf- oder Fußende anzuzeigen. // QUILTING: verschiedene Flechtbänder, Rosetten.

Lit. u. a.: Pellman Rachel u. Kenneth, The World of Amish Quilts. Intercourse/Pa. 1984, 43, Abb. 81 / [Kalender] Moments – A Book of Special Days. People's Place Quilt Museum, Intercourse/Pa. 1991, September 8–14 (m. Abb.)

Tuscarawas County is in eastern Ohio and borders on Holmes County. This area, too, was originally settled – around the mid-18th century – by Amish who migrated from Lancaster County, Pennsylvania. // This Midwestern quilt, notable for its free, undogmatic distribution of color, was made in the last year of the Second World War. Unlike the Chain of no. 29, the Triple Chain here has been smoothed by the addition of small triangles. This not only makes the quilt bright and colorful but the organization of the small elements creates an entirely different, very lively effect. It is not continuous Chains that are perceived but rather arrangements of minuscule One Patches, which sometimes form chessboard motifs and then again Four Patches. Sometimes the little red triangles edging some of the empty Diamonds leap out to meet your eye. // This is another quilt with one side of the border area made in a different color, perhaps to distinguish either the head or the foot end. // QUILTING: cable variants, rosettes.

References include: Pellman, Rachel and Kenneth, The World of Amish Quilts. Intercourse/Pa. 1984, 43, fig. 81 / [Calendar] Moments – A Book of Special Days. People's Place Quilt Museum, Intercourse/Pa. 1991, September 8–14 [with illus.]

028

CENTER DIAMOND / DIAMOND IN THE SQUARE

CA 1932
AMISCHE QUILTMACHERIN BARBARA E. LANTZ / **AMISH QUILT-MAKER BARBARA E. LANTZ**, LANCASTER COUNTY, PENNSYLVANIA
RÜCKSEITIG BESCHRIFTET (WÄSCHEBAND): BARBARA E. LANTZ / **BACKING INSCRIBED (NAME TAPE): BARBARA E. LANTZ**
WOLLE, RAYON / **WOOL, RAYON** / RÜCKSEITE: BRAUNSCHWARZ GEMUSTERTER STOFF / **BACKING: BROWNISH BLACK PRINTED CLOTH** /
219 x 219 CM

Nach der Familienüberlieferung soll Barbara E. Lantz dieses Stück zur Hochzeit ihres Sohnes in den dreißiger Jahren gefertigt haben. Ungewöhnlich für einen Diamond in the Square aus Lancaster County ist die Vielzahl der Farben – es sind fünf – und die so großflächige Verwendung von sehr auffälligen Farben wie Senfgelb und Altrosa. Ähnlich wie bei Nr. 62 sind auch hier Rahmen und Eckquadrate eingesetzt, wo immer es möglich ist. Und wie dort bekommt der zentrale Diamond, der sonst meist prononciert für sich steht, Konkurrenz durch die farblich identischen Eckquadrate seines Rahmens. Allesamt Merkmale, die die relativ späte Datierung unterstreichen. // AUFWÄNDIGES QUILTING: Federranken, Kreuzblüten-Rauten-Leiste, Rosetten, Diagonalgitter; innen: Federkranz, achtzackiger Stern, geometrisches Blütenmuster aus einander überschneidenden Kreisen.

As family tradition has it, Barbara E. Lantz made this quilt for her son's wedding in the 1930s. The number of colors – five – is unusual for a Lancaster County Diamond in the Square quilt and so is the use of very striking colors such as mustard yellow and dusty pink over a wide surface. As in no. 62, borders and corner blocks are inset wherever possible. And, as there, the central Diamond, which usually stands out boldly by itself, faces competition from the corner squares of its identically colored border. All these are features that confirm the relatively late date. // ELABORATE QUILTING: feather scrolls, Starflower-lozenge strip, rosettes, diagonal grid; inner field: feather wreath, Eight-Pointed Star, geometric floral patterns formed of intersecting circles.

029

TRIPLE IRISH CHAIN

CA 1940
AMISCHE QUILTMACHERIN / **AMISH QUILT-MAKER**, LANCASTER COUNTY, PENNSYLVANIA
FEINE WOLLE, WOLLKREPP / **FINE WOOL, WOOL CREPE** / RÜCKSEITE: GEMUSTERTER WOLLKREPP /
BACKING: PATTERNED WOOL CREPE / 207 x 201 CM

Keine Doppelkette wie bei Quilt Nr. 64, sondern sogar eine Dreifachkette bildet hier die diagonalen Reihen. Und im Unterschied zu Quilt Nr. 64 ist das Innenfeld mit Eckquadraten auf der Gesamtfläche verankert. In geradezu königlicher Festlichkeit strahlt das Rot des Hintergrundes. // Es gibt zwar keinen Innenrahmen, aber die Quiltmacherin hat darauf geachtet, dass jene kleinen Chain-Quadrate, die an den Außenrahmen grenzen, farblich von denjenigen weiter innen unterschieden sind. Beim genauen Hinschauen ist außerdem zu sehen, dass die Rahmenbalken und die getreppten inneren Diamonds farblich leicht voneinander abweichen – eine sehr raffinierte Differenzierung, die immer wieder bei amischen Quilts zu sehen ist. Und noch eine Besonderheit ließ sich die Gestalterin einfallen: Zwei der Schachbretter, die an den Kreuzungen der Dreifachketten entstehen, sind durch eine andere Farbzusammensetzung hervorgehoben. Möglicherweise sollte diese Seite am Kopfende liegen. // QUILTING: Rosenranken, geometrisch aus Halbkreisen konstruierte große Blüten, Diagonalkreuze.

This is not a Double Chain as in quilt no. 64 but in fact a Triple Chain, formed by diagonal rows. And unlike quilt no. 64, this one boasts an inner field anchored to the overall field by corner blocks. The red of the background is almost regal in its festive solemnity. // There is no inner border but the quilt-maker ensured that the little Chain squares adjacent to the outer border were of a different color to those further inside. Moreover, if you look closely, you notice that the border strips and the stepped inner Diamonds vary slightly in color – a highly sophisticated differentiation that is frequently found on Amish quilts. And the maker had yet another trick up her sleeve: two of the checkerboards created where the Triple Chains intersect are emphasized by being of a different color scheme. This side may represent the head end. // QUILTING: rose scrolls, large flowers constructed geometrically of semicircles, diagonal crosses.

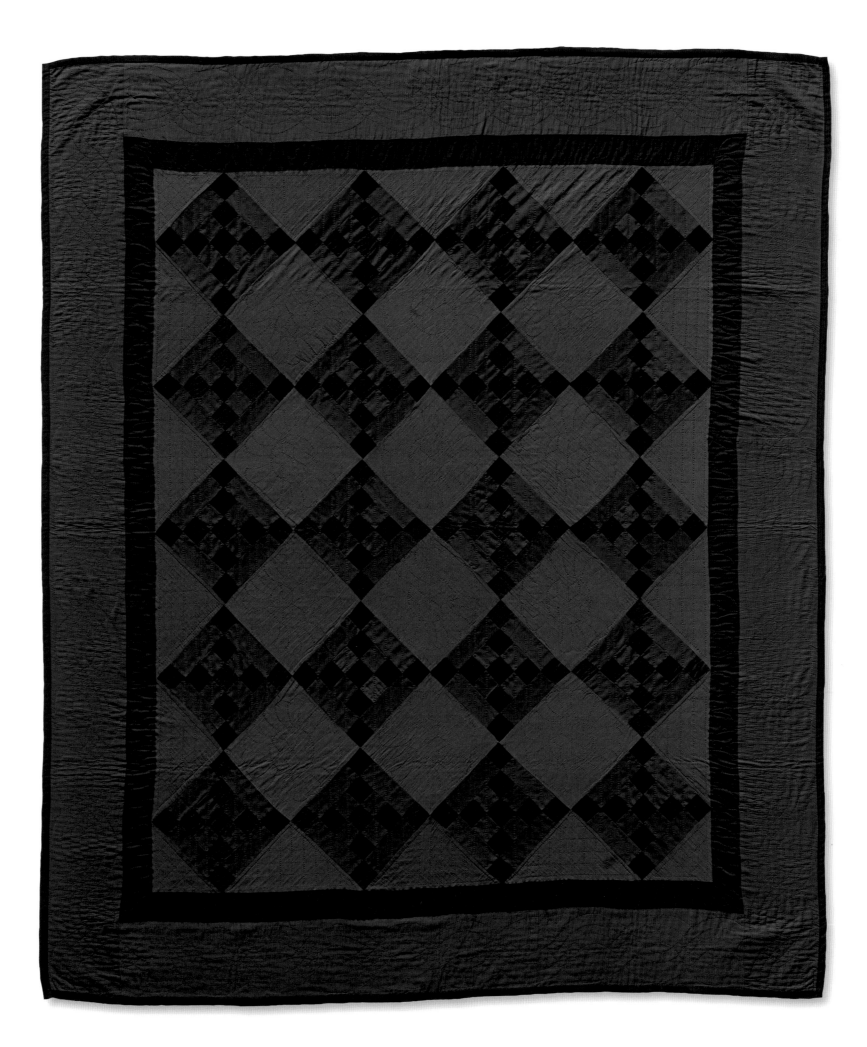

030

IRISH CHAIN – NINE PATCH BLOCKWORK

CA 1937
AMISCHE QUILTMACHERIN DER FAMILIE SWARTZENTRUBER / **AMISH QUILT-MAKER FROM**
THE SWARTZENTRUBER FAMILY, HOLMES COUNTY, OHIO
BAUMWOLLE / **COTTON** / RÜCKSEITE: BLAUER BAUMWOLLSTOFF / **BACKING: BLUE COTTON CLOTH** /
207 x 177 CM

Lancaster County in Pennsylvania wurde als erstes Gebiet in Nordamerika von Amischen aus Europa besiedelt – dies begann etwa 1720/30 – und weist noch heute eine sehr große Siedlungsdichte an Amischen auf. Ohio – zwischen Pennsylvania und Indiana gelegen – ist jedoch heute der Bundesstaat mit den meisten Amischen und Berlin in Holmes County mit 3500 Einwohnern die größte Stadt der Amischen in den USA. // Die Swartzentruber-Amischen zählen zu den orthodoxesten Gruppen der Old Order Amish, und dementsprechend ist dieser Quilt in extrem zurückhaltenden Farben komponiert. Man denkt an die ganz schlichten Open Window-Quilts in Schwarz und Dunkelblau (Nrn. 69 und 73), von denen einer ebenfalls von einer Swartzentruber-Frau gemacht wurde. Eine einfache Irish Chain in Brauntönen läuft hier nicht diagonal, sondern parallel zu den Rändern. Dunkelblaue Stückchen (quadratisch und rechteckig) ergänzen die Chain zu Diamonds oder Nine Patches – je nachdem, wie man das Muster „liest", könnte man es auch als Nine Patch Blockwork bezeichnen. // QUILTING: Flechtbänder, Sonnenblumen mit einbeschriebenem sechszackigem Stern.

Lancaster County in Pennsylvania was the first area in North America to be settled by the Amish from Europe – settlement began about 1720/30 – and still boasts a very high settlement density of Amish. Ohio – situated between Pennsylvania and Indiana – is, however, the US state with the largest Amish population and Berlin, in Holmes County, with a population of 3,500, is the largest US Amish town. // The Swartzentruber Amish are among the most orthodox of all Old Order Amish groups and this quilt is, accordingly, composed in extremely reticent colors. It recalls the very simple Open Window quilts in black and dark blue (nos. 69 and 73), one of which was also made by a woman from the Swartzentruber family. Here a simple Irish Chain in browns runs parallel to the edges rather than diagonally. Small dark blue blocks (square and rectangular) complete the Chain to form Diamonds or Nine Patches – depending on how the pattern is 'read', it might also be called Nine Patch Blockwork. // QUILTING: cable, Sunflowers with an inset Six-Pointed Star.

031

DOUBLE NINE PATCH

CA 1920
AMISCHE QUILTMACHERIN / **AMISH QUILT-MAKER**, LANCASTER COUNTY, PENNSYLVANIA
WOLLE „HENRIETTA" / **WOOL 'HENRIETTA'** / RÜCKSEITE: BAUMWOLL-RAYONSTOFF MIT STREIFENMUSTER /
BACKING: COTTON-RAYON CLOTH WITH A STRIPED PATTERN / 195 x 192 CM
PROVENIENZ / **PROVENANCE**: DAVID WHEATCROFT, WESTBOROUGH, MASSACHUSETTS

Abstrakte geometrische Muster, die auf Quadrat und Rechteck basieren, bilden das Repertoire der meisten amischen Quilts. Am stärksten fokussiert auf das Thema Quadrat sind die Lancaster-Quilts. Center Square und Diamond in the Square stellen gleichsam die elementarste Ausprägung dieser Leidenschaft dar – der Diamond ist ja nichts anderes als ein auf die Spitze gestelltes Quadrat. Dazu kommt das Bars-Muster, ebenfalls großflächig angelegt. Aus kleinen quadratischen Stoffstücken bauen sich dagegen die beiden anderen Muster auf, die bei den Lancaster-Amischen besonders geschätzt werden: Sunshine and Shadow und Nine Patch. // Bei dem vorliegenden Stück sind die jeweils zweifarbigen Neunerquadrate (Nine Patches) die kleinste Einheit – auf die Spitze gestellt, geben sie gleichsam den Grundrhythmus vor. Abwechselnd mit den leeren kleinen Diamonds bilden sie wiederum Nine Patch-Elemente, die sich mit leeren, blauen Diamonds abwechseln. Das Blau von Innenfeld und Eckquadraten und das Rot des Rahmens – intensiviert durch das Grün von Innenrahmen und Einfassung – bewirken zusammen mit den undogmatischen Farbwechseln der kleinen Neunerquadrate den geradezu spektakulären Auftritt dieses besonders lebendigen Sonntagsquilts. // QUILTING: Federranken, Blumenranken, Rosetten, Federkränze, Gitterwerk, Diagonalkreuze.

Abstract geometric designs based on the square and rectangle represent the repertory drawn on for most Amish quilts. Lancaster County quilts focus most strongly on the square theme. Center Square and Diamond in the Square represent, as it were, the most elemental expression of this passion for the square – the Diamond is, after all, nothing but a square tilted to standing on a point. Another popular Lancaster County motif is the Bar pattern, which is also designed with the entire surface in mind. The two other patterns particularly appreciated by the Lancaster Amish, on the other hand, are built up of small, square pieces of cloth: Sunshine and Shadow and Nine Patch. // On the present quilt, bichrome Nine Patches are the smallest unit – placed on end, they determine the underlying rhythm. Alternating with empty small Diamonds, they in turn form Nine Patch elements, which alternate with empty blue Diamonds. The blue of the inner field and the corner blocks and the red of the border – made more intense by the green of the inner border and edging – along with the undogmatic alternation of color in the small Nine Patches ensure that this particularly vivid Sunday quilt looks so spectacular. // QUILTING: feather scrolls, floral scrolls, rosettes, feather wreaths, waffle grids, diagonal crosses.

032

CENTER DIAMOND / DIAMOND IN THE SQUARE

CA 1930
AMISCHE QUILTMACHERIN LYDIA LAPP / **AMISH QUILT-MAKER LYDIA LAPP**, LEOLA, LANCASTER COUNTY, PENNSYLVANIA
MONOGRAMMIERT AUF DER RÜCKSEITE: JB / **MONOGRAMMED ON THE BACK: JB**
FEINE WOLLE / **FINE WOOL** / RÜCKSEITE: DUNKELGRÜNE BAUMWOLLE / **BACKING: DARK GREEN COTTON** /
204 x 201 CM

Mit seiner geradezu glühenden Farbigkeit schlägt dieser Quilt den Betrachter in Bann. Die Rottöne dominieren, umgrenzt und intensiviert durch das Grün der drei Rahmungen. Wie bei Nr. 33 sind der zentrale Diamond und die Balken des Außenrahmens durch ihre gleiche Farbe aufeinander bezogen, und eine diagonale Farbgleichheit verbindet das Innenquadrat mit den Eckquadraten von Innen- und Außenrahmen. // Der Diamondrahmen besitzt eigene Eckquadrate, ein Merkmal, das auch bei anderen Quilts aus dieser Zeit zu finden ist, etwa Nrn. 13, 28 und 62. Die Frau in Leola, die diesen Quilt gemacht haben soll – vielleicht für JB, wie das Monogramm auf der Rückseite angibt –, hat sich jedoch noch etwas Besonderes einfallen lassen. Sie verwendete für diese kleinen Quadrate denselben Stoff wie für die angrenzenden Drei-ecke, so dass sie farblich ineinander übergehen. Diese Verschmelzung lässt nicht nur das Innenfeld als zusammenhängende Quadratfläche stärker in Erscheinung treten, sondern der Quilt bekommt darüber hinaus auch etwas Vexierbildhaftes – eine sehr aparte Variante. // QUILTING: Federranken, Bogenborten, Rosenranken, Rosetten, Tulpen-Rose-Zweige; innen: Federkranz, achtzackiger Stern, geometrisierte Blüten aus einander überschneidenden Kreisen.

Its smoldering colors make this quilt truly captivating. Reds dominate, enclosed and intensified by the green of the three borders. As in no. 33, the central Diamond and the bars of the outer border are related by being the same color and a diagonal identity of color links the inner block with the corner blocks of the inner and outer borders. // The Diamond border has corner blocks of its own, a feature that occurs in other quilts of this date, for instance, in nos. 13, 28 and 62. The woman in Leola who is said to have made this quilt – perhaps for JB, whose monogram may appear on the back – thought up something special for this one. For these small blocks she used the same material as for the adjacent triangles so that they lead into one another colorwise. This merging of color not only makes the inner field stand out more sharply as a continuous square surface but also lends this quilt something of an optical illusion – a very distinctive variant. // QUILTING: feather scrolls, scallop, rose scrolls, roses and tulips; inner field: feather wreath, Eight-Pointed Star, geometric flowers formed of intersecting circles.

033

CENTER DIAMOND / DIAMOND IN THE SQUARE

1920ER JAHRE / **1920S**
AMISCHE QUILTMACHERIN / **AMISH QUILT-MAKER**, LANCASTER COUNTY, PENNSYLVANIA
FEINE WOLLE / **FINE WOOL** / RÜCKSEITE: BAUMWOLL-KALIKO MIT BLÜMCHENMUSTER /
BACKING: COTTON CALICO WITH FLORAL PRINT / 200 x 199 CM

Die kraftvolle Ausstrahlung dieses Stückes entsteht durch seine kühne Farbigkeit mit nahezu gleich intensivem Blutrot, Grün und Blau. Die Einfassung ist in die Farbenpracht nicht einbezogen, sondern umschließt das Ganze mit feiner, aber deutlicher Grenze. Wie ganz anders es ausschaut, wenn – bei sonst gleicher Komposition – das Innenquadrat nicht über die Ecken auf der Gesamtfläche verankert ist, zeigt zum Vergleich der Floating Diamond Nr. 9. Bei beiden Quilts stimmen jeweils der zentrale Diamond und die Balken des Außenrahmens farblich überein. Rot ist sogar in beiden Fällen die Farbe von Diamondrahmen und Innenrahmen. Trotzdem ergeben sich stark unterschiedliche Wirkungen. // QUILTING: Federranken, Rosetten, Kreuzblüten-Rauten-Leiste, sechszackige Sterne, Rosen-Tulpen-Zweige; innen: Federkranz, Rosetten, achtzackiger Stern, kleine sechszackige Sterne.

The powerful vibrancy of this quilt results from bold colors, blood red, green and blue, all being of equal intensity. The edging is not included in the splendor of the other colors but rather encloses the whole with a fine yet clear boundary. How different things look when – the composition being otherwise identical – the inner square is not anchored to the whole field via the corners is shown by a comparison with Floating Diamond no. 9. In these two quilts the central Diamond and the strips of edging are of the same color. In both, red is even the color of the Diamond border and the inner border. Nevertheless, the effect created is very different in each. // QUILTING: feather scrolls, rosettes, Starflower-lozenge strip, Six-Pointed Star, roses and tulips; inner field: feather wreath, rosettes, Eight-Pointed Star, small Six-Pointed Stars.

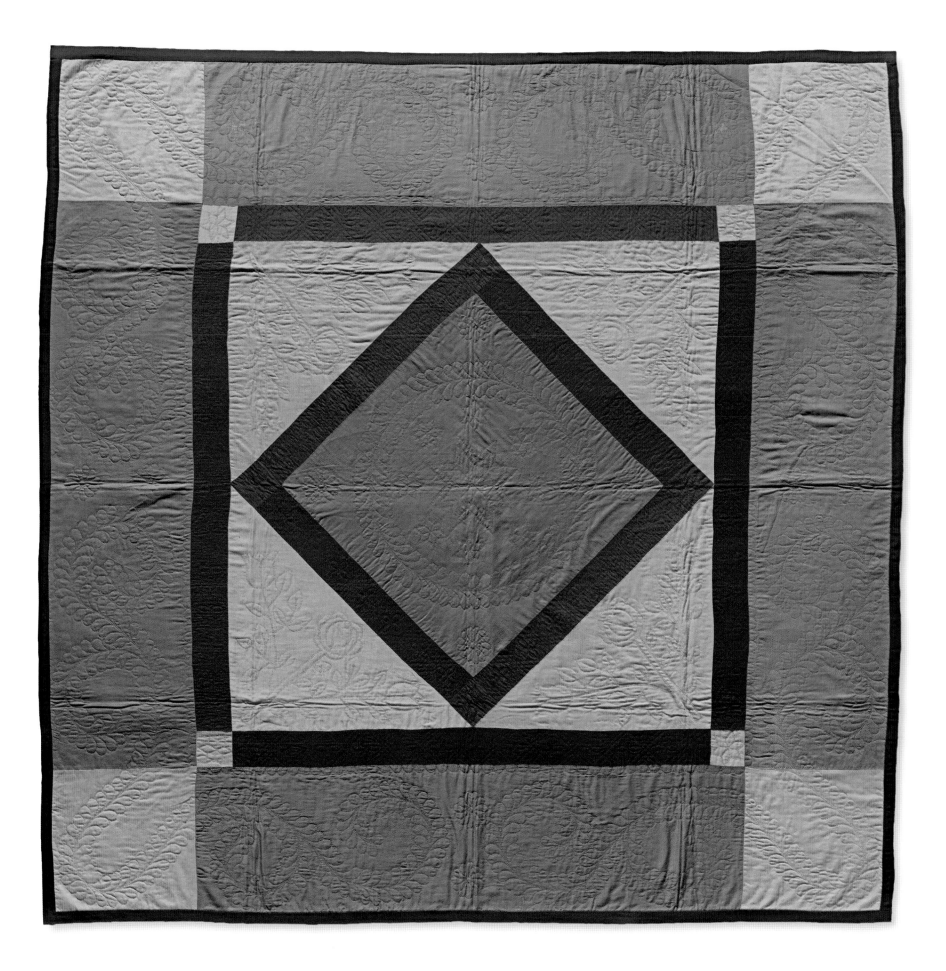

034

LONE STAR

CA 1890
AMISCHE QUILTMACHERIN DER FAMILIE SAMUEL ZOOK / **AMISH QUILT-MAKER FROM THE**
FAMILY OF SAMUEL ZOOK, EPHRATA, LANCASTER COUNTY, PENNSYLVANIA
RÜCKSEITE MIT AUFGENÄHTEM WÄSCHEBAND, BESCHRIFTET: CORA SCHACHT / **BACKING WITH SEWN ON NAME TAPE, INSCRIBED: CORA SCHACHT**
WOLLE, BAUMWOLLE, BAUMWOLLCHINTZ / **WOOL, COTTON, CHINTZ** / RÜCKSEITE: BAUMWOLLCHINTZ MIT BLÜTEN-STREIFEN-DEKOR /
BACKING: CHINTZ WITH FLORAL STRIPE DECORATION / 210 x 207 CM

Wie Tumbling Blocks sind auch die meisten Sternmuster aus kleinen Rauten aufgebaut. Das Motiv Lone Stars – auch als Star of Bethlehem bekannt – kommt in Lancaster County selten vor – vielleicht, wie Julie Silber vermutet, weil seine pulsierende Energie die üblicherweise ruhige Gesamtstimmung gefährdet (Amish: The Art of the Quilt. New York 1990, Taf. 82). Die Proportionen dieses Quilts mit seinem relativ schmalen Rahmen und das Fehlen einer Einfassung (der rote Stoff des Rahmens wurde einfach nach hinten umgenäht) erlauben die Annahme, dass seine Macherin ursprünglich nicht aus Lancaster County stammte, sondern aus einer anderen Gegend kam, denn natürlich gab es bei den Amischen – nicht zuletzt durch Einheirat – auch „Wanderungen" von Mustern. // Der in Tinte auf das Wäscheband geschriebene Name bezieht sich wohl auf die Besitzerin. Sie muss aber nicht unbedingt die Macherin des Quilts gewesen sein, sondern war vielleicht die Beschenkte – möglicherweise handelte es sich bei dem aufwändig gearbeiteten Quilt mit seiner lebensfrohen Ausstrahlung um ein Hochzeitsgeschenk. // QUILTING MIT WEISSEM GARN: Diagonalgitter, Rauten.

Like Tumbling Blocks, most Star patterns are built up of small lozenges. The Lone Star motif – also known as Star of Bethlehem – is rarely encountered in Lancaster County – perhaps, as Julie Silber conjectures, because its pulsing vigor shatters the otherwise calm overall mood of the design (Amish: The Art of the Quilt. New York 1990, pl. 82). The proportions of this quilt, which has a relatively narrow border and lacks edging (the red material used for the border was simply doubled over to the backing), suggest that its maker did not originally come from Lancaster County but instead from another region. After all, patterns did 'migrate' among the Amish – often through marriages made between people from different settlements. // The name written in ink on the name tape probably refers to the owner. She need not have been the maker of the quilt; instead, she may have been given this elaborately worked quilt, which feels so cheerful, as a wedding present. // QUILTING WITH WHITE YARN: diagonal grids, lozenges.

035

SUNSHINE STAR

CA 1890/95
AMISCHE QUILTMACHERIN / **AMISH QUILT-MAKER**, MIFFLIN COUNTY, PENNSYLVANIA
WOLLE / **WOOL** / RÜCKSEITE: ZWEI VERSCHIEDENE BAUMWOLLSTOFFE, GEBLÜMT UND KARIERT /
BACKING: TWO DIFFERENT TYPES OF COTTON CLOTH, FLORAL AND CHECKED / 184 x 165 CM

Dieser sehr eigenwillige Quilt kann in die Zeit vor 1900 datiert werden. Abgesehen von den gelben Stoffstücken weist er die typische Farbigkeit der White Topper-Amischen auf. Äußerlich charakterisiert durch die weißen Dächer ihrer Pferdekutschen („Dachwägle"), ist diese recht orthodoxe Gruppe eine von zahlreichen amischen und mennonitischen Gemeinschaften im Big Valley von Mifflin County. Die Farbe der Buggy-Dächer ist aber nur ein Teil der strengen Codes, die die religiösen Differenzen signalisieren: „Die Amischen aus dem Big Valley wiederum treffen sich zum Gottesdienst reihum zuhause. Nirgendwo sonst in Nordamerika [...] leben so viele verschiedene Gruppen von Amischen so eng beieinander. [...] [Es gibt] unter den Buggy-Amischen von Mifflin County White Topper (Old Order Nebraska Amische), Black Topper und Yellow Topper, wobei jede Gruppe ihre eigenen Regeln bezüglich Kleidung und Lebensführung befolgt. Dann gibt es noch die amischen Mennoniten, die schwarze Autos fahren, und die Valley View Amischen, die Autos und Lastwagen fahren, die nicht schwarz sind. In jeder Gruppierung gibt es beliebig viele Gemeinden." Ann E. Diviney, in: Central PA (magazine), Juni 2005. // Die Stoffstückchen sind farblich so organisiert, dass sich das Sunshine and Shadow-Muster zu einem großen achtzackigen Stern ordnet, in dessen Mitte ein kleiner Sunshine and Shadow-Diamond steht. Erkennen lassen sich die strukturierten Drillichstoffe von Männerhosen der White Topper-Amischen, aber auch andere Stoffe mit feinen Webmustern sind verwendet worden. // QUILTING: geometrisches Kreuzblütenmuster aus einander überschneidenden Kreisen, Diagonalgitter; die kleinen Quadrate sind über Eck an zwei Seiten nachgesteppt.

This very quirky quilt can be dated to before 1900. The yellow pieces of cloth notwithstanding, it reveals the color scheme typical of the White Topper Amish. Characterized externally by the white tops of their horse-drawn conveyances ('buggies'), this quite strict orthodox group is one of numerous Amish and Mennonite congregations in the Big Valley of Mifflin County. The color of the buggy tops, however, is only a part of the strict code that signalizes religious differentiation: 'The Big Valley Amish, for their part, meet for worship in each other's homes. Nowhere else in North America [...] do so many different groups of Amish live so closely together. [...] among Mifflin County's buggy Amish are the white-toppers (Old Order Nebraska Amish), black-toppers and yellow-toppers, each observing their own rules as to dress and lifestyle. Then there are the Amish Mennonites, who drive black cars, and the Valley View Amish, who drive cars and trucks that are not black. Within each order, any number of congregations exist.' (Ann E. Diviney, in: Central PA [magazine], June 2005). // The pieces of cloth are organized by color so that the Sunshine and Shadow pattern is arranged in a large Eight-Pointed Star, at the center of which stands a small Sunshine and Shadow Diamond. The textured denim materials used for men's trousers by the White Topper Amish are discernible but other materials with finely woven patterns have also been used. // QUILTING: geometric Starflower pattern formed of intersecting circles, diagonal grids; the small squares have been traced in stitching across the corners on two sides.

036

FANS, CRIB QUILT

CA 1900
AMISCHE QUILTMACHERIN / **AMISH QUILT-MAKER**, LANCASTER COUNTY, PENNSYLVANIA
WOLLE, BAUMWOLLE, BAUMWOLLSATIN / **WOOL, COTTON, COTTON SATEEN** /
RÜCKSEITE: BAUMWOLLE / **BACKING: COTTON** / 70 x 43 CM

Nicht nur Quilts für die Betten von Erwachsenen, sondern auch solche in kleinem Format fertigten die amischen Frauen, und sie widmeten sich diesen Stücken für Wiegen, Kinderbetten oder Puppen mit derselben Sorgfalt, verschiedentlich sogar mit recht großem Aufwand, wie einige Beispiele in der Sammlung Schlumberger zeigen. Fast jedes der üblichen Motive kommt auch bei Crib Quilts vor. Von Bars (siehe Nr. 2 und S. 14) und Diamond in the Square (siehe S. 200 und 201) bis zu Sunshine and Shadow und seiner Variante Grandmother's Dream, die auch „Trip around the world" genannt wird. // Bei den prachtvollen Stücken aus Lancaster County ist normalerweise nicht erkennbar, ob mit Stoffresten gearbeitet wurde. Von der Vielzahl an Quilts, die es insgesamt gegeben haben muss, blieben im Wesentlichen nur diejenigen erhalten, die als etwas Besonderes – Sonntagsquilts, Hochzeitsgeschenke etc. – gestaltet und für bewahrenswert gehalten wurden. // Dazu zählt sicher auch der Kinderquilt Nr. 36. Mit diesem und Rail Fence (Nr. 37) sind in der Sammlung Schlumberger auch Crib Quilts mit recht seltenen Motiven vertreten (siehe ebenso Nr. 2). Ob Rail Fence (Bahnschranke – auch Streak of Lightning, Blitzschlag) oder Fans (vgl. auch Nr. 38) – beide bieten sich mit auffallender Komposition, intensiver Farbigkeit und nachdrücklicher Wirkung dar. Die prächtigen stilisierten Fächer weisen eine Besonderheit auf: Rote Steppstiche folgen ihren Bögen – normalerweise gibt es kein farbiges Quilting bei den Amischen. Bei dem exotischen Motiv der Fächer wie auch bei Crazy Quilts (siehe Nr. 43) wurden jedoch anscheinend Ausnahmen von der Regel akzeptiert. // Keines der Muster auf amischen Quilts ist genuin amisch – auch Fans taucht zuerst auf den Quilts der „Englischen" im 19. Jahrhundert auf. Die Übernahme und Abwandlung der Muster durch amische Quilterinnen erfolgte deutlich später, und zwar meist erst dann, wenn diese Muster bei den angloamerikanischen Nachbarn bereits wieder unmodern und unüblich geworden waren – ein zeitlicher Abstand, der offenkundig willentlich war, um sich klar abzugrenzen.

Amish women made quilts in small formats as well as bedcovers for adults and they devoted themselves to these covers for cradles, cribs or doll beds with the same care, on occasion taking great pains indeed over them, as is shown by some examples in the Schlumberger Collection. Nearly all the usual motifs occur in crib quilts as well. From Bars (see no. 2 and p. 14) and Diamond in the Square (see p. 200 and 201) to Sunshine and Shadow and the variants called variously by the non-Amish 'Grandmother's Dream' or 'Trip around the World'. // In the magnificent Lancaster County quilts it is usually impossible to see whether the maker worked with scraps or not. Of the many quilts that must have existed, only those have come down to us that were designed for some special purpose – Sunday Quilts, quilts as wedding presents, etc. – and were, consequently, regarded as worth keeping. One of these must certainly have been the child's quilt no. 36. // In nos. 37 and 36 crib quilts with quite rare motifs are represented in the Schlumberger Collection (see also no. 2). Whether Rail Fence (also known as Streak of Lightning) or Fans (see also no. 38) – both stand out with striking compositions and intense colors that make a memorable impact. And the magnificently stylized Fans reveal another special feature: red quilting stitches trace their arcs – normally there is no colored quilting stitching among the Amish. However, exceptions to the rule were apparently acceptable in the case of such exotic motifs as Fans and also Crazy Quilts (see no. 43). // None of the patterns on Amish quilts are genuinely Amish. The Fans, too, appear first on 'English' quilts in the 19th century. Amish quilt-makers took them over and varied them considerably later, in fact not until these patterns had already gone out of fashion and become unusual among their Anglo-American neighbors – a time lapse that was evidently deliberate, an Amish way of clearly demarcating their culture from the mainstream.

037

RAIL FENCE / STREAK OF LIGHTNING, CRIB QUILT

CA 1940
AMISCHE QUILTMACHERIN / **AMISH QUILT-MAKER**, LAGRANGE COUNTY, INDIANA
BAUMWOLLE / **COTTON** / RÜCKSEITE: BAUMWOLLE / **BACKING: COTTON** / 118 X 91 CM

„Ordnung", „Schlichtheit" und die Abkehr von allem „Weltlichem", d. h. dem Treiben und den Errungenschaften der nicht-amischen modernen Welt, gehören zu den zentralen Prinzipien, von denen das Leben der amischen Gemeinden durchdrungen ist und die für jedes ihrer Mitglieder gelten. Dies schlägt sich auch in den Quilts für die Kinder nieder, ja, sogar in denen für die Puppen. Dieselben abstrakten Motive wie für die großen Quilts werden auch für die kleinen verwendet, und es gibt auch keine niedlichen Details oder – vermeintlich – kindgerechten Farben. Einzig das florale Quilting lockert die geraden Kanten und strenge Geometrie ein wenig auf; aber auch dies ist nicht anders als beim großen Format. // Bars kommen ebenso bei Kinderquilts vor (siehe Nr. 2) wie Diamond in the Square (S. 201) und fast alle anderen Muster – so auch das seltene Rail Fence-Motiv (Bahnschranke), auch Streak of Lightning (Blitzschlag) genannt. Dieser auffällige Quilt besitzt zudem ein für solch kleine Stücke recht aufwändiges Quilting: einander überschneidende Wellenbänder, Flechtband und Diagonalkreuze.

Lit. u. a.: Pellman Rachel u. Kenneth, The World of Amish Quilts. Intercourse/Pa. 1984, 109, Abb. 212 [nah verwandtes Motiv]

'Order', 'simplicity' and the rejection of all 'worldly' things, i.e., the goings-on and achievements of the non-Amish modern world, are among the pivotal principles informing life in Amish communities and binding on each member of the congregation. This is also shown in quilts for children, even in quilts made for dolls. The same abstract motifs were used for both large and small quilts and there are no cute details or – presumably – colors deemed suitable for children. The floral quilting is all that loosens up the straight edges and stringent geometry a bit; but this feature, too, does not differ from the large format. // Bars occur in Crib quilts as well (see no. 2) as do Diamond in the Square (p. 201) and virtually all the other patterns, including the rare 'Rail Fence' (also known as Streak of Lightning). This striking piece boasts very elaborate quilting for such a small piece: intersecting scallops, interlaced bands and diagonal crosses.

References include: Pellman, Rachel and Kenneth, The World of Amish Quilts. Intercourse/Pa. 1984, 109, fig. 212 [closely related motif]

038

FANS, CRIB QUILT

CA 1930
AMISCHE QUILTMACHERIN / **AMISH QUILT-MAKER**, HOLMES COUNTY, OHIO ODER INDIANA
BAUMWOLLE / **COTTON** / RÜCKSEITE: BLAUER BAUMWOLLSTOFF / **BACKING: BLUE COTTON CLOTH** / 142 x 114 CM

Merkmale wie das Fächer-Muster, der helle Hintergrund, die abgerundeten Ecken und das einfache Quilting verweisen auf den Mittleren Westen als Herkunftsgebiet dieses Quilts, der – die geringe Größe zeigt es – für das Bett eines Kindes gemacht wurde. Fächer-Motive tauchen in der europäischen und später auch amerikanischen Kunstgeschichte mit Erschließung des Orients immer wieder auf. Mode wurden sie aber erst seit den Weltausstellungen im 19. Jahrhundert – und ganz besonders seit der Ausstellung zur Hundertjahrfeier der USA 1876 in Philadelphia, bei der der Japanische Pavillon großes Aufsehen erregte. // Das gebogte Fächermotiv ist hier in Diamonds eingefügt; die diagonalen Reihen bilden eine vom Prinzip her gleiche Komposition wie beim Crib Quilt Nr. 36. // QUILTING MIT WEISSEM GARN: Streifendreiecke, Zickzack; im Innenfeld zeichnet das Quilting die Umrisse der Fächer und Restflächen nach.

Features such as the Fan pattern, the light background, the rounded corners and the simple quilting suggest that this quilt came from the Midwest. It was made – as its small size indicates – for a child's bed or crib. Fan motifs recurred in European and later also American art after the Orient was opened up. They did not, however, become fashionable until the world fairs of the 19th century – and particularly from the time of the US centennial celebration in Philadelphia in 1876, where the Japanese Pavilion caused quite a stir. // Here the arced Fan motif is set into Diamonds that form diagonal rows, a composition on the same principle as that used on Crib quilt no. 36. // QUILTING WITH WHITE YARN: triangles in strips; in the inner field the quilting traces the outlines of the Fans and the other fields.

039

LOG CABIN – BARN RAISING

CA 1935
AMISCHE QUILTMACHERIN / **AMISH QUILT-MAKER**, HOLMES COUNTY, OHIO
WOLLE, BAUMWOLLE, BAUMWOLLSATIN / **WOOL, COTTON, COTTON SATEEN** / RÜCKSEITE: BAUMWOLLE (BIBERSTOFF)
MIT KAROMUSTER / **BACKING: CHECKED COTTON TWILLED CLOTH (BEAVERTEEN)** / 192 x 165 CM

Damit ging es los: der erste Quilt der Sammlung Schlumberger. // Noch mehr als die Sunshine and Shadow-Quilts (etwa Nr. 4) lebt der Typus Log Cabin mit seinen Varianten von der Komposition aus helleren und dunklen Stoffstücken, durch deren sorgfältige Anordnung die übergreifenden Musterstrukturen entstehen. Bilden dort kleine Quadrate identischer Größe das Muster, so sind es hier Stoffstreifen gleicher Breite, jedoch unterschiedlicher Länge. Sie werden zu jenen quadratischen Blocks aneinandergenäht, aus denen sich der Quilt zusammensetzt. Dieses Beispiel ist sehr klar gestaltet, mit entschiedenen, harten Farbkontrasten, wie sie durchaus typisch sind für Quilts der Ohio-Amischen – ganz anders wirkt dagegen Quilt Nr. 41. // Bei Lancaster-Amischen wurden die Rückseiten der Quilts häufig aus gemusterten Stoffen genäht – sonst strikt verboten –, während die Schauseite immer aus einfarbigen Stoffstücken besteht. Im Mittleren Westen – Ohio und Indiana – und in Kanada hingegen waren in manchen Gemeinden klein und unauffällig gemusterte Stoffe auch für die Vorderseite erlaubt. Die Rückseite ist meist einfarbig – hier ist sie jedoch aus kariertem Flanell. // QUILTING: Flechtband, doppelte Wellenlinie, Rauten.

This is what started it all off: the first quilt in the Schlumberger Collection. Even more than Sunshine and Shadow quilts (for example no. 4), the Log Cabin type and variants are built on a composition of light and dark patches, which are carefully arranged to structure the overall design. Whereas small squares of identical size form the Sunshine and Shadow pattern, here it is created by strips of material, all of the same width yet of varying lengths. They are sewn together to form the square blocks of which the quilt is composed. The present example is very clearly designed, with definitive, even harsh, color contrasts of a kind entirely typical of quilts made by Ohio Amish – an utterly different effect has, on the other hand, been created in quilt no. 41. // The Lancaster Amish often sewed the backing of their quilts from printed material – something that was otherwise strictly forbidden – whereas the show side always consists of monochrome pieces of cloth. In the Midwest – Ohio and Indiana – as well as Canada, on the other hand, materials with small, reticent designs on them were also permitted for the front of quilts. The backing is usually monochrome – here, however, it is of checked flannel. // QUILTING: cable, double scallops, diamonds.

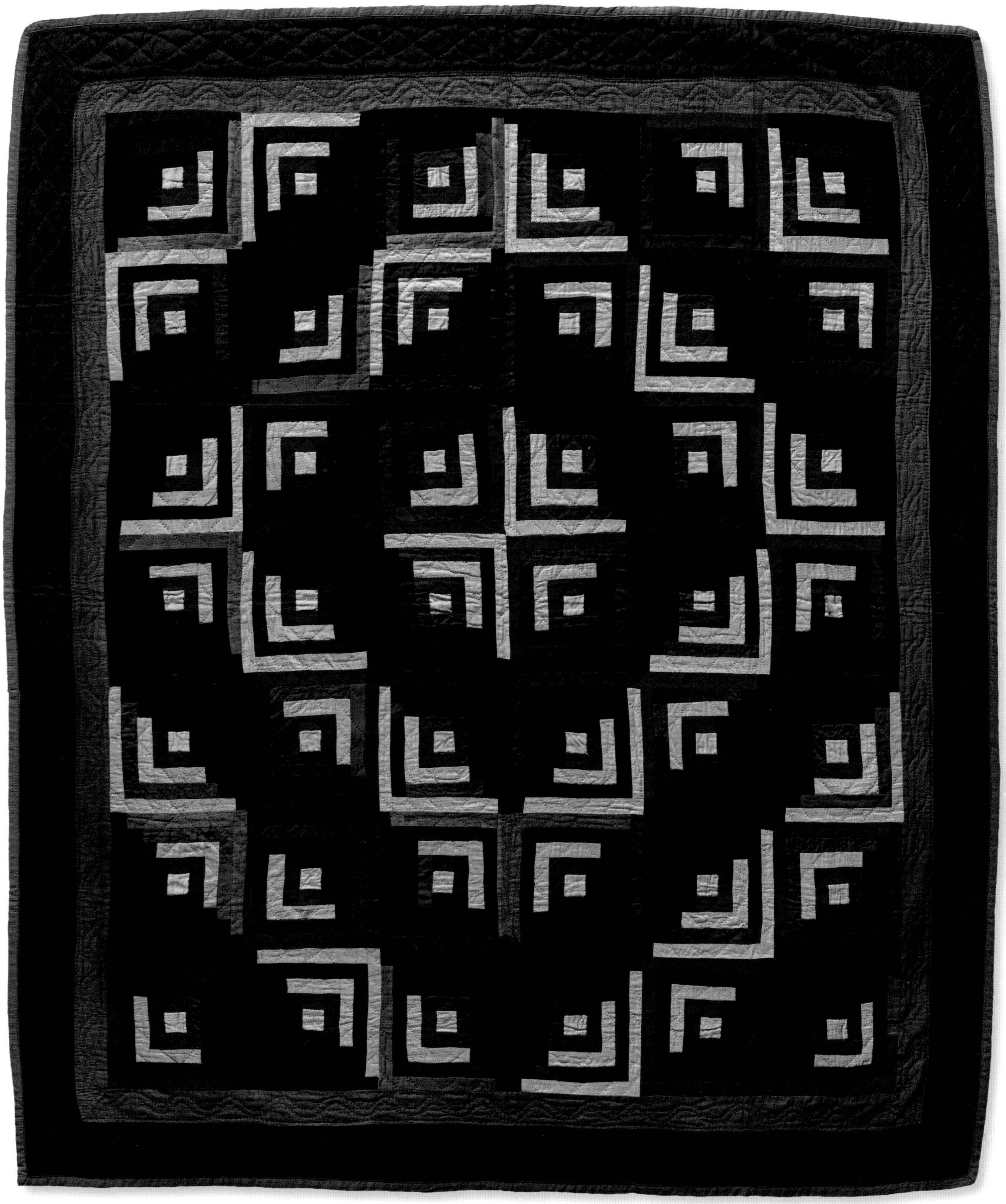

040

LOG CABIN – COURTHOUSE STEPS

CA 1925
AMISCHE QUILTMACHERIN / **AMISH QUILT-MAKER**, HOLMES COUNTY, OHIO
WOLLE, SATIN, BAUMWOLLE / **WOOL, SATIN, COTTON** / RÜCKSEITE: WOLLE / **BACKING: WOOL** / 220 x 182 CM

Eine Variante des Log Cabin ist Courthouse Steps – schmale Stoffstreifen unterschiedlicher Länge sind hier nicht wie bei Straight Furrow oder Barn Raising (Nrn. 6, 39 und 41) im Karree, sondern parallel angeordnet, und zwar so, dass getreppte Diamonds entstehen: die „Stufen des Gerichtsgebäudes". // Die Strenge des Rot-Schwarz-Kontrastes bei diesem Quilt ist sehr reizvoll durch Farbabweichungen innerhalb der Grundtöne gemäßigt. Neben verschiedenen Schwarz- und Rotschattierungen tauchen auch Dunkelblau und Grau auf: Kaum ein anderes Muster ist so geeignet, ohne ästhetische Einbuße Stoffreste aufzubrauchen. Auffällig ist nicht nur das Fehlen eines Rahmens, sondern auch die gestalterische Betonung der Ecken – wie stilisierte Baluster, die dem Stück geradezu tektonischen Charakter verleihen. // QUILTING: parallele Diagonallinien.

Courthouse Steps is a variant of the Log Cabin pattern – narrow strips of material of varying length are not arranged here in a square as they are in Straight Furrow or Barn Raising (nos. 6, 39 and 41) but instead are aligned in parallel so that stepped Diamonds are created: the 'Courthouse Steps' in fact. // The astringent contrast between red and black has been moderated very attractively in this quilt by color variations on the ground tone. Dark blue and gray appear alongside varying shades of black and red: hardly any other pattern is so suited to using up scraps of cloth without suffering aesthetically. A striking feature is the lack of a border; another is the emphasis placed on the corners in this pattern – they are like stylized balusters, which lend this piece a really tectonic character. // QUILTING: parallel diagonal lines.

041

LOG CABIN – BARN RAISING

1916
AMISCHE QUILTMACHERIN HANNAH STECKLE (STECKLY) GINGERICH / **AMISH QUILT-MAKER HANNAH STECKLE (STECKLY) GINGERICH,**
SAMUEL STECKLY DISTRICT, ONTARIO, KANADA
WOLLE, SEIDE, BAUMWOLLE, BAUMWOLLSATIN / **WOOL, SILK, COTTON, COTTON SATEEN /**
RÜCKSEITE: GROSSGEMUSTERTER BAUMWOLLCHINTZ MIT BLUMEN UND PAPAGEIEN / **BACKING: CHINTZ WITH A PATTERN**
OF LARGE FLOWERS AND PARROTS / 200 x 176 CM

Den Gewährsleuten zufolge hatte Alvin Gingerich diesen Quilt von seiner Mutter Hannah Steckle Gingerich zur Hochzeit geschenkt bekommen;
er verstarb 1991 im Alter von 97 Jahren. // Schmale Stoffstreifen – darunter auch zahlreiche Stücke mit kleinen Webmustern (siehe Quilt
Nr. 39) – legen sich rechtwinklig um einen kleinen quadratischen Kern und lassen so quadratische Felder (blocks) entstehen – jene Log
Cabins, also „Blockhütten", die dem Muster seinen Namen geben. Sie sind diagonal halbiert: halb aus helleren, halb aus dunkleren Farben
zusammengesetzt. Im Unterschied zu Nr. 6 sind die Blocks hier jedoch nicht auf die Spitze gestellt. Stattdessen verbinden sie sich farblich
zu einem die gesamte Fläche übergreifenden Rautenmuster – dem „Barn Raising"-Motiv, das auf eines der zentralen Geschehnisse amischer
Gemeinden verweist: das gemeinschaftliche Errichten einer Scheune. In seiner dunkel leuchtenden Farbigkeit ein prächtiges Stück von ein-
dringlicher Vitalität. // QUILTING: seitliche Rahmenstreifen: geometrisches Muster aus einander überschneidenden Kreisen; schmalere
Streifen oben und unten: Kreise; innen: Diagonallinien.

**According to informants, Alvin Gingerich was given this quilt as a wedding present by his mother, Hannah Steckle Gingerich. He died in
1991 at the age of ninety-seven. // Narrow strips of cloth – including numerous pieces with small woven patterns (see quilt no. 39) –
are arranged at right angles around a small square core so that square fields (blocks) are created – the eponymous 'Log Cabins' that
give the design its name. They are diagonally bisected: composed of colors, half of which are light and half of which are darker. Unlike
no. 6, however, the blocks do not rest on their points. Instead they are linked by color to form an overall lozenge pattern that covers
the entire field – the 'Barn Raising' motif that alludes to one of the most important events in Amish communities: building a barn by
communal. A magnificent piece that is invigoratingly stunning in a dark, vibrant color scheme. // QUILTING: side borders: geometric
design of intersecting circles; narrower strips top and bottom: circles; inner field: diagonal lines.**

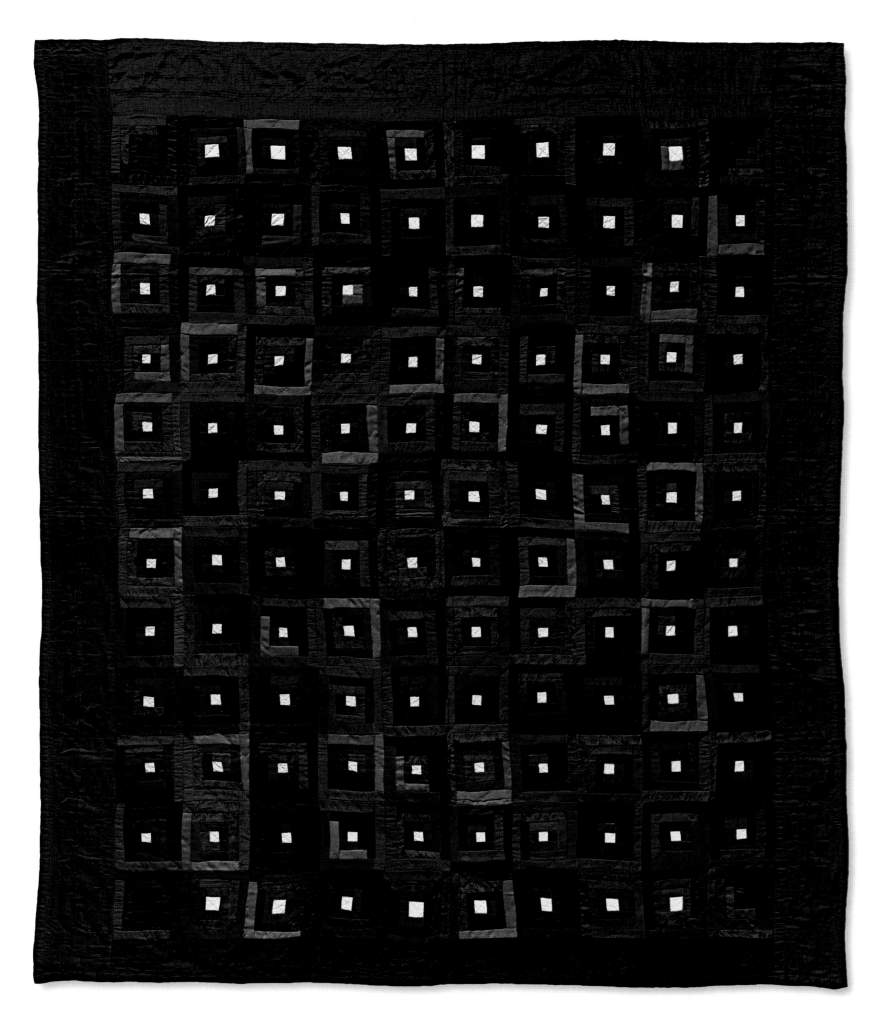

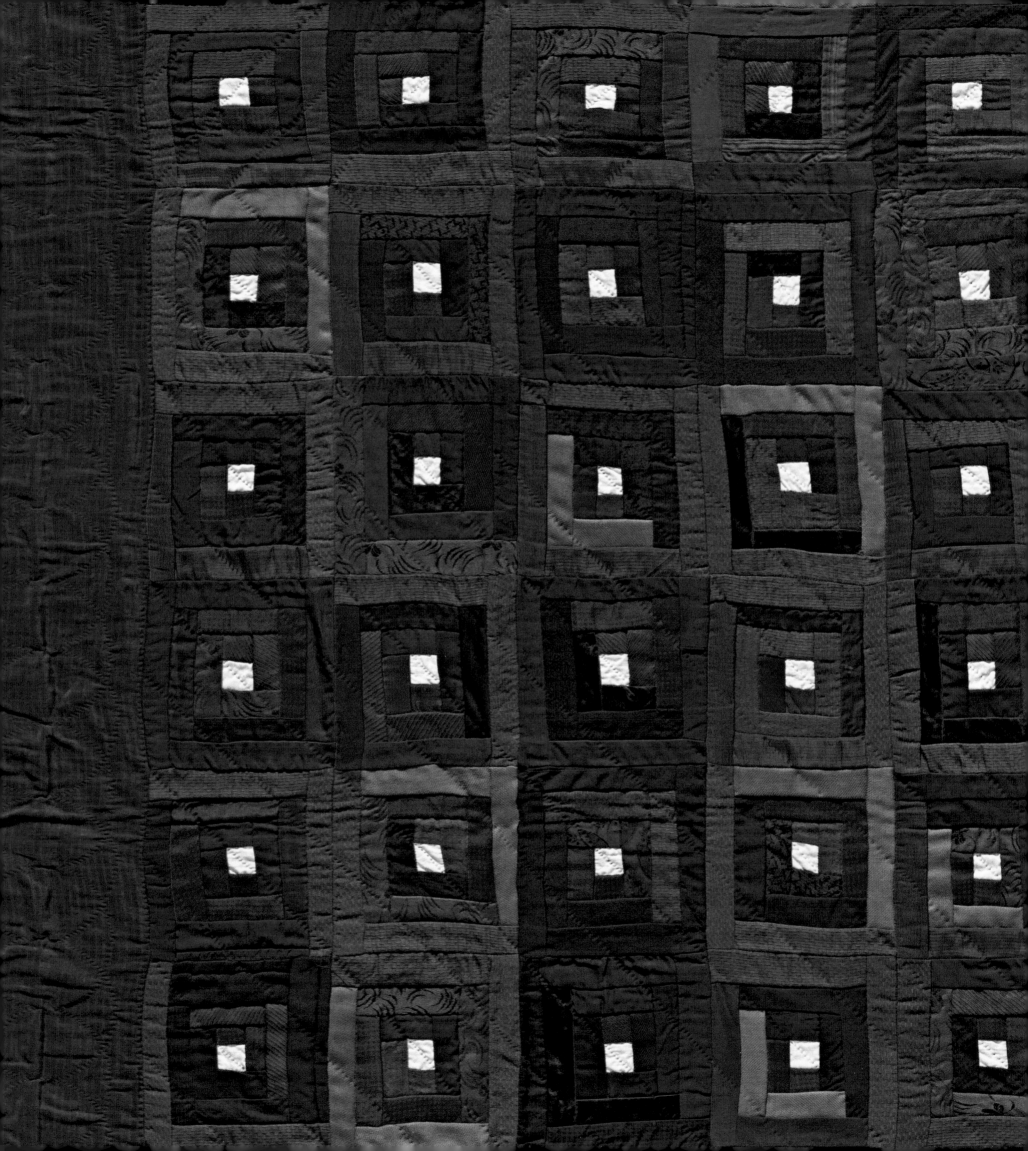

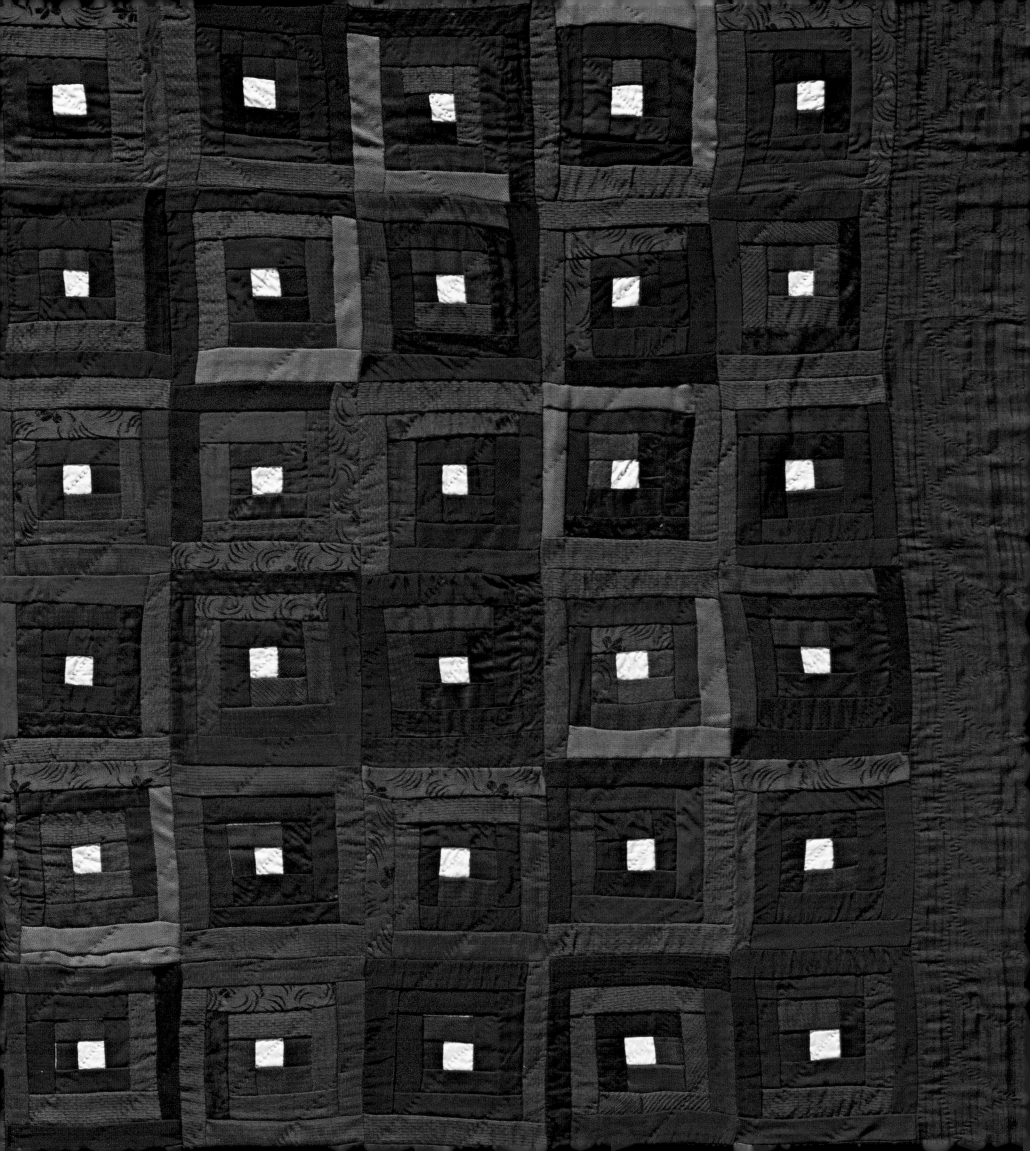

042

VARIABLE STARS / OHIO STARS

CA 1910/15
AMISCHE QUILTMACHERIN / **AMISH QUILT-MAKER**, HOLMES COUNTY, OHIO
BAUMWOLLSATIN, BAUMWOLLE / **COTTON SATEEN, COTTON** / RÜCKSEITE: ZWEI VERSCHIEDENE
BAUMWOLLSTOFFE, ROSA-BRAUN GESTREIFT UND EINFARBIG BLAU / **BACKING: TWO DIFFERENT**
TYPES OF COTTON CLOTH, REDDISH BROWN STRIPED AND MONOCHROME BLUE / 208 x 166 CM
PROVENIENZ / **PROVENANCE**: CRAFT AND FOLK ART MUSEUM, LOS ANGELES

Der Schatz an Mustern ist bei den Ohio-Amischen weit reicher als bei Quilts aus Pennsylvania – und speziell aus Lancaster County. Während sich dort die gestalterische Neigung auf den Typus mit großem zentralem Motiv – Diamond in the Square oder Sunshine and Shadow – konzentriert, gilt hier das Interesse vor allem Reihenmustern, z. B. solchen aus sternförmigen Elementen. // Mit starker graphischer Wirkung stehen die hellen Ohio Stars frei auf dem schwarzen Grund, der in die Gestaltung der Sterne einbezogen ist. Das Motiv besteht aus Dreiecken und einem kleinen, auf der Spitze stehenden Innenquadrat. Gekonnt sind wenige farblich hervorstechende Sterne in Rot und Blau asymmetrisch über die Fläche verteilt. // QUILTING MIT HELLEM UND DUNKLEM GARN: Wellenbänder, geometrisches Muster aus einander überschneidenden Halbkreisen in der Art eines Astragal, Gitterwerk, Parallellinien.

The repertory of patterns is far richer among the Ohio Amish than on Pennsylvania quilts, especially Lancaster County. And whereas in Lancaster County designs tend to be concentrated on the type with a large central motif – Diamond in the Square or Sunshine and Shadow – in Ohio the interest is mainly in row patterns, for instance rows of star-shaped elements. // Markedly graphic in appearance like a print, the light Ohio Stars stand out free on the black ground, which is incorporated in the design of the Stars. The motif consists of triangles and a small inner square standing on end. A few stars in striking red and blue are distributed asymmetrically across the field, a distinctive touch. // QUILTING WITH BRIGHT AND DARK YARN: scallop bands, geometric patterns formed of intersecting semicircles rather like bead and reel, waffle grids, parallel lines.

043

CRAZY QUILT

CA 1930
AMISCHE QUILTMACHERIN / **AMISH QUILT-MAKER**, MIFFLIN COUNTY, PENNSYLVANIA
WOLLE, BAUMWOLLE, SEIDE / **WOOL, COTTON, SILK** / RÜCKSEITE: BAUMWOLLE /
BACKING: COTTON / 195 x 198 CM

Crazy Quilts waren bei den „Englischen" eine Mode der Viktorianischen Zeit. Mit zeitlicher Verzögerung taucht das verblüffende Muster auch bei den Amischen auf. Nicht nur die Stoffstücke sind völlig unregelmäßig in Größe und Form, sondern es werden auch viele verschiedene Stoffarten verwendet, und wilde Ziernähte in kontrastierendem Garn überziehen die Komposition mit einer Art Spinnennetz. In vielen Varianten wird die Verrücktheit gewissermaßen gebändigt – etwa, indem die unregelmäßigen Stoffstücke zu Diamonds geordnet werden, die sich streng mit leeren Diamonds abwechseln. Recht ungezähmt wirkt dagegen dieser Crazy Quilt der Sammlung Schlumberger. Trotzdem: Auf den zweiten Blick ist zu sehen, dass hier auch Reihen aus großen quadratischen Blocks die Struktur bilden. Ein kräftiger schwarzer Rahmen gibt dem Innenfeld festen Halt. // QUILTING: Fächer.

Crazy Quilts were in fashion among the 'English' in the Victorian era. The astonishing pattern also appeared among the Amish after some time had lapsed. Not only are the pieces of cloth entirely irregular in size and shape; many different kinds of cloth are used and crazy decorative seams in contrasting yarn cover the composition to form a sort of spider web. In many variants the craziness is to a certain extent watered down – the irregular pieces of cloth have been arranged in Diamonds alternating regularly with empty Diamonds. This Crazy Quilt in the Schlumberger Collection, on the other hand, looks pretty much untamed. Nevertheless, at second sight, it becomes clear that rows of large square blocks form a structure here, too. A powerful black border firmly anchors the inner field. // QUILTING: Fans.

044

BARS

CA 1880/90
AMISCHE QUILTMACHERIN DER FAMILIE SAMUEL STOLTZFUS / **AMISH QUILT-MAKER**
FROM THE FAMILY OF SAMUEL STOLTZFUS, LANCASTER COUNTY, PENNSYLVANIA
WOLLE / **WOOL** / RÜCKSEITE: KLEINGEMUSTERTER BAUMWOLLSTOFF / **BACKING: COTTON CLOTH**
WITH A SMALL PATTERN / 210 x 200 CM
PROVENIENZ / **PROVENANCE**: DAVID WHEATCROFT, WESTBOROUGH, MASSACHUSETTS

Durch aufgestickte Jahreszahlen zweifelsfrei datierbare Quilts gibt es relativ selten. Insgesamt sind nur wenige Stücke erhalten, für die eine Entstehung vor 1900 angenommen werden kann. Für eine frühe Entstehung dieses Stückes, das aus der Familie Samuel Stoltzfus kommt, sprechen der im Verhältnis zum Innenfeld sehr breite Außenrahmen, die geringe Zahl der Bars, die Erdtöne der Farben und das exakte, feine, sehr differenzierte und sorgsam stilisierte Quilting. // Dass jedoch relativ viele Farben verwendet wurden, könnte eine spätere Datierung vermuten lassen, ebenso der Aufbau mit Innenrahmen und Eckquadraten. Denkbar wäre aber auch, dass um 1900 eine ältere Frau diesen Quilt hergestellt hat – noch geübt in der einstigen Nadelfertigkeit, an den in ihrer Jugend gebräuchlichen Proportionen festhaltend, aber bei der Komposition inspiriert durch einen moderneren Stil. // Den Old Order Amish, und vor allem jenen in Lancaster County, waren gemusterte Stoffe verboten – auf den Rückseiten ihrer Quilts tauchen sie allerdings trotzdem auf; ganz offenkundig wurde diese Meterware eigens dafür gekauft. // QUILTING: Federranken mit Rosetten, große Sonnenblumenmotive, Weinranken, sechszackige Sterne; auf den weißen Bars nochmals Weinranken, jedoch in größeren Wellen; farnartige Ranken mit kleinen Blütchen.

There are relatively few quilts that can be objectively dated by embroidered date numerals. Only a few quilts have survived that can be dated with assurance to before 1900. The following features suggest an early date for this quilt, which comes from the family of Samuel Stoltzfus: the outer field being very wide compared to the inner, the low number of Bars, the earthy color tones and the precise, fine, very sophisticated and meticulously stylized quilting. // Nevertheless, the fact that a relatively large number of colors was used might also suggest a later date as might also the structure with an inner frame and corner blocks. It is also conceivable that an elderly woman made this quilt around 1900 – a quilt-maker still handy with her needle, who clung to the proportions usual in her youth but who let herself be inspired by a more modern style in her approach to composition. // Printed and patterned materials were forbidden to the Old Order Amish, especially to those living in Lancaster County – but they do appear on the backs of their quilts; obviously these bolts of cloth were bought especially for the use to which they were put. // QUILTING: feather scrolls with rosettes, large Sunflower motifs, grape vines, Six-Pointed Stars; on the white Bars again grape vines but in larger scrolls; fern-like scrolls with tiny flowers.

045

CENTER DIAMOND / DIAMOND IN THE SQUARE

CA 1920
AMISCHE QUILTMACHERIN / **AMISH QUILT-MAKER**, LANCASTER COUNTY, PENNSYLVANIA
WOLLE / **WOOL** / RÜCKSEITE: BLAUWEISS MELIERTE BAUMWOLLE / **BACKING: BLUE-AND-WHITE MOTTLED COTTON** /
183 x 184 CM

Bauern inmitten fruchtbaren Landes, sind die Amischen in Lancaster County meist wohlhabende Leute. Daher konnten sie nicht nur darauf verzichten, bei ihren Quilts Stoffreste zu verwerten – im Gegenteil, oft scheint es, als seien die Stoffe eigens für diese großflächigen Stücke erworben. // Dieser Quilt ähnelt in seiner Komposition Nr. 11: Es gibt keine Eckquadrate im Innenrahmen und keine diagonale Farbverbindung vom Zentrum zu den Ecken – im Gegensatz zu vielen anderen Center Diamonds der Sammlung Schlumberger, etwa Nrn. 17, 25 und 33, um nur diejenigen zu nennen, bei denen Diamond und Innenrahmen ebenfalls rot sind. Bei Nr. 45 wie bei Nr. 11 wiederholt sich zudem das Rot auch in den Eckquadraten des Außenrahmens. Sich solche Details bewusst zu machen, kann sehr reizvoll sein, wenn man versucht, den Gründen für die Wirkung eines Quilts nachzuspüren. Mittels der Eckquadrate ist das quadratische Zentrum bei diesem Diamond in the Square besonders stark – noch stärker als bei Nr. 11 – mit dem Gesamtformat verbunden, da die Gestalterin für die übrigen Flächen ungewöhnliche helle, und damit äußerst zurückhaltende Farben gewählt hat. Der Farbton der Dreiecke im Innenfeld wiederholt sich bei der Umfassung des Quilts und intensiviert ebenfalls den vorherrschenden Ausdruck von großer Ruhe, Entschiedenheit und klarer Organisation – kurz: „Ordnung", einer der zentralen Werte amischer Weltauffassung. // QUILTING: Federranken, Kreuzblüten-Rauten-Leiste, Bogenborte, Diagonalgitter; großer achtzackiger Stern, Federkranz, Blüten.

Since they farm in the midst of lushly fertile countryside, the Lancaster County Amish are usually prosperous people. Hence they not only can eschew using scraps of left-over material for their quilts – on the contrary, it often seems as if the materials used were acquired for the express purpose of making these large pieces. // In composition this quilt resembles no. 11: there are no corner squares in the inner frame and no diagonal color links between the center and the corners – unlike many other Center Diamonds in the Schlumberger Collection, including nos. 17, 25 and 33, to name just a few examples with Diamond and inner borders both in red. Moreover, in no. 45, as in no. 11, the red is repeated in the corner blocks of the outer border. Becoming aware of such details is fun and challenging when one is trying to track down why a particular quilt makes such an impact. By means of the corner blocks, the square center of this 'Diamond in the Square' is particularly firmly – even more emphatically so than in no. 11 – tied into the overall format since the designer chose unusually light as well as extremely reticent colors for the other fields. The color tone of the triangles in the inner field is repeated in the edging of the quilt and also heightens the prevailing impression of great repose, resolve and clear organization – in brief: 'order', a pivotal value in the Amish world-view. // QUILTING: feather scroll, Starflower-lozenge strips, scallop, diagonal grid; large Eight-Pointed Star, feather wreath, flowers.

046

TUMBLING BLOCKS

2. HÄLFTE 19. JAHRHUNDERT / **EARLY 2ND HALF 19TH CENTURY**
AMISCH-MENNONITISCHE QUILTMACHERIN LYDIA JANTZI, GEB. NAFZIGER / **AMISH MENNONITE QUILT-MAKER LYDIA JANTZI,**
NÉE NAFZIGER, MILVERTON, ONTARIO, KANADA
WOLLE, SEIDE, BAUMWOLL-SEIDE-MISCHGEWEBE, WOLLE-SEIDE-MISCHGEWEBE; EINIGE SPÄTERE AUSBESSERUNGEN MIT KUNSTFASERSTOFF /
WOOL, SILK, MIXED COTTON AND SILK, MIXED WOOL AND SILK; SOME LATER REPAIRS CARRIED OUT IN SYNTHETIC FIBER /
RÜCKSEITE: LEINEN IN DREI BAHNEN VON CA. 60 CM BREITE / **BACKING: LINEN IN THREE PANELS, EACH APPROX. 60 CM WIDE /**
190 x 189 CM

Der Familientradition zufolge soll dieser Quilt, dessen spezielle Form für ein Himmelbett, das four-poster bed, gemacht war, um 1851/52 entstanden sein. Da amische Quilts aus der Zeit vor 1880 extrem selten sind, wäre dies ein sensationell frühes Entstehungsdatum. Die noch manufaktur-gewebten Stoffe, die pflanzlichen Farben und die Handarbeit – es wurde keine Nähmaschine verwendet – sprechen tatsächlich für eine Entstehung im 19. Jahrhundert. Der Quilt ist mit grüner Wolltresse umfasst; auffällig ist die Nachlässigkeit des sehr einfachen Quiltings, das die Rautenumrisse nachzeichnet. // Christian Nafziger aus Bayern war der erste amische, genauer: amisch-mennonitische Einwanderer in Kanada. Nach langer Reise via Amsterdam, New Orleans und Lancaster County, Pennsylvania, kam er 1822 in Waterloo

According to Jantzi family tradition, this quilt, which was made in a shape to fit a canopied four-poster bed, dates from ca 1851/52.
Since Amish quilts made before 1880 are extremely rare this would be a sensationally early date indeed. The factory loom-woven
materials, the vegetable dyes and the sewing and quilting done by hand – a sewing machine was not used – actually do argue for a 19th-
century date. The quilt is edged with green woolen braid; the carelessness with which the very simple quilting was executed to trace
the outlines of the lozenges is very apparent. // Christian Nafziger of Bavaria was the first Amish, more precisely, Amish Mennonite,
emigrant to Canada. After a long roundabout voyage via Amsterdam, New Orleans and Lancaster County, Pennsylvania, he arrived in

County, Ontario, an, um Land für seine Glaubensgefährten zu kaufen. 1824 ließen sich dort die ersten Amish Mennonites nieder, darunter auch die ebenfalls aus Bayern stammende Jantzi-Familie, in die Lydia Nafziger (geb. 1798 in Regensburg) 1830 einheiratete. Sie soll diesen äußerst prächtigen, festlichen Quilt zur Hochzeit ihres Sohnes Samuel, eines ihrer sechs Kinder, gefertigt haben. // Der Siegeszug der Nähmaschine begann mit ihrer Markteinführung 1856; sehr rasch eroberte sie auch amische Haushalte. Die Arbeitserleichterung durch die pedalbetriebene „Singer" fiel in eine Zeit, in der selbstgewebte Stoffe oder solche aus Manufakturen mehr und mehr durch industriell produzierte ersetzt wurden – Textilien, die in den Manufakturen oder Fabriken zunächst noch mit natürlichen Farbstoffen, zunehmend aber mit chemischen gefärbt wurden. Der bei aller Kleinteiligkeit aufsehenerregend für Fernwirkung komponierte Quilt der Sammlung Schlumberger könnte aus jener Umbruchsphase in der 2. Hälfte des 19. Jahrhunderts stammen. // Der sechszackige Stern, der stets im Tumbling-Blocks-Muster enthalten ist, wurde – seine farbliche Betonung zeigt es – bewusst als Mitte des Stückes eingesetzt. Von dort aus entwickelt sich das Muster wie bei einer Explosion; farblich sind die kleinen Rautenelemente so geordnet, dass eine innere Fläche durch ein großes Hexagon umfasst wird. So klingt das Center Medaillon-Kompositionsschema an, das um die Mitte des 19. Jahrhundert bei nicht-amischen Quiltmacherinnen „en vogue" war. Es ist vorstellbar, dass im relativ liberalen mennonitischen Umfeld damals ein solch „modisches" Muster toleriert wurde.

Waterloo County, Ontario, in 1822 to purchase land for his fellow Amish Mennonites. In 1824 the first Amish Mennonites settled there, including the Jantzi family, who also came from Bavaria. Lydia Nafziger (b. in Regensburg in 1798), who married into the Jantzi family in 1830, is said to have made this utterly magnificent, festive quilt for the wedding of her son Samuel, one of her six children. // The all-conquering sewing machine was an immediate success when it was launched on the market in 1856; it very soon became a staple commodity in Amish households as well. The labor-saving convenience of the treadle-driven Singer became available just at a time when home-loomed cloth or textiles loom-woven in factories were being increasingly replaced by industrially manufactured products – natural dyes were at first still used at textile mills but they were soon replaced by chemical dyes. This quilt in the Schlumberger Collection could very well date from this transitional period in the early second half of the 19th century. // Its intricate pattern was designed to be viewed at a distance – a very fascinating feature. The Six-Pointed Star, which is always integrated in the Tumbling Blocks pattern, was – the colors emphasize this – deliberately planned to form the center of the quilt. The pattern explodes outwards from there; the small lozenge elements are arranged by color so that an inner field is framed by a large hexagon. Thus the Center Medallion composition scheme is ushered in, that was very much en vogue among non-Amish quilt-makers in the mid-19th century. Conceivably, a 'fashionable' pattern of this kind was tolerated then in the relatively liberal Mennonite environment.

047

ONE PATCH – VARIATION

CA 1900
AMISCHE QUILTMACHERIN / **AMISH QUILT-MAKER**, TUSCARAWAS COUNTY, OHIO
BAUMWOLLE, WOLLE / **COTTON, WOOL** / RÜCKSEITE: BAUMWOLLE /
BACKING: COTTON / 227 x 193 CM

Datierung und Lokalisierung dieses sehr ungewöhnlichen Quilts, über den nichts Genaueres bekannt ist, erfolgen aufgrund seiner nahen Verwandtschaft mit einem Stück aus der Sammlung Monika Müller, Wetzikon/Schweiz. Das Muster ist ohne Parallele und bisher unbenannt. // In beiden Fällen handelt es sich um ein Reihenmuster auf der Basis von One Patches, kleinen Quadraten. Einige davon sind durch zwei kleine Dreiecke ersetzt, und die Verteilung der Farben ist so organisiert, dass der Eindruck von abwechselnd dunklen und hellen Zickzackbändern entsteht, die über das Innenfeld laufen. Umgrenzt wird das Innenfeld von einem schmalen grünen Rahmen, den ein nur geringfügig breiterer Rahmen aus kleinen Dreiecken umfasst, während der Außenrahmen ästhetisch völlig zurückgenommen ist. // Die große Ähnlichkeit der beiden Quilts in den Sammlungen Schlumberger und Monika Müller erlaubt die Vermutung, dass sie von ein und derselben Person gestaltet wurden; siehe auch Nrn. 5, 51/52 und 66/72. // QUILTING: Wellenbänder, Gitterwerk.

Lit. u. a.: [Kat. Ausst.] Amish Quilts 1870–1920. Collection Monika Müller Zurich. Musée d'art et d'histoire. Genève 1975, Nr. 21, Titel-Abb. [Vergleichsstück, hier 1880 datiert und „Villages" benannt] / [Kat. Ausst.] Quilts des Amish 1870–1930. Musée des arts décoratifs de la Ville de Lausanne. Lausanne 1988, Taf. 38 [Vergleichsstück der Sammlung Müller]

This highly unusual quilt, about which nothing precise is known, was dated and localized on the grounds of its close affinities with a piece from the Monika Müller Collection, Wetzikon, Switzerland. The pattern is without parallels and, therefore, unnamed. // Both quilts boast a row pattern based on One Patches, small squares. Some of them have been replaced by two small triangles and the distribution of color is organized to create an impression of alternating dark and light zigzag strips running across the inner field. The inner field in turn is surrounded by a narrow green frame, edged by an only slightly broader border composed of small triangles, whereas the outer frame is, aesthetically speaking, of less importance. // The close resemblance of the two quilts in the Schlumberger Collection and the Monika Müller Collection suggests that they were designed by the same person; see also nos. 5, 51/52, and 66/72. // QUILTING: scallops, waffle grid.

References include: [Exhib. cat.] Amish Quilts 1870–1920. Collection Monika Müller Zurich. Musée d'art et d'histoire. Genève 1975, no. 21, cover picture [Piece for comparison, here dated to 1880 and called 'Villages'] / [Exhib. cat.] Quilts des Amish 1870–1930. Musée des arts décoratifs de la Ville de Lausanne. Lausanne 1988, pl. 38 [piece for comparison from the Müller Collection]

048

STAIRWAY TO HEAVEN

1899
AMISCHE QUILTMACHERIN / **AMISH QUILT-MAKER**, MIFFLIN COUNTY, PENNSYLVANIA
MONOGRAMMIERT UND DATIERT, INNENRAHMEN MITTE UNTEN: KJY BY KY 1899 / **MONOGRAMMED AND DATED,**
INNER BORDER, BOTTOM CENTER: KJY BY KY 1899
LEICHTE WOLLE, BAUMWOLLE, SATIN / **LIGHTWEIGHT WOOL, COTTON, SATIN** /
RÜCKSEITE: BAUMWOLLE / **BACKING: COTTON** / 203 x 177 CM

Auch Stairway to Heaven kann – wie Chinese Coins (Nr. 66) – als Variante des Typus Bars angesehen werden. Schräggestellte, rechteckige Stoffstücke, die in die hellen Balken gefüllt sind, bilden die Himmelsleitern. Der gedämpfte Dreiklang aus sattem Blau, Goldocker und Rot bestimmt die Wirkung dieses Stückes. Oben und unten ist der Innenrahmen durch einen weiteren, roten Rahmenstreifen verdoppelt, was sehr ungewöhnlich ist. Auf dem unteren dieser Streifen sind in der Mitte die Jahreszahl und die Monogramme eingesteppt, die sich lesen wie die Initialen von drei Personen. // QUILTING: Farnranken, Wellenband, Kreuzblüten-Rauten-Muster, Fächer.

Stairway to Heaven – like Chinese Coins (no. 66) – can be regarded as a variant of the Bars type. Rectangular pieces of cloth arranged diagonally to fill the light bars form the ladders to heaven. A muted chord of saturated blue, gold ochre and red is what creates the effect made by this piece. At top and bottom the inner border is doubled by another, red border, a highly unusual feature. The center of the lower edge of these strips bears a quilted date and monograms which read as if they were the initials of three people. // QUILTING: ferns, scallop, Starflower-lozenge pattern, Fans.

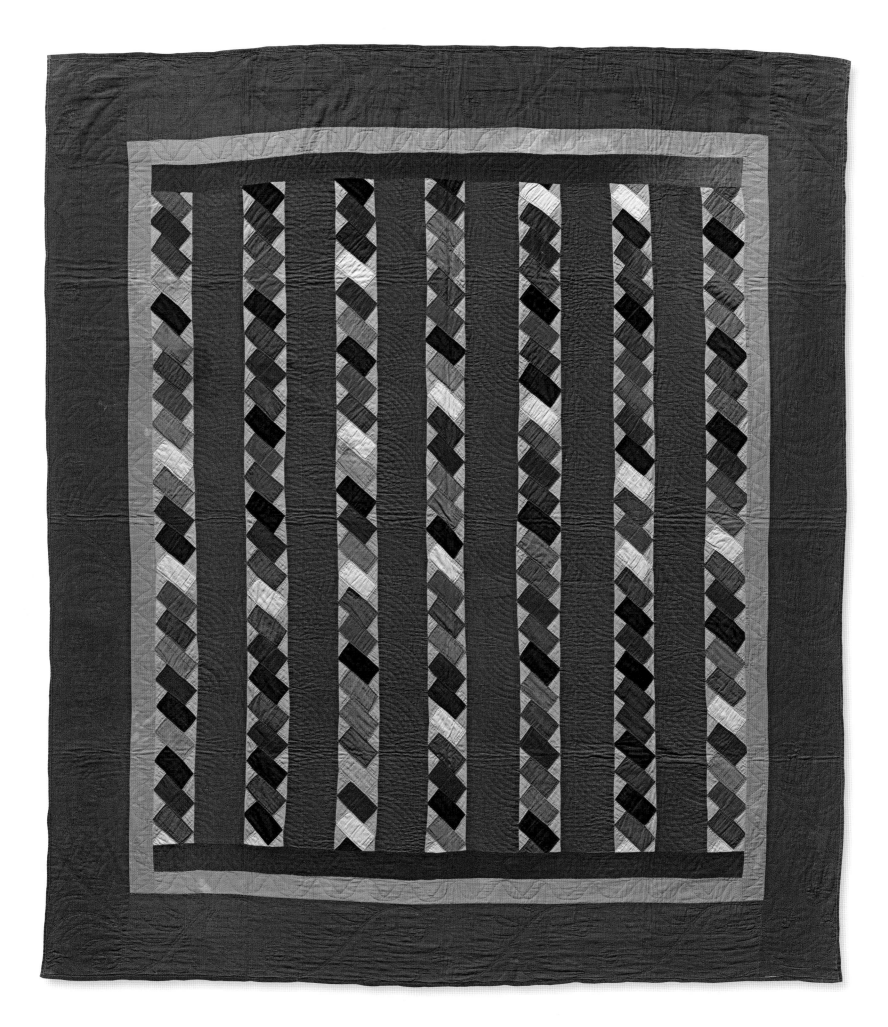

049

TUMBLING BLOCKS – COLUMBIA STARS VARIATION

CA 1915
AMISCHE QUILTMACHERIN / **AMISH QUILT-MAKER**, ELKHART COUNTY, INDIANA
BAUMWOLLE / **COTTON** / RÜCKSEITE: BLAUER BAUMWOLLSTOFF / **BACKING: BLUE COTTON CLOTH** / 184 x 172 CM

Wie nah verwandt Tumbling Blocks und Stars sein können, zeigt dieser Quilt aus dem Mittleren Westen. Beide Muster bestehen aus rauten-förmigen Stoffstückchen – für die Columbia Stars ist sogar die Anordnung identisch. Während jedoch bei Tumbling Blocks die optische Täuschung aufeinandergestapelter Würfel durch eine exakte Abstimmung von hellen, mittleren und dunklen Farbtönen entsteht, ist bei Columbia Stars das Muster flächig, das Auge nimmt sechszackige Sterne wahr. Bei diesem Stück scheinen sie inmitten von Hexagonen zu stehen – eine recht wilde Komposition. Dennoch ist eine gewisse Ordnung erkennbar: Helle Zonen, in denen Weißtöne und Schwarz domi-nieren, wechseln ab mit dunkleren, in denen Blau- und Rottöne vorherrschen. // Das Quilting, bei dem das Fächermotiv Außenrahmen und Innenrahmen unterschiedslos übergreift, differenziert im Innenfeld genau und legt gleichsam eine zweite Ebene über die Sterne und Hexa-gone: In wechselnden Reihen sind entweder die Umrisse der rautenförmigen Stoffstückchen nachgesteppt oder es durchziehen Parallellinien die hexagonalen Felder.

This Midwestern quilt shows how closely related Tumbling Blocks and Stars may be. Both patterns are composed of lozenge-shaped pieces of cloth – the arrangement is even identical in Columbia Stars. However, whereas the optical illusion of piled up cubes is created in Tumbling Blocks by light, medium and dark color tones being precisely attuned, in Columbia Stars the pattern is two-dimensional and the Six-Pointed Stars are what is noticed. In the present quilt, they seem to stand in the midst of hexagons – a rather wild composition. Nevertheless, a certain order is recognizable: light zones, in which shades of white and black are dominant alternate with darker zones in which blues and reds predominate. // The quilting, in which the Fan motif spans equally the outer and the inner borders, precisely differentiates in the inner field, overlaying, as it were, the stars and hexagons with a second plane: in alternating rows the outlines of the lozenge-shaped pieces of cloth are either traced in the quilting or parallel lines run through the hexagonal fields.

050

BROKEN DISHES

CA 1930
AMISCHE QUILTMACHERIN / **AMISH QUILT-MAKER**, GEAUGA COUNTY, OHIO
BAUMWOLLE / **COTTON** / RÜCKSEITE: DUNKELBLAUER BAUMWOLLSTOFF /
BACKING: DARK BLUE COTTON CLOTH / 202 x 167 CM

Amische Quilts aus dem Mittleren Westen – Ohio oder Indiana – zeigen eine weit größere Vielfalt an Mustern als die aus Pennsylvania stammenden Quilts. Broken Dishes ist wie Ocean Waves, Ohio Stars, Shoofly, Birds in the Air, Railroad Crossing und viele andere aus kleinen dreieckigen Stoffstücken aufgebaut. Hier bilden sie, dicht an dicht nebeneinander gesetzt, Reihen von Quadraten. Auf den ersten Eindruck von gedämpfter Farbigkeit, entfaltet sich bei genauerem Hinsehen eine erstaunlich reichhaltige Palette von Blau-, Braun- und Grüntönen; dazu kommt das bei den Ohio-Amischen bevorzugte Schwarz. // QUILTING: Fächer, Rautenleiste; bei den Dreiecken sind die Umrisse jeweils an zwei Seiten winkelförmig nachgesteppt.

Lit. u. a.: [Kat. Ausst.] Amish Quilts 1880 to 1940 from the Collection of Faith and Stephen Brown. Michigan Museum of Art. Ann Arbor / Mich. 2000, Taf. 11 [nah verwandter Crib Quilt, circa 1930, vermutlich Holmes County, Ohio]

Amish quilts from the Midwest – Ohio and Indiana – reveal a far greater diversity in patterns than quilts from Pennsylvania. Broken Dishes is, like Ocean Waves, Ohio Stars, Shoofly, Birds in the Air, Railroad Crossing and many other Midwestern patterns, built up of small triangular pieces of cloth. Here, densely arrayed, they form rows of squares. At first sight the palette seems muted but on closer scrutiny it is revealed as an astonishingly rich one of blues, browns and greens, plus black, which was so popular with the Ohio Amish. // QUILTING: Fans, Diamond strip; the outlines of the triangles are traced in stitching to form angles on two sides.

References include: [Exhib. cat.] Amish Quilts 1880 to 1940, from the Collection of Faith and Stephen Brown. Michigan Museum of Art. Ann Arbor / Mich. 2000, pl. 11 [a closely related Crib quilt, 'circa 1930, probably Holmes County, Ohio']

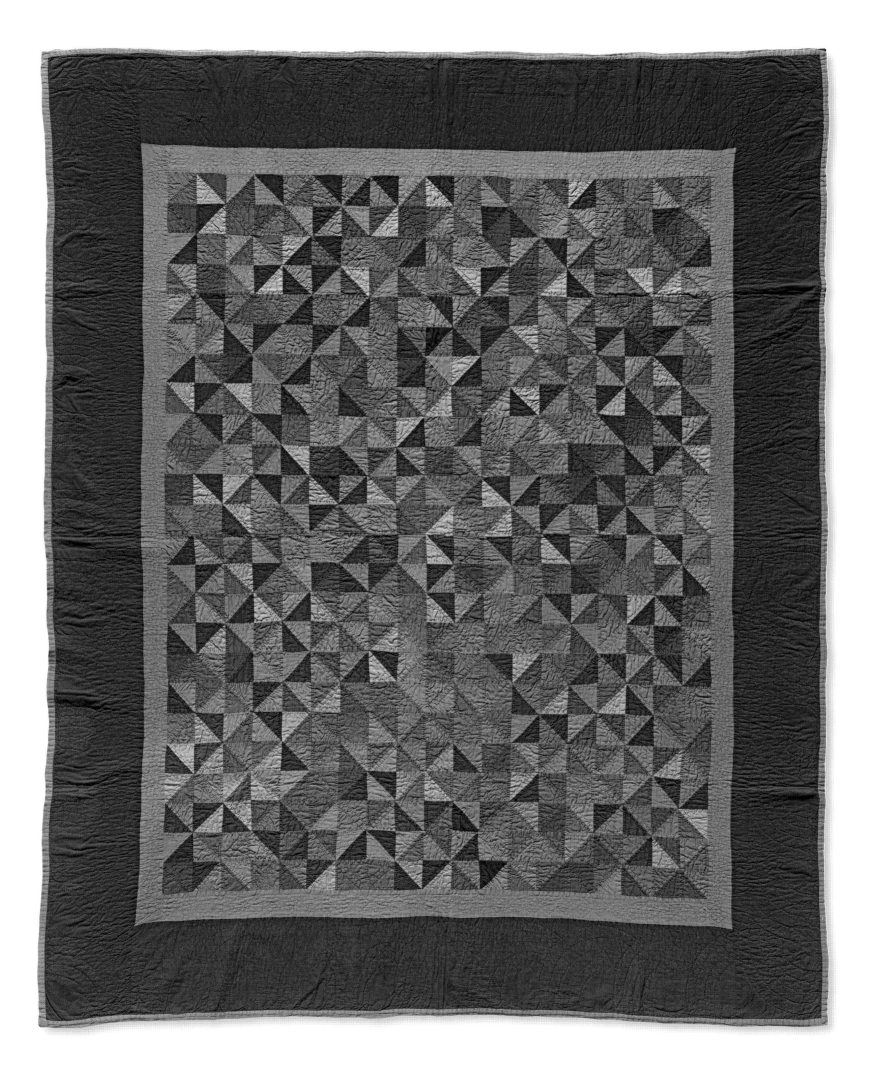

051

TUMBLING BLOCKS, YOUTH-SIZE QUILT

CA 1937
AMISCHE QUILTMACHERIN DER FAMILIE SIMON SCHMUCKER / **AMISH QUILT-MAKER**
FROM THE FAMILY OF SIMON SCHMUCKER, ELKHART COUNTY, INDIANA
BAUMWOLLE / **COTTON** / RÜCKSEITE: GRAUER BAUMWOLLSTOFF / **BACKING: GRAY COTTON CLOTH** / 175 x 137 CM

Die optische Illusion aufeinandergestapelter Würfel entsteht durch die sorgfältige Farbverteilung der kleinen Stoffrauten in hellen, mittleren und dunklen Tönen. Anscheinend war aber nicht immer die genau richtige Schattierung zur Hand, und so springt das Muster manchmal um, die Dreidimensionalität geht verloren, und andere, flächige Motive sind wahrnehmbar, so etwa ein Hexagon, oder es gibt Zickzacks anstelle von Treppen. Ganz offensichtlich ein Quilt, in dem Stoffreste verarbeitet wurden, und dennoch ist eine sorgfältig ausbalancierte Farbkomposition gelungen. // Dieselbe Quilterin scheint Roman Stripes Nr. 52 gefertigt zu haben. // QUILTING: parallele Doppellinien, einfaches Wellenband, Rosetten; einfache Linien wiederholen den Umriss der Rauten.

The optical illusion created by stacked-up cubes is created by the painstaking distribution of color in the small lozenge-shaped pieces of cloth in light, medium and dark shades. Apparently, however, just the right shade was not always available; as a result, the pattern sometimes flops over, the three-dimensional effect is lost and other, flat motifs come to view, such as a hexagon, or there are zigzags instead of steps. This is very obviously a quilt for which scraps of material were used yet the color composition is meticulously balanced. // The same quilt-maker seems to have made Roman Stripes no. 52. // QUILTING: parallel double lines, simple scallop, rosettes; simple lines repeating the outline of the lozenges.

052

ROMAN STRIPES, YOUTH-SIZE QUILT

CA 1937
AMISCHE QUILTMACHERIN DER FAMILIE SIMON SCHMUCKER / **AMISH QUILT-MAKER FROM THE FAMILY OF SIMON SCHMUCKER,**
ELKHART COUNTY, INDIANA
BAUMWOLLE / **COTTON** / RÜCKSEITE: BAUMWOLLE / **BACKING: COTTON** / 155 x 111 CM

Die große Vielfalt, die aus einem kleinen Repertoire erlaubter Muster, ja einem einzigen Mustertyp erarbeitet wurde, zeigt sich auch bei Roman Stripes. Von extrem strengen oder gravitätischen Beispielen über Kompositionen wie diese, die ihre Lebhaftigkeit vor allem aus der freien Verteilung der roten Streifen gewinnt, bis hin zu „wilden" Stücken gibt es unzählige Varianten. // Aus derselben Familie und Zeit wie dieser Roman Stripes stammt Tumbling Blocks Nr. 51. Die Übereinstimmungen bei einigen Stoffen sowie in Farbigkeit und Quilting lassen vermuten, dass dieselbe Frau beide Quilts gestaltet hat – vielleicht für zwei ihrer Kinder. // QUILTING: Parallellinien, Knospen, einfaches Wellenband, parallele Linien auf den leeren Dreiecken.

The enormous variety which can be produced from a small repertory of permitted patterns, indeed from a single pattern, is also revealed in Roman Stripes. There are innumerable variants, ranging from extremely stringent or ponderous examples through compositions like the one shown here, whose liveliness is primarily due to the free distribution of the red stripes, to rather wild patterns. // Tumbling Blocks no. 51 comes from the same family and is of the same date as this Roman Stripes quilt. Some of the materials as well as the colors and quilting are virtually identical, which suggests that they were made by the same woman – perhaps for two of her children. // QUILTING: parallel lines, buds, simple scallop, parallel lines on the empty triangles.

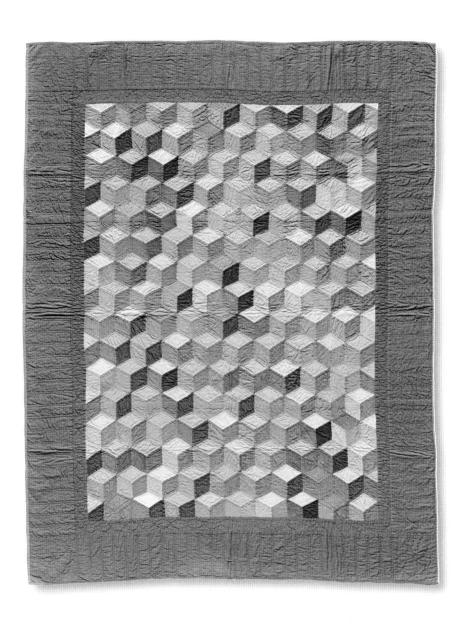

053

TUMBLING BLOCKS – VARIATION OF SEVEN SISTERS

CA 1940
AMISCHE QUILTMACHERIN / **AMISH QUILT-MAKER**, HOLMES COUNTY, OHIO
BAUMWOLLE / **COTTON** / RÜCKSEITE: BLAUER BAUMWOLLSTOFF / **BACKING: BLUE COTTON CLOTH** / 200 x 170 CM

Die Pole von freier Komposition und sehr exakter Ordnung werden besonders deutlich beim Vergleich der Quilts Nrn. 49 und 51 mit diesem Stück. Die perspektivisch wirkenden Würfel sind hier gleichsam zu kleinen Bauwerken gestapelt – Pyramiden in quadratischen Feldern, die durch kräftige schwarze Balken voneinander getrennt sind. Ebenso wie die strenge Geometrie lässt die reduzierte, wenngleich sehr elegante Farbigkeit von Braun, Blautönen und Petrolgrün auf Schwarz vermuten, dass die Quilterin einer recht konservativen amischen Gemeinde angehörte. // QUILTING: Dreieckslinien, Herzen; Innenrahmen: geometrisches Muster aus einander überschneidenden Halbkreisen (an einen Astragal erinnernd), ähnliche Eierstab-Motive auf den schwarzen Balken im Innenfeld, Sterne, Rauten.

The polar opposites represented by free composition and precise arrangement are particularly apparent when quilts nos. 49 and 51 are compared to this piece. The cubes look three dimensional and are stacked up to form small buildings as it were, pyramids in square fields demarcated by strong black borders. Like the stringent geometry, the reduced yet very elegant palette of browns, blues and petroleum green on black suggests that the maker belonged to a rather conservative Amish community. // QUILTING: triangular lines, hearts, inner borders: geometric designs formed of intersecting semicircles (reminiscent of bead and reel), similar egg and dart motifs on the black bars in the inner field, stars, lozenges.

054

VARIABLE STARS / OHIO STARS

1932
AMISCHE QUILTMACHERIN AMANDA SCHLABACH / **AMISH QUILT-MAKER AMANDA SCHLABACH**, BURTON DISTRICT, GEAUGA COUNTY, OHIO
MONOGRAMMIERT UND DATIERT, UNTEN IM INNENRAHMEN: AAS FEB 15 1932 /
MONOGRAMMED AND DATED, IN THE INNER FRAME, BOTTOM: AAS FEB 15 1932
BAUMWOLLE / **COTTON** / RÜCKSEITE: BLAUER BAUMWOLLSTOFF / **BACKING: BLUE COTTON CLOTH** / 200 x 180 CM

Monogramme und Datierungen auf Quilts kommen bei den Ohio-Amischen häufiger vor als in anderen Gebieten. Sie beziehen sich selten auf die Macherin, sondern fast immer auf die Person, die mit dem Stück beschenkt wurde, etwa zur Hochzeit. // Trotz ähnlichem Muster wie bei dem schwarzgrundigen Quilt Nr. 42 hat dieser Quilt einen ganz anderen Ausdruck. Auf dem khakifarbenen Grund besitzt jeder Stern ein eigenes schwarzes Feld in Form eines Diamond – jedenfalls, soweit der Stoff gereicht hat, denn ganz offensichtlich gab es zu wenig Schwarz. Im Unterschied zu Nr. 42 sind alle Sterne farbig und so gedreht, dass die Strahlen nicht diagonal, sondern kreuzförmig gerichtet sind. In raffinierter Ordnung der Farben entsteht eine Zentrierung, doch wirkt der Quilt trotz dieser Symmetrie sehr lebendig und undogmatisch. // SCHÖNES QUILTING: Wellenbänder, Flechtband, Diagonalgitter; bei den Sternen folgen die Steppstiche den Umrissen der Dreiecke.

Monograms and dates on quilts occur more frequently among the Ohio Amish than among Amish of other regions. They rarely refer to the maker but instead almost invariably to the person who was given the quilt, perhaps as a wedding present. // Although the pattern on this quilt is similar to quilt no. 42, which has a black ground, the present quilt expresses something quite different. Each star boasts its own black field in the form of a Diamond on the khaki-colored ground – at least as long as there was enough material since evidently there was not enough black. Unlike the Stars on no. 42, the Stars on this quilt are in color and turned so that their rays are in a cruciform arrangement rather than diagonally arrayed. The sophisticated composition of the colors creates a centered effect; however, despite the symmetry, this quilt still looks very lively and 'undogmatic' in design. // HANDSOME QUILTING: scallops, cable, diagonal waffle grids; the stitching traces the outlines of the triangles in the Stars.

055

JACOB'S LADDER

CA 1920
AMISCHE QUILTMACHERIN ELISABETH YODER / **AMISH QUILT-MAKER ELISABETH YODER**, WAYNE COUNTY, PENNSYLVANIA
SIGNIERT IM QUILTING AUF DER VORDERSEITE, MITTE UNTEN: E.Y. / **SIGNED IN THE QUILTING ON THE FRONT, BOTTOM CENTER: E.Y.**
BAUMWOLLE / **COTTON** / RÜCKSEITE: HELLGRAUER BAUMWOLLSTOFF WIE AUF DER VORDERSEITE /
BACKING: LIGHT GRAY COTTON CLOTH AS ON THE FRONT / 195 x 168 CM

Während in Lancaster County Signaturen versteckt auf der Rückseite der Umrandung – häufig im Hexenstich – eingestickt wurden, sind bei anderen Amischen Monogramme und Jahreszahlen häufiger auf der Vorderseite zu lesen, innerhalb des Quiltings. Allerdings sind derartige Kennzeichnungen bei den Amischen selten. Zwar ist der hier abgebildete Grisaille-Quilt sehr ruhig und zurückhaltend – „schlicht" würden Amische vielleicht sagen –, aber seine Macherin, eine Elisabeth Yoder aus Wayne County im äußersten Nordosten von Pennsylvania, hat ihn dennoch mit ihren Initialen auf der Vorderseite gekennzeichnet. // Wie Chains besteht die „Jakobsleiter" aus aneinandergehängten kleinen Quadraten. Dabei ergibt sich jedoch kein Gitter, sondern durch die Farborganisation entstehen durchgängige Diagonalstreifen – hier in zwei Grautönen. // QUILTING: Federranke, geometrisches Blütenmuster aus einander überschneidenden Halbkreisen.

Whereas signatures in Lancaster County were hidden – often embroidered in hex stitching – on the back of the border, among the Amish from other places monograms and date numerals can be read more often on the front, within the quilting. However, such marks are rare among the Amish on the whole. Although the grisaille quilt shown here is very reticent and subdued – 'plain' as the Amish might say – its maker, one Elisabeth Yoder from Wayne County in the north-eastern corner of Pennsylvania, nevertheless marked it on the front with her initials. // Like Chains, 'Jacob's Ladders' are composed of little adjacent squares. However, they do not create a waffle pattern but rather continuous diagonal stripes are formed by the organization of the colors – here in two shades of gray. // QUILTING: feathers, geometric floral pattern formed of intersecting semicircles.

056

BOW TIES

1914/20
AMISCHE QUILTMACHERIN DER FAMILIE JONAS HERSHBERGER / **AMISH QUILT-MAKER**
FROM THE FAMILY OF JONAS HERSHBERGER, BURTON, GEAUGA COUNTY, OHIO
WOLLE, BAUMWOLLE / **WOOL, COTTON** / RÜCKSEITE: BLAUER BAUMWOLLSTOFF /
BACKING: BLUE COTTON CLOTH / 205 x 184 CM
PROVENIENZ / **PROVENANCE**: DAVID WHEATCROFT, WESTBOROUGH, MASSACHUSETTS /
THE PEOPLE'S PLACE QUILT MUSEUM, INTERCOURSE, PENNSYLVANIA

Bow Ties – ein Motiv mit fünfeckigen Elementen – wurden häufig in einander überkreuzenden, diagonalen Reihen angeordnet, so dass zwischen den „Fliegen" achteckige Zwischenfelder entstehen. Nicht so bei diesem relativ frühen, einfacheren Stück, das nur parallele Reihen aufweist. Wie bei dem Muster üblich, sitzt jede „Fliege" diagonal in einem kleinen Quadratfeld, dessen beide anderen Ecken mit braunen Stoffstückchen gefüllt sind. Die unregelmäßige Verteilung einer Vielzahl von Farben – manche der Stoffe sind sogar gemustert – und das vorherrschende Rotbraun erlauben dem Auge keine klare Unterscheidung von Vorder- und Hintergrund. Aus der lebhaften Komposition blitzen in der Mittelzone eine rote und eine cremeweiße Fliege hervor. // QUILTING MIT HELLEM UND DUNKLEM GARN: schräge Parallellinien, Doppellinien auf dem Innenrahmen; im Innenfeld von Horizontalreihe zu Horizontalreihe wechselnde Richtung der Parallellinien.

Lit. u. a.: The People's Place Quilt Museum Address Book of Amish Folk Art. Intercourse/Pa. 1987 (m. Abb.)

The Bow Tie motif – formed of pentagonal elements – was often arranged in criss-crossing, diagonal rows so that octagonal fields were created between the 'Bow Ties'. This is not the case with this relatively early, quite simple quilt, which only boasts parallel rows. As is usual with this pattern, each 'Bow Tie' sits diagonally in a small square field, whose other two corners are filled with little bits of brown cloth. The irregular distribution of a wide variety of colors – some of the materials are even patterned – and the predominant reddish brown make it difficult to distinguish clearly between foreground and background. A red and cream-colored Bow Tie leaps startlingly out of the lively composition in the center zone to meet the eye. // QUILTING WITH LIGHT AND DARK YARN: oblique parallel lines, double lines on the inner border; in the inner field the parallel lines change direction from horizontal row to horizontal row.

References include: The People's Place Quilt Museum Address Book of Amish Folk Art. Intercourse/Pa. 1987 (with illus.)

057

OLD MAID'S PUZZLE / GARDEN PATH

CA 1932
AMISCHE QUILTMACHERIN DER FAMILIE NOAH TROYER / **AMISH QUILT-MAKER**
FROM THE FAMILY OF NOAH TROYER, HOLMES COUNTY, OHIO
BAUMWOLLE, RAYON / **COTTON, RAYON** / RÜCKSEITE: BAUMWOLLE / **BACKING: COTTON** / 197 x 190 CM

Ein bei den Amischen ungewöhnliches Muster, das – auch Love Rings genannt – fast nur in der Welt der „Englischen" vorkommt. Zentralisiert und mit Elementen, die sich zu übergreifenden Diamonds zusammenfügen, erinnert es an die Komposition von Sunshine and Shadow. Allerdings wird das „Puzzle der alten Jungfer" nicht aus identischen kleinen Quadraten gebildet, sondern durch eine geometrische Figur, die den Elementen bei Bow Ties (siehe Nr. 56) ähnelt: ein Quadrat, dem mit rundbogigem Schnitt eine Ecke entnommen und in anderer Farbe wieder eingesetzt wird. Die Farbverteilung lässt rund um eine kreisförmige Mitte konzentrisch abstrahlende Diamonds mit geschweiften Umrissen entstehen. Mehrere Rahmenleisten – abwechselnd einfarbig und mit Dreiecksmuster – fassen das Innenfeld ein. Ein sehr aufwändig und präzise gearbeitetes Stück. // Bisher ist nur ein einziges amisches Vergleichsstück bekannt – in der Sammlung Faith and Stephen Brown. Um 1930 datiert, soll es aus Ohio oder Indiana stammen. // QUILTING: Blütenranken, schräge Parallellinien, bei den Dreiecken und den Elementen des Innenfeldes sind die Umrisse nachgesteppt.

Lit. u. a.: [Kat. Ausst.] Amish Quilts 1880 to 1940 from the Collection of Faith and Stephen Brown. Michigan Museum of Art. Ann Arbor/Mich. 2000, Taf. 17 [Vergleichsstück]

An unusual pattern – also called Love Rings – for the Amish, one that occurs almost exclusively in quilts by 'English' makers. Centralized and boasting elements that fit together to form overlapping Diamonds, it is reminiscent of the Sunshine and Shadow composition. However, the Old Maid's Puzzle is not formed of identical little squares but rather of a geometric figure similar to the elements of the Bow Tie pattern (see no. 56): a square, from which a round-arched cut has removed a corner that is set in again in a different color. The distribution of colors creates Diamonds with curvilinear outlines radiating concentrically from a circular center. Several framing borders – alternately monochrome and with a triangular design – surround the inner field. A very elaborate and precisely worked quilt. // Only a single other example has previously come to light, from Ohio or Indiana, dating to ca 1930 (Faith and Stephen Brown Collection). // QUILTING: floral scrolls, oblique parallel lines; the outlines of the triangles and elements of the inner field are traced in the quilting.

References include: [Exhib. cat.] Amish Quilts 1880 to 1940 from the Collection of Faith and Stephen Brown. Michigan Museum of Art. Ann Arbor/Mich. 2000, pl. 17 [similar quilt]

058

SHOOFLY, YOUTH-SIZE QUILT

CA 1910
AMISCHE QUILTMACHERIN DER FAMILIE ELI LEHMANN / **AMISH QUILT-MAKER**
FROM THE FAMILY OF ELI LEHMANN, LAGRANGE COUNTY, INDIANA
LEICHTE WOLLE / **LIGHTWEIGHT WOOL** / RÜCKSEITE: WEINROTER BAUMWOLLSTOFF /
BACKING: MAROON COTTON CLOTH / 237 x 171 CM

Der Name des Musters bezieht sich auf ein nicht nur bei den Amischen, sondern überhaupt bei den Pennsylvania-Deutschen beliebtes Gebäck: Melassekuchen, der angeblich deshalb Shoofly heißt, weil man immer wieder die Fliegen von ihm verscheuchen muss: shoo! shoo! // Dieser sehr diszipliniert wirkende Quilt soll noch vor dem Ersten Weltkrieg entstanden sein. Er beschränkt sich auf zwei Farben und eine strenge, ohne Abweichung eingehaltene Komposition aus kleinen Dreiecken und Rechtecken. Allerdings ist das Rot so stark, dass das Auge eher die Diagonalkreuze mit ihren aus Dreiecken gebildeten T-Balken wahrnimmt als das blaue Shoofly-Motiv auf rotem Grund. Das Quilting ist besonders sorgfältig. So differenziert es im Innenfeld klar zwischen den leeren Diamonds (horizontale Linien) und jenen mit dem Shoofly-Motiv (vertikale Linien); auch die vier Ecken sind unterschieden (diagonale Linien). // Abgerundete Ecken kommen bei Mid West-Quilts gelegentlich vor. Bei diesem Stück wurde außerdem die Umrandung an ihrer Außenkante rundum mit der Nähmaschine im Zickzackstich eingefasst – vielleicht eine nachträgliche Ausbesserung, als der Rand auszufransen begann. // QUILTING: Schuppenmuster, geometrisches Blütenband aus einander überschneidenden Halbkreisen, Parallellinien.

The name of this pattern alludes to a pie that is popular not just with the Amish but throughout the 'Dutch Country', where the Pennsylvania Germans (called 'Dutch' from 'Deutsch') live: featuring a filling layer of usually sticky molasses, the pie is said to have been given its name because swarms of flies always had to be shooed away from it: shoo! shoo! // This very disciplined-looking quilt is said to have been made before the First World War. It is limited to two colors and an austere composition undeviatingly made up of small triangles and rectangles. However, the red is so vibrant that the viewer's eye tends to perceive the diagonal crosses with their T-Bars formed of triangles rather than the blue Shoofly motif on a red ground. The execution of the quilting is particularly meticulous. The stitching clearly differentiates in the inner field between empty Diamonds (horizontal lines) and Diamonds filled with the Shoofly motif (vertical line); even the four corners are set apart (diagonal lines). // Rounded-off corners occur sporadically, primarily on Midwestern quilts. Moreover, the border of this quilt is edged in turn by zigzag stitches executed by a sewing machine – possible a later repair done when the original edging began to fray. // QUILTING: scale pattern, geometric floral strip formed of intersecting semicircles, parallel lines.

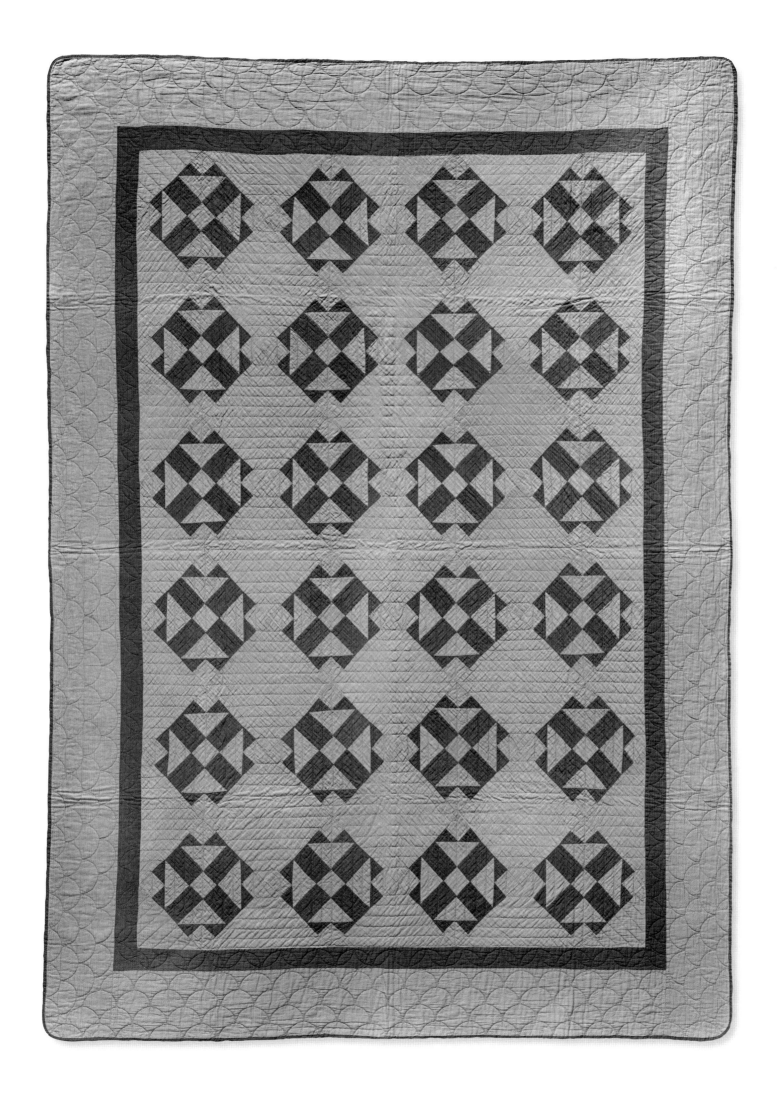

059

CENTER DIAMOND / DIAMOND IN THE SQUARE

CA 1925
AMISCHE QUILTMACHERIN SUSAN BEILER / **AMISH QUILT-MAKER SUSAN BEILER**, BIRD IN HAND, LANCASTER COUNTY, PENNSYLVANIA
WOLLE, BAUMWOLLE / **WOOL, COTTON** / RÜCKSEITE: GRÜNER BAUMWOLLSTOFF / **BACKING: GREEN COTTON CLOTH** / 205 x 206 CM

Dieser kraftvolle Quilt war der erste Center Diamond in der Sammlung Schlumberger und entfachte die besondere Leidenschaft der Sammlerin für diesen Typus. Er wurde auf einer Auktion in Zürich erworben und soll in den zwanziger Jahren von Susan Beiler in dem Ort mit dem
schönen Namen „Bird in Hand" gefertigt worden sein. // Wie bei Nrn. 17 und 25 besitzen der zentrale Diamond, der Innenrahmen und die
Einfassung dieselbe Farbe. Und auch hier wiederholt sich die Farbe des Innenquadrates in den quadratischen Ecken des Innen- und Außenrahmens. Mit dem gedämpften Akkord aus Violett und Blau entsteht trotzdem ein ganz anderer, feierlicher Ausdruck. // QUILTING MIT
HELLVIOLETTEM GARN: Federranken, Rautenmuster, Andreaskreuze, Federkränze und Gitterwerk; innen: doppelter Federkranz, Gitterwerk.

**This powerful quilt was the first Center Diamond in the Schlumberger Collection and sparked off the collector's passion for this type.
Bought at an auction in Zurich, Switzerland, it is said to have been made by Susan Beiler in the 1920s in a hamlet with the pleasing
name of 'Bird in Hand'. // As in nos. 17 and 25, the central Diamond, the inner border and the outer border are all the same color.
And here, too, the color of the inner square is repeated in the square fields of both the inner and the outer borders. Nevertheless, an
entirely different solemnity is expressed in the muted accord of purple and blue. // QUILTING WITH LAVENDER YARN: feather scrolls,
lozenge designs, crosses of St Andrew, feather wreaths and waffle grid; inside: double feather wreath, waffle grid.**

060

SUNSHINE AND SHADOW

CA 1935
AMISCHE QUILTMACHERIN LYDIA BEILER / **AMISH QUILT-MAKER LYDIA BEILER**, LANCASTER COUNTY, PENNSYLVANIA
WOLLE, BAUMWOLLE, RAYON / **WOOL, COTTON, RAYON** / RÜCKSEITE: RAYON / **BACKING: RAYON** / 218 x 214 CM

Dieses dekorative Stück erinnert daran, dass die amischen Frauen in Lancaster County keineswegs nur dunkle Kleider in gedeckter Farbigkeit trugen. Und so tauchen intensiv leuchtende Farben auch in ihren Bettüberwürfen auf, die ja meist aus Kleiderstoffen gefertigt wurden. Bei späteren Quilts werden zunehmend auch hellere Töne verwendet, und man sieht, dass eine breitere Farbpalette zur Verfügung stand – entsprechend dem wachsenden Angebot an chemisch gefärbten Stoffen. Die Stoffe wurden entweder in größeren Orten gekauft oder in Versandhauskatalogen geordert – etwa bei Sears, Roebuck & Company oder kleineren regionalen Mail-Order-Unternehmen. Es gab aber auch verschiedene jüdische Stoffhändler, die von Haus zu Haus zogen und den Amischen ihre Ware anboten. // QUILTING: gegenständige Gitterkörbe mit Rosengirlanden, die von den Blumenmotiven in den Ecken ausgehen, Diagonalkreuze.

This decorative piece is a reminder that Amish women in Lancaster County did not just wear dark clothing in subdued colors. And intensely vibrant colors also appear in the bedcovers they designed, most of which were, after all, made from the same bolts of material used for making clothes. Lighter shades were increasingly used in later quilts and it is apparent that a broader palette became available, matching the wider range of chemically dyed materials on the market. Bolts of cloth were either bought in larger towns or ordered through mail-order catalogs – from Sears, Roebuck & Company or smaller regional mail-order businesses. There were also Jewish peddlers who went from house to house hawking their wares to the Amish. // QUILTING: waffle-grid baskets with garlands of roses, which face each other and start at the floral motifs in the corners, diagonal crosses.

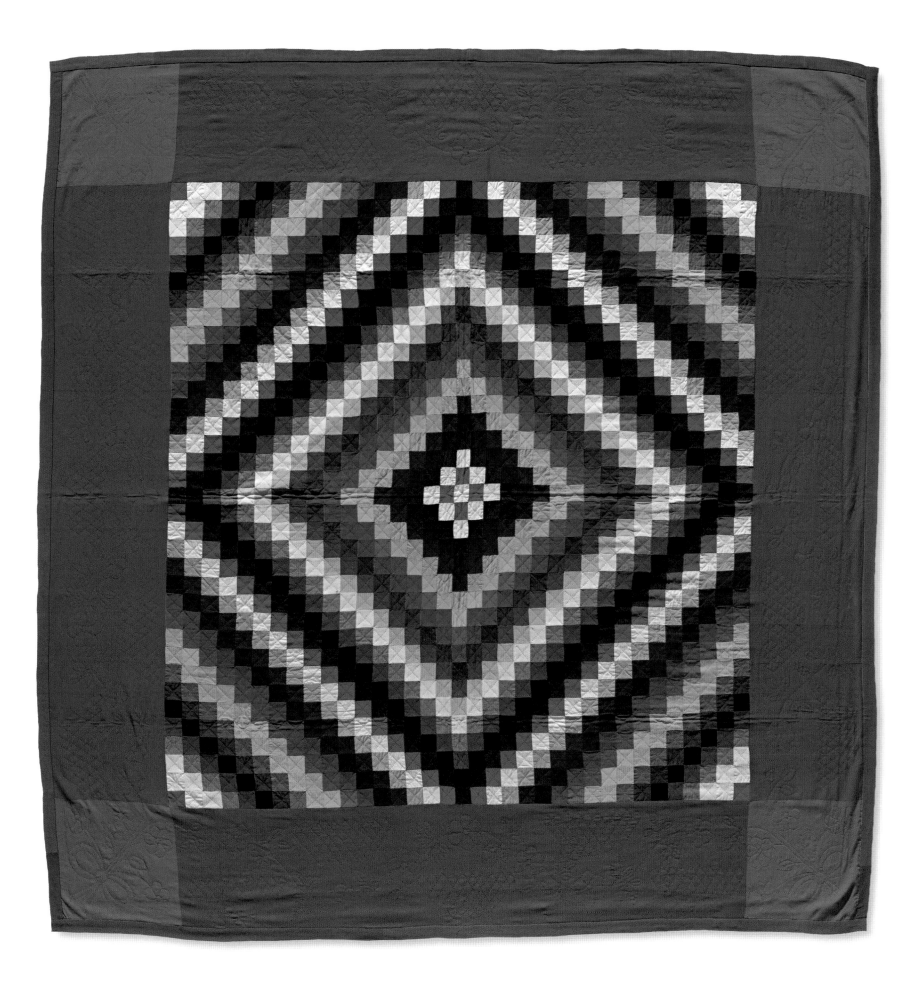

061

BASKETS

CA 1920
AMISCHE QUILTMACHERIN / **AMISH QUILT-MAKER**, HOLMES COUNTY, OHIO
BAUMWOLLE, BAUMWOLLSATIN / **COTTON, COTTON SATEEN** /
RÜCKSEITE: DUNKELBLAUE BAUMWOLLE / **BACKING: DARK BLUE COTTON** / 207 x 210 CM
PROVENIENZ: SAMMLUNG SUSAN C. KOLKER / **PROVENANCE: SUSAN C. KOLKER COLLECTION**

Wie bei den Quilts Nrn. 70 und 71 wurde auch hier das unterschiedliche Schwarz von normaler Baumwolle und Satin für die Komposition genutzt und im Innenfeld eine Differenzierung zwischen den leeren Diamonds und denjenigen mit Baskets (auch „Hands" genannt) erreicht. Vor diesem sublimen Rautenhintergrund verlaufen als zweite Ebene die vertikalen Reihen der Körbe – vertikal nicht nur, weil diese Gegenstände im Gegensatz zu abstrakteren Mustern ein Oben und Unten haben, sondern auch durch die Anordnung der Farben. // Außergewöhnlich ist die Umrandung mit ihrem Sägezahnmuster. Beim drittobersten Korb der rechten Außenreihe hat die Gestalterin außerdem das korrekte Schema durchbrochen: Zwei Dreiecke „fliegen davon", anstatt den Korb zu schließen – ein geradezu kapriziöser Akzent. // QUILTING: Wellenbänder, Flechtband, Gitterwerk, parallele Linien in Dreiergruppierung.

Lit. u. a.: Bishof Robert u. Elizabeth Safanda, A Gallery of Amish Quilts. New York 1976, 77, Abb. 120 [dort Angabe der damaligen Besitzerin]

As in quilts nos. 70 and 71, the two different blacks of normal cotton cloth and cotton sateen have been used in the composition to differentiate on the inner field between empty Diamonds and Diamonds filled with Baskets (also known as 'Hands'). Against this sublime lozenge background run the vertical rows of Baskets as a second plane – in the vertical not just because these representational figurations, unlike the abstract patterns, have a top and bottom but also due to the arrangement of colors. // The Sawtooth edging is an unusual feature. And the designer departed from the correct schema in the third Basket from the top in the right-hand outer row: two triangles 'fly away' instead of closing the Basket: a truly capricious touch. // QUILTING: scallops, cable, waffle grids, parallel lines in groups of three.

References include: Bishof, Robert and Safanda, Elizabeth, A Gallery of Amish Quilts. New York 1976, 77, fig. 120 [with information on the then owner]

062

CENTER DIAMOND / DIAMOND IN THE SQUARE

CA 1935
AMISCHE QUILTMACHERIN MARY GLICK / **AMISH QUILT-MAKER MARY GLICK**, LANCASTER COUNTY, PENNSYLVANIA
SIGNIERT AUF DER RÜCKSEITE: MG / **SIGNED ON THE BACK: MG**
WOLLE, WOLLKREPP / **WOOL, WOOL CREPE** / RÜCKSEITE: BUNT GEBLÜMTER BAUMWOLLSTOFF /
BACKING: COTTON CLOTH PRINTED WITH A BRIGHT-COLORED FLORAL PATTERN / 214 x 209 CM

Dieser Quilt ist mit den Initialen seiner Macherin versehen: die Signatur ist auf der Rückseite der Umrandung mit andersfarbenem Garn eingestickt. // Alle Elemente eines klassischen Center Diamond aus Lancaster County sind hier vorhanden, und doch hat Mary Glick das Schema aufgebrochen. Entgegen dem Üblichen existiert zwischen Innenfeld und Außenrahmen keine farbliche Verbindung. Die Konzentration auf das Innenfeld ist dadurch verstärkt und wird zusätzlich gesteigert durch das leuchtende Violett im Außenrahmen. Der zentrale Diamond besitzt – wie bei Nrn. 13, 28 und 32 – einen eigenen Rahmen mit kleinen Eckquadraten. Deren Grün verankert den Diamond mit dem Grün des Innenrahmens; und es ist das helle Rosa des Diamondrahmens, das – ebenso wie das Hellblau der restlichen Flächen – die Wirkung des Spiels mit den grünen Flächen intensiviert. // QUILTING: Federranken, Weinranken, Rosenzweige, Schuppenmuster; innen: Federkranz, achtzackiger Stern, kleine Sterne.

This quilt bears the initials of its maker: the signature is embroidered on the back of the edging in a different color. // All elements of a classic Lancaster County Center Diamond are on show here yet Mary Glick has loosened up the scheme. Unlike the usual Center Diamond, this one has no color link between the inner and outer fields. This concentrates the focus on the inner field and this effect is enhanced by the glowing purple of the outer field. The Central Diamond – as in nos. 13, 28 and 32 – boasts a border of its own with small corner blocks. The green of these blocks anchors the Diamond with the green of the inner field border. It is the light pink of the Diamond border that – like the light blue of the other surfaces – intensifies the interplay of the Diamond and the green fields. // QUILTING: feather scrolls, grape vines, rose sprays, scale pattern; inner field: feather wreath, Eight-Pointed Star, small stars.

SUNSHINE AND SHADOW

CA 1910
AMISCHE QUILTMACHERIN ELISABETH LAPP / **AMISH QUILT-MAKER ELISABETH LAPP**, LANCASTER COUNTY, PENNSYLVANIA
BAUMWOLLE / **COTTON** / RÜCKSEITE: BAUMWOLLE / **BACKING: COTTON** / 188 x 188 CM

Bei den Amischen taucht das Muster Sunshine and Shadow erst um 1900 auf, obwohl es bei den „Englischen", also den nicht-amischen Nachbarn, schon sehr viel früher gebräuchlich war. Und es blieb bei den Amischen bis in die 1960er Jahre „en vogue", als sich angelsächsische Quilterinnen längst anderen Mustern zugewandt hatten. Derartige chronologische Verschiebungen sind charakteristisch für den Stil der Amischen, die nicht nur Neuerungen ablehnend gegenüberstanden, sondern sich auch ganz dezidiert von den „Englischen" absetzen wollten. // Generell lässt sich das Motiv als Ableitung des Diamond in the Square verstehen, nur dass der zentrale Rhombus und die ihn zum Quadrat ergänzenden Dreiecke in unzählige kleine, einfarbige Quadrate aufgelöst sind. Diese Stoffstückchen, dicht an dicht gesetzt, sind farblich so geordnet, dass hellere und dunklere Zonen entstehen – Sonnenschein und Schatten. Bei diesem Stück, das nach Aussage der früheren Besitzer eine Elisabeth Lapp vor dem Ersten Weltkrieg gefertigt haben soll, sind die Sonnen- und Schattenzonen besonders aufwändig und genau geplant: Es gibt von innen nach außen Verläufe innerhalb einer Farbe von hellen zu dunklen Tönen – äußerst effektvoll. Winzige, aber auffällige Akzente bilden die Stücke in den Ecken des großen Quadrates: das einzige kräftige Rot, wie kleine Ziernägel. // UNGEWÖHNLICHES QUILTING: Ranke mit Rosetten und Zweiglein; in den Ecken lyraförmig gelegt.

The Sunshine and Shadow design does not appear among Amish quilt-makers until about 1900 although it was widespread much earlier among the 'English', i.e. the non-Amish neighbors. And it stayed en vogue among the Amish until the 1960s, long after English American quilt-makers had turned to other designs. Chronological lags of this kind are characteristic of the Amish style, whose exponents not just rejected innovations but wanted to differentiate themselves explicitly from the 'English'. // On the whole, the motif can be viewed as deriving from the 'Diamond in the Square' except that the central rhombus and the triangles completing it as a square have been dissolved into countless tiny, monochrome squares. These little patches of cloth, in dense array, are arranged so that lighter and darker colored zones are created – hence sunshine and shadow. In this piece, which, according to the former owner, is said to have been made by one Elisabeth Lapp before the First World War, the sun and shadow zones are particularly lavishly and precisely planned. As a result, within a row running from inside to out range from light to dark shades of a single color – an extremely striking approach to color. The pieces in the corners of the large square form minute yet highly noticeable touches: the only vibrant red, like little decorative studs. // UNUSUAL QUILTING: scrolls of rosettes and stalks; lyre-shaped arrangement at the corners.

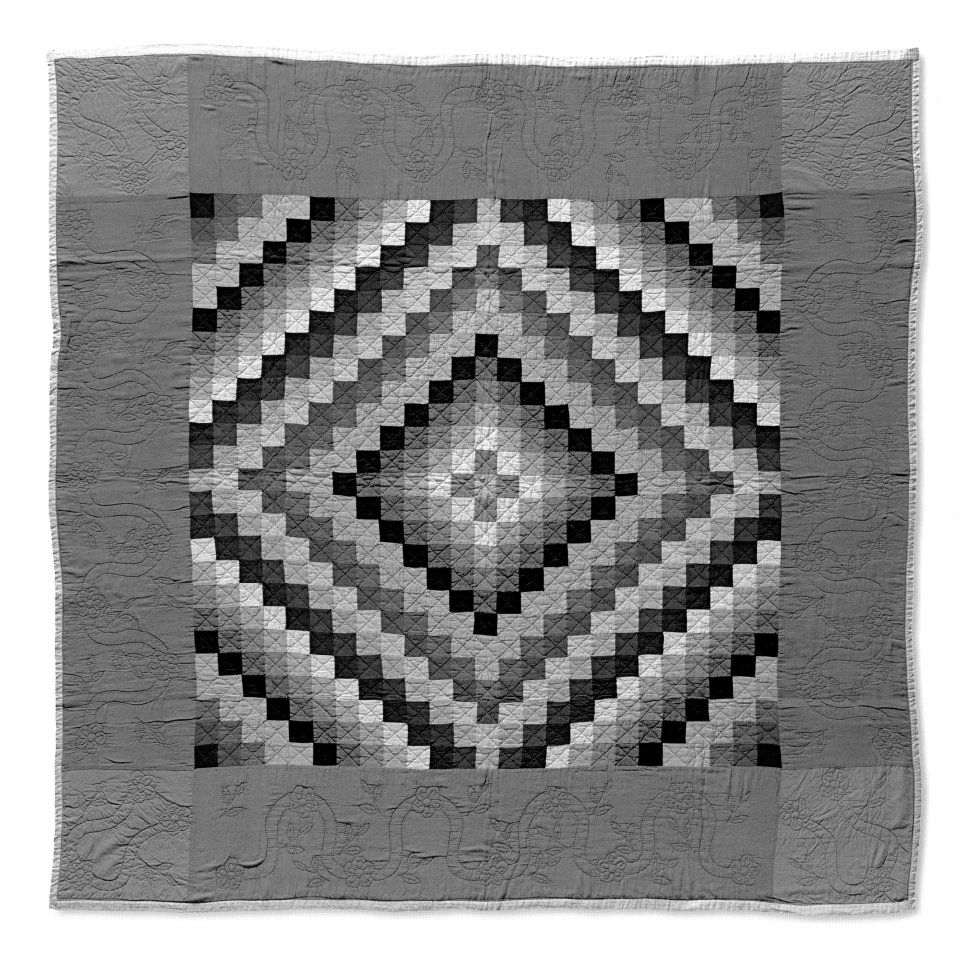

064

DOUBLE IRISH CHAIN – FLOATING

CA 1920
AMISCHE QUILTMACHERIN / **AMISH QUILT-MAKER**, LANCASTER COUNTY, PENNSYLVANIA
WOLLE / **WOOL** / RÜCKSEITE: BAUMWOLLSTOFF MIT STREUBLÜTENDEKOR /
BACKING: COTTON CLOTH WITH STREWN FLOWERS DECORATION / 198 x 195 CM

Kleine, an ihrer Spitze aneinandergehängte Quadrate bilden die Irish Chain. Auch bei den „Englischen" sehr beliebt und dort bedeutend früher verwendet, scheint das Muster aus dem „alten Europa" in die Neue Welt mitgebracht worden zu sein – ob es wirklich aus Irland stammt, wird allerdings bezweifelt. // Bei Double Irish Chain sind zwischen zwei Ketten dunklerer Farbe stets Quadrate in hellerem Ton eingefügt – hier in Lachsrosa zwischen roten Ketten. Außer dem Diagonalgitter dieser Ketten gibt es nichts, was das Innenfeld definieren würde, da ein Innenrahmen oder Eckquadrate fehlen (vgl. etwa Nr. 29). Nur das Quilting ist anders, und so erscheinen das Blau der getreppten Diamonds und das Blau des Rahmens unterschiedlich. Die Umrandung ist – ungewöhnlich für einen Lancaster-Quilt – farblich nicht unterschieden; um so intensiver kommen die Chains auf dem leuchtend blauen Fond zur Geltung. // Wie Nine Patch oder Sunshine and Shadow gehört Irish Chain zu den Mustern, die aus identisch geformten, kleinen Elementen entwickelt werden – meist aus Quadraten. Es können aber auch Drei- ecke sein, wie bei Broken Dishes (siehe Nr. 50) und Ocean Waves (siehe Nr. 65) oder Rauten wie bei Tumbling Blocks (u. a. Nrn. 46, 51, 67) und Lone Stars (siehe Nr. 34). // FEINES QUILTING: Federranken, Rosetten, Diagonalkreuze.

Small squares connected at the corners form the Irish Chain. Also very popular with the 'English' and used by this group considerably earlier, the pattern seems to have been brought by settlers from 'the Old Country' to the New World – it is doubtful, however that it really came from Ireland. // The Double Irish Chain consists in two chains of a darker color interspersed with squares in a lighter shade – here in salmon pink between red Chains. Apart from the diagonal grille formed by these Chains, there is nothing that might define an inner field since both an inner border and corner squares are lacking (cf., for instance, no. 29). Only the quilting is differenti- ated so the blue of the stepped Diamonds and the blue of the border look different. The outer border is – unusual in a Lancaster County quilt – not of a different color; thus the Chains stand out all the more intensely on the glowing blue ground. // Like Nine Patch and Sunshine and Shadow, Irish Chain is one of those patterns developed out of identically formed, small elements, usually squares. They may also, however, be triangles, as in Broken Dishes (see no. 50) and Ocean Waves (see no. 65) or lozenges as in Tumbling Blocks (inter alia nos. 46, 51, 67) and Lone Stars (see no. 34). // FINE QUILTING: feather scrolls, rosettes, diagonal crosses.

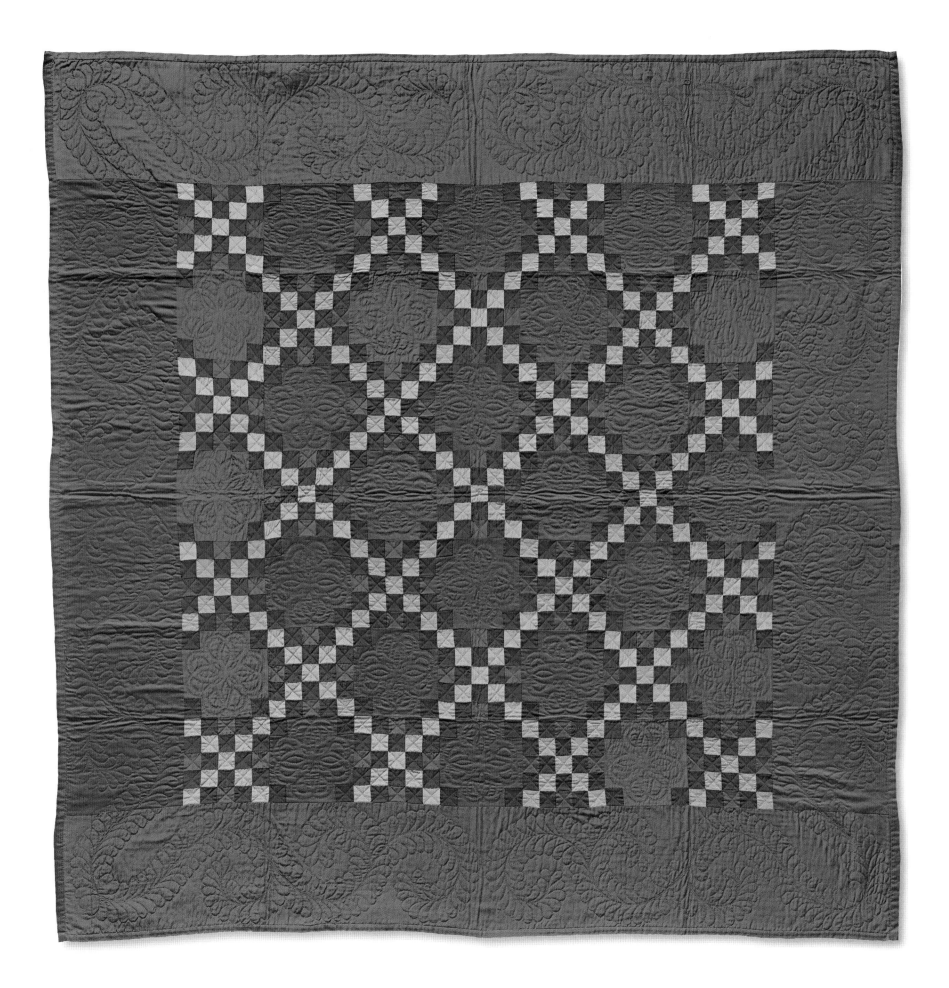

065

OCEAN WAVES

CA 1935
AMISCHE QUILTMACHERIN / **AMISH QUILT-MAKER**, HOLMES COUNTY, OHIO
BAUMWOLLE, BAUMWOLLSATIN / **COTTON, COTTON SATEEN** / RÜCKSEITE: HELLBLAUER BAUMWOLLSTOFF /
BACKING: LIGHT BLUE COTTON CLOTH / 199 x 196 CM
PROVENIENZ / **PROVENANCE**: PEOPLE'S PLACE QUILT MUSEUM, INTERCOURSE, PENNSYLVANIA

Schwarz findet sich häufig in den Quilts der Ohio-Amischen, und es steigert die Intensität der anderen Farben. Hier ist es Hintergrund für das akkurat ausgeführte Muster aus kleinen Dreiecken, die sich zu einander überkreuzenden Sechserreihen formieren. Ocean Waves kann auch aus mehreren Farben bestehen, und manche Stücke besitzen keine diagonalen Reihen, sondern waagrechte und senkrechte. Wie das Muster zu seinem Namen kam, führt dieses Beispiel mit seinem ruhelosen, endlosen Hin und Her der geometrisch stilisierten Meereswogen besonders schön vor Augen. // QUILTING IN DUNKLEM UND WEISSEM GARN: Federranken mit einzelnen Blättern, Blattranke, Sonnenblumen, parallele Linien.

Lit. u. a.: Amish Quilts – Calendar 1989. People's Place Quilt Museum. Intercourse/Pa., Juni-Blatt

Black occurs frequently on Ohio Amish quilts and it enhances the intensity of the other colors used. Here it is the background of a meticulously executed pattern of small triangles formed into criss-crossing rows of six. Ocean Waves can consist of several colors. Further, some quilts of this design boast horizontal and vertical rows rather than diagonals. However, with the restless, ceaseless back and forth of the geometrically stylized waves of the sea, this particular example compellingly illustrates how the pattern came by its name. // QUILTING IN DARK AND WHITE YARN: feather scrolls with individual leaves, foliate scroll, Sunflowers, parallel lines.

References include: Amish Quilts – Calendar 1989. People's Place Quilt Museum. Intercourse/Pa., June calendar sheet

066

CHINESE COINS

CA 1935
AMISCHE QUILTMACHERIN DER FAMILIE RUDOLF MILLER / **AMISH QUILT-MAKER**
FROM THE FAMILY OF RUDOLF MILLER, HOLMES COUNTY, OHIO
BAUMWOLLE / **COTTON** / RÜCKSEITE: DUNKELBLAUER BAUMWOLLSTOFF /
BACKING: DARK BLUE COTTON CLOTH / 200 x 169 CM

An bunte Glasmosaiken oder die leuchtende Farbigkeit von Kirchenfenstern erinnern viele der Ohio-Quilts, bei denen immer wieder Schwarz als – dominierende – Farbe des Hintergrundes zu finden ist (vgl. etwa Nrn. 50, 53, 61, 65, 74). // Nicht exakt gleich hoch, aber doch ziemlich regelmäßig sind die aufeinander gestapelten Stoffstreifen, die das Muster Chinese Coins bilden. Wie Stairway to Heaven (siehe Nr. 48) ist es eigentlich eine Variante von Bars. // Aus derselben Familie Rudolf Miller kommt der ungefähr gleichzeitig entstandene Quilt Nr. 72. Die verwendeten Stoffe und ihre Farben, aber auch der Stil der Farbkomposition, die Proportionen und das Quilting sind in beiden Stücken so nah verwandt, dass sich die Vermutung aufdrängt, beide Stücke stammen von derselben Quiltmacherin. // QUILTING: Fächer, Schuppenmuster; Flechtband, parallele Linien.

Many Ohio Amish quilts are reminiscent of brightly colored glass mosaics or the glowing colors of stained-glass church windows. Black frequently occurs as – the dominant – background color (cf., for instance, nos. 50, 53, 61, 65, 74). // The Chinese Coins pattern is built up of strips of cloth, that are not all of precisely the same length yet are fairly regular, piled one above the other. Like Stairway to Heaven (see no. 48), Chinese Coins is actually a variant of Bars. // Quilt no. 72, made at about the same time, is also from the Rudolf Miller family. The materials used and the colors, as well as the style of the color composition, the proportions and the quilting in the two quilts are so closely related that all these factors strongly suggest both were made by the same woman. // QUILTING: Fans, scale pattern; cable, parallel lines.

067

TUMBLING BLOCKS

CA 1915/20
AMISCHE QUILTMACHERIN / **AMISH QUILT-MAKER**, LAGRANGE COUNTY, INDIANA
BAUMWOLLE / **COTTON** / RÜCKSEITE: BAUMWOLLE / **BACKING: COTTON** / 216 x 181 CM

Eines der spektakulärsten Muster bei amischen Quilts ist Tumbling Blocks mit seiner Anmutung von Dreidimensionalität. Ungeachtet seiner ganz modernen Wirkung taucht es bereits im 19. Jahrhundert auf nicht-amischen Quilts auf, und das Prinzip dieses Ornamentmotives war bereits seit Antike und Renaissance bekannt. Hier handelt es sich um ein Muster aus gleichgeformten Stoffstückchen, wie bei One Patch, Nine Patch, Broken Dishes, Log Cabin etc. Die einzelnen Elemente sind jedoch nicht kleine Quadrate, Dreiecke oder Streifen, sondern Rauten, die so zusammengesetzt werden, dass ein heller, ein mittlerer und ein dunkler Farbton einen kleinen, perspektivisch gesehenen Würfel bilden. // QUILTING: Flechtbänder.

Tumbling Blocks, which evokes an optical illusion of being three-dimensional, is one of the most spectacular Amish quilt patterns. Although it looks so utterly modern, it had surfaced on non-Amish quilts by the 19th century. The principle underlying this ornamental motif was known to Greco-Roman antiquity and the Renaissance. In the present instance, the pattern is built up of uniform pieces of cloth, as it is in One Patch, Nine Patch, Broken Dishes, Log Cabin, etc. However, the individual elements are not small squares, triangles or strips but rather lozenges arranged to create the effect of cubes made up of a light, medium and dark shade each viewed in perspective. // QUILTING: cable.

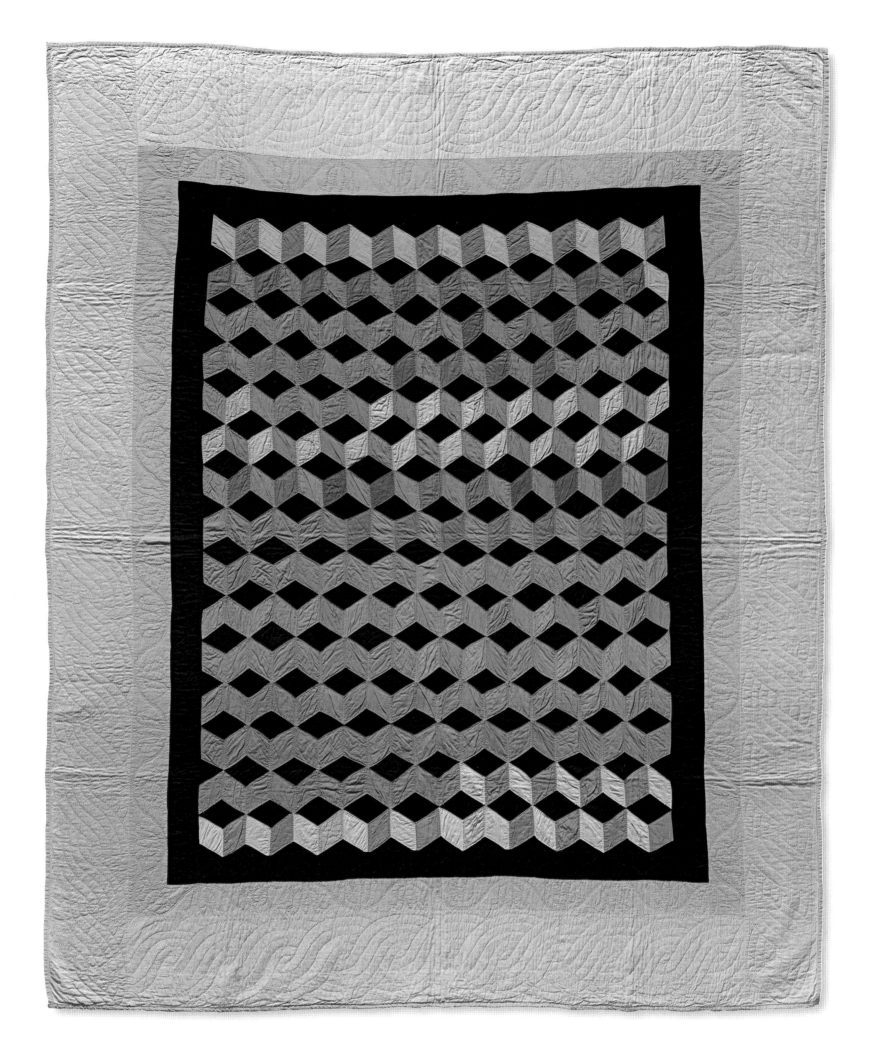

068

CROWN OF THORNS

CA 1940
AMISCHE QUILTMACHERIN / **AMISH QUILT-MAKER**, HOLMES COUNTY, OHIO
BAUMWOLLE / **COTTON** / RÜCKSEITE: DUNKELBLAUER BAUMWOLLSTOFF /
BACKING: DARK BLUE COTTON CLOTH / 198 x 166 CM

Eine große Vielfalt an Mustern wurde bei den Mid West-Amischen aus der Kombination von kleinen Dreiecken mit weiteren geometrischen Formen wie kleinen Quadraten oder größeren Dreiecken gewonnen. Crown of Thorns ist nur ein Beispiel, und die Namen all dieser Muster beschwören eine ganz eigene Welt herauf: Shoofly, Hole in the Barndoor (auch: Monkey Wrench), Goose in the Pond, Fox and Geese (auch: Crosses and Losses), Old Maid's Puzzle, Fence Row, Bear Paw, Pinwheels, Baskets etc. // Zwar sollte man sich davor hüten, den bildhaften Namen übergroße Bedeutung zuzuschreiben – es handelt sich <u>nicht</u> um Abbildungen, und Realismus war nicht angestrebt – im Gegenteil. Dennoch lassen sich bei einigen Mustern die Assoziationen nachvollziehen; so ist die Dornenkrone bei diesem Stück mit einiger Phantasie gut erkennbar. Die Schlichtheit der „Fassung" mit blauem Rahmen auf schwarzem Grund erinnert an die Plain Quilts sehr konservativer Amisch-Gruppen (etwa Nr. 73), und dies scheint dem ernsten Thema ebenso zu entsprechen wie die gedämpfte Palette der Farben – die im übrigen völlig frei, aber ruhig ausbalanciert verteilt sind. // QUILTING: Fächer, geometrisches Blütenmuster aus einander überschneidenden Halbkreisen, Weinblätter, parallele Linien, Kreuze, bei den inneren Elementen sind die Umrisse nachgesteppt.

Lit. u. a.: [Kat. Ausst.] Abstraktion und Farbe. Die Kunst der Amischen: Quilts der Sammlung Ziegler. Die Neue Sammlung. München 1991, 32–33 [m. Abb.]

The Midwestern Amish produced a wide variety of patterns by combining small triangles with other geometric forms such as small squares or larger triangles. Crown of Thorns is just one example and the names of all these patterns evoke a world apart: Shoofly, Hole in the Barn Door (also: Monkey Wrench), Goose in the Pond, Fox and Geese (also: Crosses and Losses), Old Maid's Puzzle, Fence Row, Bear Paw, Pinwheels, Baskets, etc. // One should avoid over-interpreting these metaphorical names – they do <u>not</u> stand for representations and realism was not the aim – quite the contrary. Nevertheless, the associations are intelligible in some patterns; with a bit of imagination, the Crown of Thorns is easy to spot on this quilt. The simplicity of the 'frame' with a blue border on a black ground is reminiscent of the plain quilts made by very conservative Amish groups (no. 73, for instance) and this approach seems to be just as appropriate to the serious theme as the muted palette is – the colors, incidentally, are entirely freely distributed but tranquil and harmoniously balanced. // QUILTING: Fans, geometric floral pattern formed of intersecting semicircles, grape leaves, parallel lines, crosses; the outlines of the elements of the inner field are traced in the stitching.

References include: [Exhib. cat.] Abstraktion und Farbe. Die Kunst der Amischen: Quilts der Sammlung Ziegler. Die Neue Sammlung. Munich 1991, 32–33 [with illus.]

069

OPEN WINDOW

CA 1935
AMISCHE QUILTMACHERIN DER FAMILIE TROYER / **AMISH QUILT-MAKER**
FROM THE TROYER FAMILY, SUGAR CREEK, HOLMES COUNTY, OHIO
BAUMWOLLE / **COTTON** / RÜCKSEITE: GRAUER BAUMWOLLSTOFF / **BACKING: GRAY COTTON CLOTH** /
205 x 174 CM

Es wird vermutet, dass die ersten amischen Quilts einfarbig waren – Plain Quilts. „Pieced", also aus verschiedenfarbigen Stücken zusammengenäht – wie es bei den nicht-amischen Nachbarn schon längst „en vogue" war –, waren sie wohl noch nicht. Pieced Quilts kamen bei den Amischen vielleicht erst mit Einführung der Nähmaschine auf, die eine enorme Arbeitserleichterung bedeutete (vgl. Nr. 46). // Plain sind jedenfalls die frühesten erhaltenen amischen Quilts mit eingestickter Jahreszahl, die also sicher datiert werden können. Von ihnen gibt es aus der Zeit vor 1870 überhaupt nur zwei: der eine datiert 1840 (oder 1849) im People's Place Quilt Museum, Intercourse/Pa., der andere 1869 im Indiana State Museum, Indianapolis. Beide sind einfarbig blau; die ganze Fläche ist dicht mit Quilting ornamentiert. // Das gilt auch für dieses viel spätere Stück aus dem Mittleren Westen, dessen Schlichtheit und Strenge auf die Entstehung in einer sehr orthodoxen Familie verweist (vgl. auch Nr. 73). Lediglich ein innerer Rahmen in dunkelstem Grün wurde als zusätzliches Element konzediert. // Um so reicher ist das Quilting: Flechtband im Außenrahmen; geometrisches Muster aus einander überschneidenden Halbkreisen auf dem Innenrahmen; das Innenfeld weist eine andreaskreuzförmige Zone auf, in der stilisierte Bäume in quadratischen und rautenförmigen Feldern gequiltet sind, Rautengitter auf den restlichen Flächen.

Lit. u. a.: Granick Eve Wheatcroft, The Amish Quilt. Intercourse/Pa. 1989, 30–31 mit Abb. [Plain Quilts, 1849 und 1869] / [Kat. Ausst.] Amish Quilts 1880 to 1940 from the Collection of Faith and Stephen Brown. Michigan Museum of Art. Ann Arbor/Mich. 2000, 15 m. Abb., Taf. 3, 4 [Plain Quilts, 1840 und 1869]

The earliest Amish quilts are believed to have been monochrome – that is, plain quilts. However, they were probably not 'pieced', sewn together from scraps of different colors – as had long been 'fashionable' among the non-Amish neighbors of Amish settlements. Pieced quilts are thought to have surfaced among the Amish with the introduction of the sewing machine, which was an enormously labor-saving appliance (cf. no. 46). // The earliest Amish quilts bearing embroidered date numerals, that is quilts that can be dated with assurance, are in any case plain. Only two of them dating from before 1870 are in existence: one dated 1840 (or 1849) in the People's Place Quilt Museum, Intercourse, Pa., the other in the Indiana State Museum, Indianapolis, which dates from 1869. Both are monochrome blue and the entire field is decorated with dense quilting. // The same holds for this much later quilt from the Midwest, whose austere simplicity suggests that it was made in a strictly orthodox family (cf. also no. 73). The only additional element allowed was an inner frame in very dark green. // The quilting, on the other hand, is extremely lavish: cable in the outer field; geometric designs formed of intersecting semicircles on the inner field; the inner field boasts a zone in the shape of a cross of St Andrew, in which stylized trees are quilted in square and lozenge-shaped fields, lozenge-shaped waffle grids cover the rest of the surface.

References include: Granick, Eve Wheatcroft, The Amish Quilt. Intercourse, Pa. 1989, 30–31 with illus. [Plain Quilts, 1849 and 1869] / [Exhib. cat.] Amish Quilts 1880 to 1940 from the Collection of Faith and Stephen Brown. Michigan Museum of Art. Ann Arbor, Mich. 2000, 15 with illus., pls. 3, 4 [Plain Quilts, 1840 and 1869]

070

BEAR PAW

1951
AMISCHE QUILTMACHERIN / **AMISH QUILT-MAKER**, WAYNE COUNTY, PENNSYLVANIA
MONOGRAMMIERT UND DATIERT IN DEN UNTEREN ECKEN: LINKS UNTEN: MAR 24; RECHTS UNTEN: 1951 D /
MONOGRAMMED AND DATED IN THE LOWER CORNERS: BOTTOM LEFT: MAR 24; BOTTOM RIGHT: 1951 D
BAUMWOLLE (SATIN UND KÖPER) / **COTTON (SATEEN AND TWILL)** /
RÜCKSEITE: BLAUER BAUMWOLLSTOFF / **BACKING: BLUE COTTON CLOTH** / 194 x 170 CM

Mit seiner Beschränkung auf zwei Blautöne und Schwarz wirkt dieser Quilt ruhig und ernst. Die Datierung 24. März 1951 markiert vielleicht einen Festtag, zu dem er verschenkt wurde. Nicht nur der dunkle Klang und die stimmigen Proportionen, sondern vor allem auch das sehr gute, differenzierte Quilting scheinen der späten Entstehung zu widersprechen – solch feine Steppereien tauchen um die Mitte des 20. Jahrhunderts nicht mehr auf; die handwerkliche Fertigkeit war verloren gegangen. So ist zu vermuten, dass die Macherin schon eine recht alte Frau war. Was die Initiale D bedeutet, muss offenbleiben. // QUILTING: Zickzacklinien, Flechtband, geometrisiertes Spinnennetz, Parallellinien.
Limited as it is to two shades of blue and black, this quilt is both tranquil and somber in appearance. The date, 24 March 1951, may mark a festive occasion on which the quilt was given as a present. Not just the dark color scheme and the harmonious proportions but especially the very good, sophisticated quilting would seem to argue against the late date – such fine quilting no longer occurs after the mid-20th century; the needleworking skills had been lost by then. This suggests that the woman who made it was very old. What the initial 'D' refers to has not been ascertained. // QUILTING: zigzag lines, cable, geometrically stylized spider web, parallel lines.

071

BASKETS

CA 1918
AMISCHE QUILTMACHERIN DER FAMILIE BENJAMIN ADAM FISCHER / **AMISH QUILT-MAKER FROM THE FAMILY OF BENJAMIN ADAM FISCHER**, SPRINGS, SOMERSET COUNTY, PENNSYLVANIA
BAUMWOLLE, BAUMWOLLSATIN / **COTTON, COTTON SATEEN** / RÜCKSEITE: HELLBEIGER BAUMWOLLSATIN / **BACKING: LIGHT BEIGE COTTON SATEEN** / 205 x 180 CM

Auch Baskets ist kein genuin amisches Muster, sondern wurde von den „Englischen", den nicht-amischen Nachbarn, übernommen – mit der üblichen Zeitverzögerung, die klar machen sollte, dass man nichts mit „weltlichen" Gepflogenheiten gemein hatte. Nicht immer ist das Motiv so stark geometrisch wie auf diesem Quilt aus Süd-Pennsylvania mit seiner einfachen, klaren Farbigkeit aus leuchtendem Grün auf schwarzem Grund. Ohne jede Abweichung durchgeführt (vgl. Nr. 61), besitzt er eine Haltung von großer Strenge. // QUILTING: Wellenbänder, gebogene Parallellinien, Gitterwerk; Herzen, die sich zu vierblättigen Kleeblättern zusammenfügen – ein Hochzeitsquilt?

Baskets is another pattern that is not genuinely Amish. It, too, was taken over from the 'English' neighbors of the Amish – with the usual time lag that was to indicate clearly that the Amish wanted nothing to do with 'worldly' ways. The motif is not always so emphatically geometric as it is on this quilt from southern Pennsylvania, with its simple, clear color scheme of glowing green on a black ground. Executed without any deviation from the pattern (cf. no. 61), it is stringently austere in appearance. // QUILTING: scallop borders, bent parallel lines, waffle grid; hearts fitted together to form four-leaf clovers – a Wedding quilt?

072

DOUBLE WEDDING RINGS

CA 1935
AMISCHE QUILTMACHERIN DER FAMILIE RUDOLF MILLER / **AMISH QUILT-MAKER**
FROM THE FAMILY OF RUDOLF MILLER, HOLMES COUNTY, OHIO
BAUMWOLLE / **COTTON** / RÜCKSEITE: VIOLETTBLAUER BAUMWOLLSTOFF /
BACKING: BLUISH PURPLE COTTON CLOTH / 203 x 173 CM

Vielleicht hat dieselbe Frau diesen Quilt und Chinese Coins Nr. 66 gestaltet – der Stil ist jedenfalls sehr eng verwandt. // Die „Eheringe"
setzten sich stets aus bunten Stoffstückchen von nicht ganz regelmäßiger Form zusammen. Die Überschneidungen der Ringe werden durch
sorgfältige Four Patches betont. Bei diesem Exemplar wirkt das Muster besonders energiegeladen: Die Ringe mit ihren lebhaften Farben
scheinen in unablässiger Bewegung um ihre eigene Achse zu rotieren. // QUILTING: Fächer, geometrisches Blütenmuster aus einander
überschneidenden Halbkreisen; innen zeichnen die Steppstiche das Muster nach: parallele Kreislinien, konzentrische konkave Diamonds.
The maker of this quilt may also have made Chinese Coins no. 66 – in any case, they are stylistically very closely related. // The 'Wedding Rings' are composed of brightly colored, irregularly shaped pieces of cloth. The overlapping of the Rings is emphasized by meticulously worked Four Patches. The pattern appears particularly highly charged in this exemplar: the Rings in lively colors look as if they are perpetually rotating about their axes. // QUILTING: Fans, geometric floral pattern formed of intersecting semicircles; inside the quilting stitches trace the pattern: concentric circles, concentrically concave Diamonds.

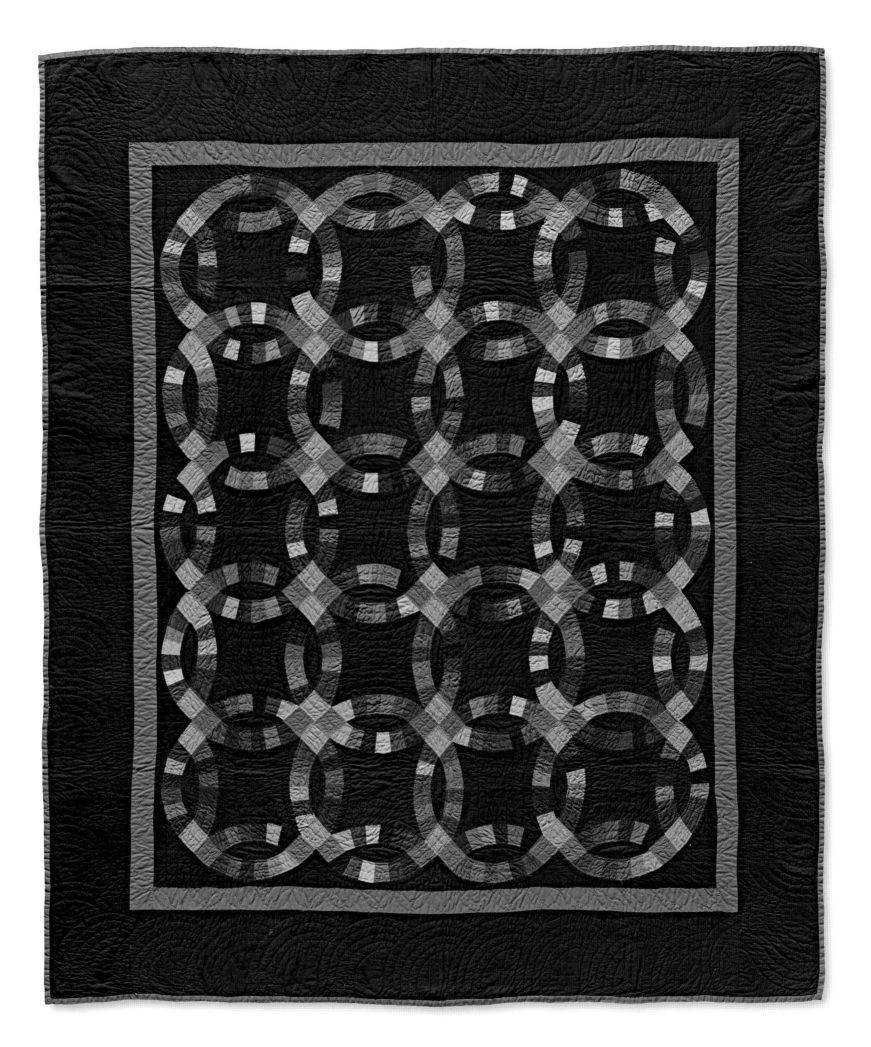

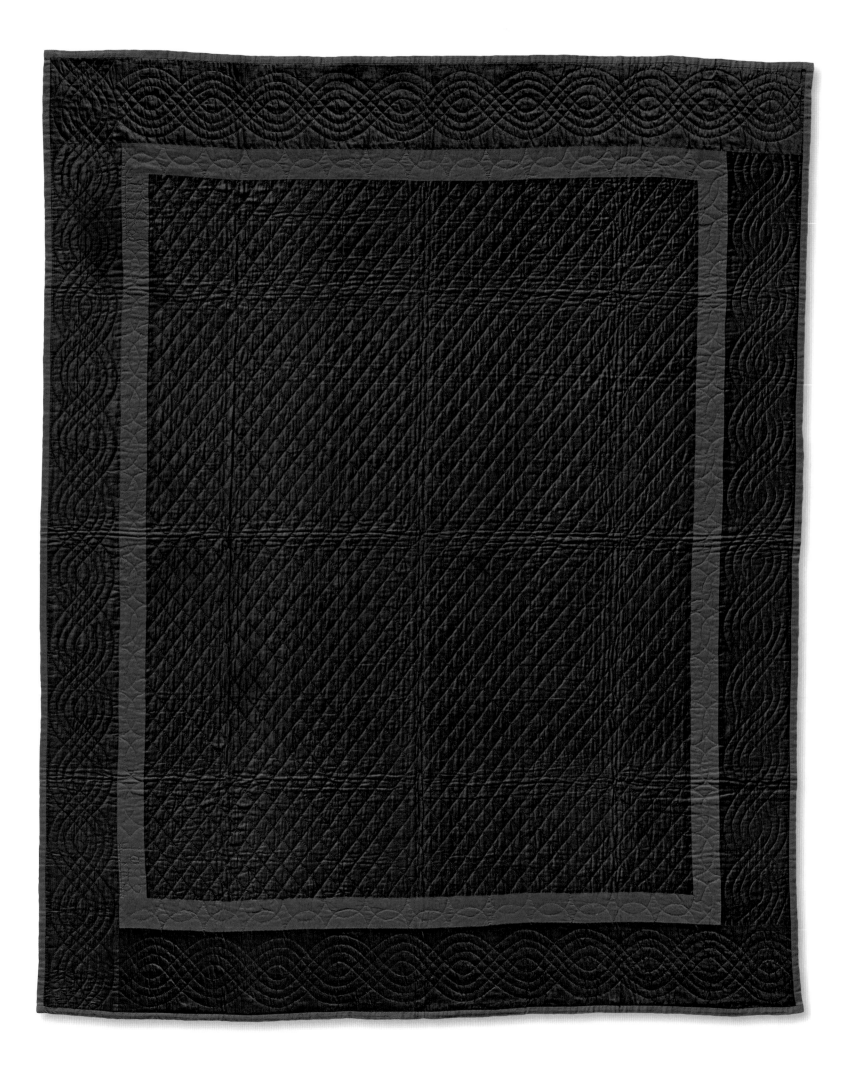

073

OPEN WINDOW

1948
AMISCHE QUILTMACHERIN DER FAMILIE SWARTZENTRUBER / **AMISH QUILT-MAKER**
FROM THE SWARTZENTRUBER FAMILY, HOLMES COUNTY, OHIO
MONOGRAMMIERT UND DATIERT AUF DER VORDERSEITE IM INNENRAHMEN: MG & 1948 / **MONOGRAMMED**
AND DATED ON THE FRONT IN THE INNER FRAME: MG & 1948
BAUMWOLLSATIN / **COTTON SATIN** / RÜCKSEITE: SCHWARZER BAUMWOLLSTOFF /
BACKING: BLACK COTTON CLOTH / 206 x 170 CM

Die Swartzentruber-Amischen gehören zu den konservativsten Gruppen der Old Order Amish, und so ist auch dieser Quilt von größter Schlichtheit und tiefem Ernst: nur Schwarz und das sparsam eingesetzte leuchtende Blau – und das lebhafte Relief des Quilting. Im Widerspruch zur betonten Schlichtheit scheint die mit rotem Garn eingestickte Signatur zu stehen, jedoch bezieht eine solche sich meistens nicht auf die Macherin, sondern benennt üblicherweise die Person, für die der Quilt als Geschenk gemacht wurde. Eigenartigerweise stehen hier die Initialen MG mit dem &-Zeichen ohne das zu erwartende zweite Monogramm – über den Grund kann man nur spekulieren. // Ein anderes Beispiel des Typus Open Window in der Sammlung Schlumberger ist Nr. 69. Eve Wheatcroft Granick (1989) zitiert eine konservative Amische der Old Order Mennonites in Pennsylvania, die sich noch in den 1970er oder 1980er Jahren in einem Interview mit Vehemenz gegen das (für Pieced Quilts nötige) Zerschneiden von Stoff, nur um ihn dann wieder zusammenzunähen, aussprach – das sei „just for pride", nur Eitelkeit. // DICHTES QUILTING: Flechtband, geometrisches Muster aus einander überschneidenden Halbkreisen (an einen Astragal erinnernd), Rautengitter.

The Swartzentruber Amish are among the most conservative of all Old Order Amish groups. No wonder, therefore, that this quilt is so simple and so profoundly solemn in tone: only black and sparingly used glowing blue – and the lively relief of the quilting. The signature, embroidered in red yarn would seem to contradict the emphatic simplicity yet such signatures do not usually refer to the maker but usually name the person for whom the quilt was made as a present. Oddly, the initials 'MG' are here with the ampersand, '&', without a second monogram as might be expected – one is left to conjecture on the reason for this seeming omission. // Another example of the 'Open Window' type in the Schlumberger Collection is no. 69. Eve Wheatcroft Granick (1989) quotes a conservative Old Order Amish Mennonite woman in Pennsylvania, who even in an interview she gave in the 1970s/1980s heatedly denounced the practice of cutting up cloth (necessary for pieced quilts) just to sew it together again – that was 'just for pride', labor in vain for vanity. // DENSE QUILTING: cable, geometric pattern (reminiscent of bead and reel) formed of intersecting semicircles, lozenge waffle grid.

074

BIRDS IN FLIGHT / FLYING BIRDS

CA 1920
AMISCHE QUILTMACHERIN RUTH MAST / **AMISH QUILT-MAKER RUTH MAST**, FREDERICKSBURG, HOLMES COUNTY, OHIO
BAUMWOLLE, BAUMWOLLSATIN / **COTTON, COTTON SATEEN** / RÜCKSEITE: BAUMWOLLE /
BACKING: COTTON / 212 x 175 CM

Kleine, identisch geformte Dreiecke bilden die Grundelemente von Mustern wie Variable Stars, Broken Dishes, Railroad Crossing, Ocean Waves, Lady of the Lake, Birds in the Air, Flying Geese, Flocks of Birds, Hour Glasses und vielen anderen. // Ungewöhnlich bei diesem Flying Birds – auch „Fence Row Variation" genannt – ist nicht nur die sehr seltene Verdopplung des Innenrahmens, sondern auch die unangestrengte Sicherheit, mit der die Farben auf dem schwarzen Grund verteilt sind. Auf den ersten Blick ohne Regel, aber bei genauerer Betrachtung entdeckt man die Symmetrie. Ein paar Mal ist sie unterbrochen, und ganz unkonventionell ist der Kunstgriff, den mittleren „Vogel" in der obersten Reihe um 90 Grad zu drehen: Er tanzt aus der Reihe. // QUILTING: Flechtband, Diagonalgitter, parallele Linien.

Small identically shaped triangles form the basic elements of patterns such as Variable Stars, Broken Dishes, Railroad Crossing, Ocean Waves, Lady of the Lake, Birds in the Air, Flying Geese, Flocks of Birds, Hour Glasses and many others. // What is unusual about this Flying Birds – also known as 'Fence Row Variation' – is not just the very rare doubling of the inner border but also the effortless assurance with which the colors are distributed on the black ground. At first glance, this quilt seems devoid of regularity in design but when scrutinized more closely, its symmetry is revealed. It is disrupted in a few places. An entirely unconventional touch is turning the central 'bird' in the uppermost row by 90 degrees: it breaks ranks. // QUILTING: cable, diagonal grid, parallel lines.

DIE RAUTE, DAS QUADRAT UND DER STREIFEN – UND ANDERE FORMEN AUS DEM SCHATZ DER GEOMETRIE / **LOZENGE, SQUARE AND STRIPE – AND OTHER FORMS FROM THE GEOMETRIC REPERTOIRE**

Corinna Rösner

Quilts sind gesteppte Bettdecken – bei den Amischen gleichbedeutend mit „pieced quilts". Sie bestehen aus Wolle, Baumwolle, Seide, Samt oder anderen textilen Materialien und besitzen drei Lagen: Unterseite, Schau- oder Oberseite und ein wärmendes Vlies als Füllung. Nach Fertigstellung der Schauseite werden die drei Lagen zunächst durch grobe Heftstiche aufeinander fixiert, dann über einen Rahmen gespannt und schließlich mit Tausenden möglichst kleiner Stiche – Heft- oder Reihstiche – zusammengesteppt, d. h. „gequiltet". Aufgrund der Weichheit des Materials erhält das Quilting-Muster neben seiner graphischen Wirkung auch Plastizität. // Je nach Konstruktion der Schauseite lassen sich drei verschiedene Arten von Quilts unterscheiden: Der „appliqué quilt", bei dem die Elemente des Dekors, meist figürliche Motive wie Blumen, Pflanzen, Häuser etc. aus farbigen Stoffstücken, auf einen durchgängigen Untergrund aufgenäht werden. Der „whole cloth quilt" oder „plain quilt", dessen Schauseite aus einem einzigen Stoff besteht. Und der „pieced quilt", dessen Schauseite aus mehreren, meist geometrisch zugeschnittenen Stücken verschiedener Stoffe zusammengenäht ist. // Die Verwendung und Herstellung gesteppter Bettdecken ist keine amische Erfindung. Rund 150 Jahre vor den ältesten amischen Quilts wurde der erste bekannte amerikanische Quilt (Saltonstall Quilt[1]) gefertigt: 1704 – angeblich durch Sarah Sedgwick Leverett, die Frau des Gouverneurs der Massachusetts Bay Colony, und ihre Tochter Elisabeth, also ein geselliger Zeitvertreib wohlhabender Leute. Damals hatte noch kein Amischer seinen Fuß auf den Boden der Neuen Welt gesetzt; das geschah erst zwanzig, dreißig

Quilts are padded bed covers – among the Amish, this means 'pieced quilts'. They are made of wool, cotton, silk, velvet or other fabrics and have three layers: the backing, the front side or top for show and insulating fleece as filling. After the show side is finished, the three layers are first roughly tacked together, then stretched over a frame and finally quilted with thousands of stitches that are as minute as possible – tacking stitches. The softness of the material lends the quilting pattern both a linear effect and plasticity. // Three different types of quilts are distinguished by the construction of the top: the 'appliqué quilt', for which decoration elements, usually figurative motifs such as flowers, plants, houses, etc., cut from pieces of colored cloth, are sewn on to a continuous ground. The second type is the 'whole cloth quilt', whose top consists in a single piece of cloth. And then there is the 'pieced quilt', whose top is sewn together from several or many pieces of different kinds of cloth, usually cut into geometric shapes. // The Amish did not invent the use and making of quilted bed coverings. Some one hundred and fifty years before the earliest Amish quilts were made, the first known American quilt (the Saltonstall Quilt[1]) was sewn: in 1704 – allegedly by Sarah Sedgwick Leverett, wife of the governor of the Massachusetts Bay Colony, and her daughter, Elisabeth, as a sociable pastime for affluent women. At that early date no Amish person had set foot in the New World. That did not happen until twenty or thirty years later and a century and a half would elapse before there was evidence of the first Amish quilts – around 1850/1860. Quilting did not, however, assume broader significance among the Amish until the 1870s and 1880s – evidently ushered in by the launch of the mechanical treadle-operated sewing machine (cf. no. 46). No wonder then that each and every feature of Amish quilts derives from the Anglo-American quilting tradition. The secret of the inimitable style of the 'classical period' that gradually came to a close in the 1940s lies in the combination and consistent composition of these elements.

Jahre später; und es dauert noch mehr als ein Jahrhundert, bis sich – um 1850/1860 – die frühesten amischen Quilts nachweisen lassen. Breitere Bedeutung erlangte das Quiltmachen bei den Amischen jedoch erst ab den siebziger und achtziger Jahren des 19. Jahrhunderts – offenbar mit Einführung der mechanischen Nähmaschine (vgl. Nr. 46). So ist es nicht erstaunlich, dass jedes einzelne der Merkmale amischer Quilts aus der angloamerikanischen Quilt-Tradition herzuleiten ist. Erst in ihrer Kombination und konsequenten Komposition liegt das Geheimnis ihres unverwechselbaren Stils, dessen „klassische Zeit" in den 1940er Jahren allmählich zu Ende ging.

In Lancaster County, rund zweieinhalb Fahrstunden von Philadelphia entfernt, lebt die Kernzelle der ursprünglich aus Europa stammenden Amish People nach den Regeln eines christlichen Fundamentalismus und in einem Lebensstil, der dem American Way of Life diametral entgegengesetzt ist. Ihr ideologischer Überbau – die theologisch begründete Verweigerung säkularer Ziele, etwa des Strebens nach Geltung und Reichtum – bedingt im sozialen und wirtschaftlichen Bereich ein Bemühen um Autarkie und Autonomie. Dies spiegelt sich vor allem auch in ihrer Geräte- und Wohnwelt wider. // Das Farmhaus als Zentrum der Wirtschaftseinheit ist ebenso wie alle Nebengebäude entweder vollständig aus Holz oder teilweise aus Naturstein errichtet. Industriell gefertigte Baustoffe finden keine Verwendung. Bei rund 500–600 qm (!) Wohnfläche ist lediglich die Küche beheizbar. Die Wohnräume sind mit selbstgezimmerten, einfachen, stabilen Holzmöbeln ausgestattet, die keinerlei Verzierungen besitzen. Auf Tapeten und Bilder wird verzichtet; die Wände sind zumeist weiß oder allenfalls einfarbig getüncht. Es fehlen Spiegel, Vorhänge oder Photographien, ebenso Radio, Fernsehgerät etc. Die Räume enthalten nichts außer Bett, Schrank, Tisch und Waschgerät; selbst Bücherregale fehlen. Den einzigen Schmuck der Häuser, das einzig farbige Element der Einrichtung bilden die Quilts, denen nicht zuletzt wegen der Minimalbeheizung der Räume zentrale Bedeutung zukommt.

The core community of the Amish of European origin lives in Lancaster County, some two and half hours' drive from Philadelphia. The Amish live by the rules of an fundamentalist Christian community and practice a lifestyle that is diametrically opposed to the American way of life. The ideological superstructure of the Amish lifestyle – theologically based rejection of such secularist goals as striving for fame and riches – is premised on an attempt to achieve cultural and social autonomy. This is also reflected in the tools and implements they make as well as their homes. // The Amish farmhouse as the center of a self-sustaining economic unit is, like all Amish outbuildings belonging to the farmstead, built entirely of wood or occasionally of unhewn stone (fieldstone). No industrially manufactured building materials are used. With farmhouses boasting some 500–600 square meters (!) of living area, the kitchen is the only room that can be heated. The rooms are furnished with homemade, simple, sturdy wooden furniture devoid of decoration. Wallpaper and pictures on the wall are eschewed. Walls are usually either white or monochrome. There are no mirrors, curtains or photographs nor are there any radios, television sets, etc. The rooms contain no furnishings other than beds, blanket chests, tables and simple washstands; there are not even any bookshelves. The quilts are the only decoration of these homes, the only touch of color in their appointments. Moreover, since the heating is so rudimentary, they are of pivotal importance.

Amish quilts are 'pieced quilts'. Materials with woven or printed patterns are eschewed on principle – the same holds for Amish clothing. The tops of 'pieced quilts' are made by sewing together pieces of various kinds of cloth, most of them relatively large and cut into geometric shapes. Decoration schemes that were too fussy and intricately detailed – non-Amish quilt-makers actually tried to outdo one another in producing quilts made up of the most pieces – were rejected by the Amish as unfunctional luxury indicative of 'pride' as were appliqués, embroidered patterns and trapunto or Italian quilting (padding to emphasize some parts). // The Lancaster Amish were the strictest observers of the prohibition against materials with patterns on them. More liberal Amish communities, for instance in the Midwest and

Amische Quilts sind „pieced quilts". Prinzipiell werden Stoffe mit eingewebten oder aufgedruckten Mustern vermieden – genau wie bei der Kleidung der Amischen. Die Schauseiten der „pieced quilts" entstehen durch Zusammennähen verschiedenfarbiger, meist relativ großer Stoffstücke geometrischen Zuschnitts. Allzu klein gestückelte Dekore – bei den Nichtamischen gab es geradezu Konkurrenzen, wer den vielteiligsten Quilt machen konnte – werden bei den Amischen ebenso als unfunktionaler Luxus und „Hochmut" abgelehnt wie Applikationen, Stickmuster oder Trapunto (das Hinterfüllen einzelner Partien). // Am strengsten befolgten die Lancaster-Amischen das Verdikt gegen gemusterte Stoffe; liberalere Gemeinden im Mittleren Westen und die Amish Mennonites in Kanada hingegen durften offenbar fein strukturierte Stoffe mit Webmustern verarbeiten (siehe Nr. 41 oder Nr. 42). Das Muster-Verbot gilt notabene für die Schauseiten. Quilts aus Lancaster County besitzen nämlich häufig Rückseiten aus gemusterten Stoffen, von schlichten Web- oder Karomustern (Nrn. 12, 44) bis zu manchmal sehr üppigen Dekoren mit Paisleymustern oder großblumigen Ranken, in denen sich Papageien tummeln (Nrn. 22, 41) – Stoffe, die eigens dafür gekauft worden sein müssen, da sie ja sonst strengstens verboten waren. Im Gegensatz dazu findet man bei den Quilts aus Mid West und Kanada fast ausschließlich einfarbige Rückseiten.

Mit Ausnahme der – allerdings stark stilisierten – „Baskets" sind die Schauseiten amischer Quilts nie gegenständlich, sondern immer abstrakt gestaltet. Ihren Benennungen liegen allerdings häufig bildliche Assoziationen zugrunde, die zu Spekulationen über den Ursprung der Muster einladen. Etwa soll das Log Cabin-Motiv auf die Blockhütte zurückgehen. Seine Variante Barn Raising ist nach jener großen gemeinschaftlichen Unternehmung des Scheunenbaus benannt (siehe Nrn. 39, 41). Auch andere Muster werden in der Quilt-Literatur gerne als Abstraktionen interpretiert. So seien die „Bars" letztlich auf die Ackerfurchen der amischen Felder zurückzuführen – oder doch eher auf das Stabwerk von Fenstergittern...? Meist sagen solche Mutmaßungen mehr über die Phantasie des Interpreten aus als über die wirkliche Herkunft eines Ornamentmotives. Dazu gehört wohl auch die Hypothese, „Diamond in the Square" leite sich vom übereck gelegten Schultertuch der amischen Frauen ab oder – die religiöse Lesart – von der Ornamentik auf dem Vorderdeckel des „Ausbunds", dem Gesangbuch der Amischen.

the Amish Mennonites in Canada, on the other hand, were evidently permitted to work fabrics that were finely textured with woven patterns (see nos. 41 and 42). The pattern prohibition, it must be observed here, applied to quilt tops. The backing of Lancaster County quilts is frequently made of materials with patterns, either woven ones or checks (nos. 12, 44), even sumptuous decorations such as paisley patterns or large flower scrolls teeming with parrots (nos. 22, 41) – fabrics that had to be bought for the express purpose of making a quilt since they would otherwise be strictly prohibited. By contrast, most Midwestern and Canadian Amish quilts feature monochrome backing.

Except for 'Baskets' – and they are highly stylized – figurative motifs never occur on the tops of Amish quilts, which are always abstract in design. However, the names given to the patterns are often based on visual associations, which invite conjecture about the origin of these patterns. The 'Log Cabin' motif, for instance, is supposed to derive from log cabins. 'Barn Raising', a variant of it, is named after the renowned Amish custom of getting together to build barns as a communal undertaking (see nos. 39, 41). There are also other patterns that are often interpreted in specialist publications as abstract. 'Bars' are said to derive from the ploughed furrows of Amish fields – or, as another interpretation has it, from the upright bars of window grilles. Such conjectures usually reveal more about the interpreter's imagination than the real origin of a decoration motif. One such hypothetical reading is that 'Diamond in the Square' derives from the way Amish women wear their shawls folded into triangles or – this is the religious interpretation – from the decoration on the front cover of the Ausbund, the Amish hymnal.

For all their simplicity, Amish quilts are distinguished by a pronounced stylistic thrust as well as surprising richness and variety of color despite the economy of the means used to make them and clear, balanced compositions shaped by

Ausgeprägter Stilwille trotz betonter Schlichtheit, überraschende Farbigkeit trotz Sparsamkeit der eingesetzten Mittel und ein klarer, ausgewogener Aufbau, der von strengen Traditionen bestimmt ist, kennzeichnen die Quilts der Amischen. // Mit ihrer charakteristischen Kombination bestimmter Merkmale sind sie auf den ersten Blick erkennbar. Die Quiltmacherinnen folgen dabei einem relativ engen Repertoire an Mustern, jedoch wurde keine (religiöse) Ikonographie entwickelt, wie sie etwa aus der europäischen Malerei bekannt ist. Vielmehr unterliegt die im einzelnen freie Gestaltung der Quilts einer größeren Gesamtordnung – einer Ordnung, von der auch das gesamte Leben der Amischen durchdrungen ist, ohne dass dabei alle Einzelheiten der Handlungsweise vorgeschrieben wären. Obwohl dieses großteils ungeschriebene Gesetz der „Ordnung", das auf wörtlicher Auslegung der Bibel basiert, mit bewusster Weltabkehr, Verteufelung jeglichen „Hochmuts", Ablehnung von Eitelkeiten und Unterordnung des Individuums unter die Gemeinschaft einhergeht, entstanden unter diesen vermeintlich widrigen Bedingungen, fernab vom aktuellen Kunstgeschehen, Werke von hoher Ausdruckskraft und großer ästhetischer Kühnheit. In ihrer formalen Reduktion und Abstraktion scheinen sie die Suche nach dem Elementaren zu verkörpern.

Das Musterrepertoire ist relativ klein. Bei den Lancaster-Amischen konzentriert es sich vorwiegend auf Diamond in the Square, Bars, Sunshine and Shadow und Nine Patch, denen jedoch in unzähligen Abwandlungen immer neue Stimmungen und Ausdrucksmöglichkeiten abgewonnen werden. Umfangreicher ist der Motivschatz im Mittleren Westen und in Kanada: neben den spektakulären Tumbling Blocks unter anderem Shoofly (Nr. 58), Broken Dishes (Nr. 50), Ocean Waves (Nr. 65), Stars (Nrn. 42, 54), Birds in Flight (Nr. 74), Crown of Thorns (Nr. 68), Baskets (Nrn. 61, 71), Chinese Coins (Nr. 66), Stairway to Heaven (Nr. 48), Rail Fence oder Streak of Lightning (Nr. 37) und viele andere. // Die Muster bauen sich allesamt aus wenigen, geometrischen Grundelementen auf. Fast ausschließlich sind es Stoffstücke von geradem Zuschnitt: Quadrat, Rechteck, gleichschenkliges Dreieck und Raute. Gelegentlich findet man auch Achtecke oder Ausschnitte davon (Bow Ties Nr. 56, S. 212), Pfeilformen (Bear Paw Nr. 70), langgestreckte Trapeze (Roman Stripes Nr. 52) etc. Kurvig ausgeschnittene Stücke tauchen seltener auf: Viertel- und Halbkreis, Kreissegment und Kreissektorenteile wie bei Fans (Nrn. 36, 38), Garden Path (Nr. 57) und Wedding Rings (Nr. 72). Aus diesen Elementen in unterschiedlichen Größen und Farben sind alle Muster der amischen Quilts zusammensetzbar – abgesehen von den Crazy Quilts mit ihren ganz unregelmäßigen Stoffstücken (Nr. 43).

strict traditions. // Their characteristic combination of particular features makes them instantly identifiable. Amish quilt-makers followed a relatively small repertory of patterns yet no (religious) iconography was developed of the kind known from European painting, for instance. On the contrary, the free design of individual quilts is subject to an overarching order – an order that informs the entire Amish way of life even though behavior is not prescribed in detail. Although this largely unwritten law of 'order' based on literal interpretation of the Bible is accompanied by the rejection of all worldly things, condemnation of any sort of 'pride', eschewal of vanity and subordination of the individual to the community, powerfully expressive works that are aesthetically very bold nonetheless grew out of what might be regarded as decidedly unfavorable conditions. In reduction of form and abstraction, they seem to embody a quest for elementals.

The repertoire of forms is relatively small. Among the Lancaster County Amish, it consists for the most part in 'Diamond in the Square', 'Bars', 'Sunshine and Shadow' and 'Nine Patch' although they can be almost infinitely varied to produce new moods and modes of expression. The Midwestern and Canadian motif repertoire is richer, including the spectacular 'Tumbling Blocks' as well as 'Shoofly' (no. 58), 'Broken Dishes' (no. 50), 'Ocean Waves' (no. 65), 'Stars' (nos. 42, 54), 'Birds in Flight' (no. 74), 'Crown of Thorns' (no. 68), 'Baskets' (nos. 61, 71), 'Chinese Coins' (no. 66), 'Stairway to Heaven' (no. 48), 'Rail Fence', 'Streak of Lightning' (no. 37) and many more. // All patterns are built up of just a few basic geometric elements. They are almost all made up of pieces of cloth cut out with straight edges: squares, rectangles,

Vor allem die strenge Komposition verleiht den amischen Quilts ihren unverwechselbaren Charakter: Der klare und feste Bezug der Einzelflächen zueinander und zur Gesamtfläche; Formen und Proportionen der kleinsten Einheiten werden innerhalb der Gesamtkomposition immer wieder aufgegriffen und variiert (Diamond in the Square Nrn. 25, 33). Es wird mit Reihungen (Jacob's Ladder Nr. 55, Seven Sisters Nr. 53), Symmetrien (Birds in Flight Nr. 74) und den Effekten von Positiv-Negativ-Formen (Shoofly Nr. 58) gearbeitet, mit Wiederholungen im kleineren Maßstab (Double Nine Patch Nr. 5) und konzentrischem Ineinanderschachteln (Garden Path Nr. 57) – und dies stets nach einem auf das Ganze bezogenen System. Schon die meist recht breiten Außenrahmen und die farblich hervorgehobenen Umfassungen der Kanten verweisen auf diese Systematisierung, betonen sie doch besonders deutlich die Anbindung des Innenfeldes an den Gesamtumriss (Bars Nr. 44, Diamond in the Square Nr. 17, Sunshine and Shadow Nr. 8).

Charakteristisch ist auch die Farbigkeit mit satten, dunklen oder intensiv leuchtenden Tönen, häufig in kühner Zusammenstellung. Grün-, Blau-, Violett- und Rottöne dominieren; auch Braun, Grau und Schwarz kommen vor, während Weiß, Gelb, Orange und andere sehr helle Töne bis um 1920 selten blieben (Bars Nr. 21, Diamond in the Square Nr. 45). Pastelltöne tauchen erst mit den dreißiger Jahren vermehrt auf (Fans Nr. 38). Nach dem Zweiten Weltkrieg, seit den fünfziger Jahren, ist ein rapides Nachlassen der Gestaltungskraft zu beobachten; das fällt vor allem bei den Farben auf. Generelle Aussagen lassen sich aber schwer treffen, gibt es doch beträchtliche Unterschiede zwischen den Gemeinden oder Siedlungsgebieten und im Lauf der Jahrzehnte. Verschiedentlich wurden von durchsetzungsstarken Individuen oder in liberaleren Gemeinden auch sonst nicht übliche Farben gegen jede Konvention gewagt. Ein in jeder Hinsicht ganz ungewöhnliches, äußerst farben-

equilateral triangles and lozenges. Octagons or octagonal elements ('Bow Ties' no. 56, p. 212) as well as arrow shapes ('Bear Paw' no. 70), elongated trapezoidal forms ('Roman Stripes' no. 52), etc., also occur occasionally. Pieces cut in curvilinear shapes surface more rarely: quarters and semicircles, segments and sectors of circles as in 'Fans' (nos. 36, 38), 'Garden Path' (no. 57) and 'Wedding Rings' (no. 72). All patterns encountered on Amish quilts are composed of the above elements in varying sizes and colors – with the notable exception of Crazy Quilts, which are made up of entirely irregular pieces of cloth (no. 43).

It is the stringent composition of Amish quilts that makes them so utterly distinctive: the clear, astringent relationship of parts of the whole surface to one another and to the entire field. The forms and proportions of the smallest units recur and are varied continually within the overall composition ('Diamond in the Square' nos. 25, 33). Patterns may be based on rows ('Jacob's Ladder' no. 55, 'Seven Sisters' no. 53) or symmetrical arrangements ('Birds in Flight' no. 74) or play with the effect created by positive and negative forms ('Shoofly' no. 58). Repetitions may occur on a smaller scale (Double Nine Patch no. 5) or be based on concentric interlocking ('Garden Path' no. 57) – and an overarching system invariably structures the whole. Even the outer borders and frames, which are usually quite broad, and the binding, which is always picked out emphatically in color, refer to this systemic ordering since they emphasize particularly clearly the linkage of the inner field and the overall outline ('Bars' no. 44, 'Diamond in the Square' no. 17, 'Sunshine and Shadow' no. 8).

Another characteristic feature is the color scheme: saturated, dark or glowing colors often in bold combinations. Greens, blues, purples and shades of red predominate. Brown, gray and black also occur whereas white, yellow, orange and other very light colors were rarely used before around 1920 ('Bars' no. 21, 'Diamond in the Square' no. 45). Pastel shades do not appear much until the 1930s ('Fans' no. 38). After the Second World War and since the 1950s quilt design has become markedly less sophisticated. This decline in quality is particularly noticeable in the colors. However, it is difficult to generalize since after all there have been considerable differences between the congregations and settlement areas down through the decades. Unusual colors that boldly defy convention have been used on occasion by

prächtiges Stück ist etwa der sehr frühe Tumbling Blocks aus Ontario (Nr. 46). // Die Farben, die ja überhaupt erst das „pieced design" konstituieren, sind der Komposition unlösbar eingebunden. Aber das Verhältnis der Farbe – oder anders gesagt: des einzelnen, so und so gefärbten Stoffstückes – zum Muster kann sehr unterschiedlich sein. // Zum einen können Farbe und Formelement identisch sein und gleichsam nichts anderes darstellen als sich selbst: bei Open Window, Center Square, Diamond in the Square und Bars sowie bei den Patch-Mustern und den meisten anderen Reihen-Mustern. // Bei der zweiten Gruppe lässt die Farbkomposition etwas anderes entstehen, ein die Formelemente übergreifendes, übergeordnetes Muster. Gut verständlich wird das bei Log Cabin. Viele schmale Stoffstreifen sind hier zu großen Quadratblöcken zusammengenäht. Allerdings nimmt der Betrachter diese Grundeinheiten keineswegs als erstes wahr, denn jeder Quadratblock ist durch die Farbigkeit seiner Stoffstreifen diagonal in eine dunklere und eine hellere Hälfte geteilt. Im Gesamteindruck dominieren die aus diesen hellen und dunklen Zonen gebildeten übergreifenden Muster, seien es die langen Ackerfurchen von Straight Furrow (Nr. 6) oder die Treppen von Courthouse Steps (Nr. 40), seien es die konzentrischen quadratischen Rahmungen von Barn Raising (Nrn. 39, 41). // Auch die Sunshine and Shadow-Quilts gehören eher zur zweiten als zur ersten Gruppe: Zwar besteht ihr Innenfeld aus einem ganz einfachen One Patch-Muster, und jedes einzelne Stoffstückchen ist farblich unterschieden von seinem Nachbarn, jedoch dominieren auch hier die übergreifenden konzentrischen Quadrate, die sich infolge der Farbanordnung bilden – abwechselnd sonnenhell und schattendunkel (Nrn. 22, 63 u. a.). // In der dritten Gruppe bewirkt das Zusammenspiel von Flächen und Farben räumliche Effekte: Die Tumbling Blocks-Quilts erwecken die Illusion übereinandergestapelter Würfel. Nur mit äußerster Konzentration erkennt man das ihnen zugrunde liegende Layout: zu sechszackigen Sternen arrangierte Rauten, deren drei Farben in ihrer Helligkeit sorgsam abgestuft sein müssen (Nr. 53), da sonst nur Flächen zu sehen sind – keine Würfel, sondern Sterne, Rautenketten, Zickzackbänder, Hexagone etc. (Columbia Stars Variation Nr. 49).

assertive individuals or more liberal congregations. An extraordinarily colorful piece that is unusual in every respect is the very early 'Tumbling Blocks' from Ontario (no. 46). // Color, the basic constituent of 'pieced design', is indissolubly linked with composition. But the relationship of color – or, in other words, the color a piece of cloth was originally dyed – to pattern can vary widely. On the one hand, color and form element can be identical and represent exactly what they are, as it were, for instance in 'Open Window', 'Center Square', 'Diamond in the Square' and 'Bars' as well as the 'Patch' patterns and most other row patterns. // In the second group, on the other hand, the color composition creates something else again: an overarching design that transcends the boundaries of a given form element. This principle is easy to grasp in 'Log Cabin'. There many narrow strips of cloth have been sewn together to form large square blocks. However, the viewer does not perceive these basic units at first glance since each square block is divided diagonally into a dark and a lighter half by the color of the strips of cloth composing it. The overall impression received is that the boundary-crossing patterns formed by these light and dark zones are dominant, be they the long furrows in 'Straight Furrow' (no. 6), the stairs of 'Courthouse Steps' (no. 40) or the concentric square framing elements of 'Barn Raising' (nos. 39, 41). // 'Sunshine and Shadow' quilts belong to the second rather than the first group. Their inner field does consist of a very simple 'One Patch' pattern and each individual piece of cloth differs in color from the ones around it. Nevertheless, here, too, a single feature is dominant: the boundary-transcending concentric squares formed by the arrangement of colors – alternately bright as sunshine and dark as shadow (nos. 22, 63, etc). // In the third group the interplay of surfaces and colors creates spatial effects: the design of 'Tumbling Blocks' quilts creates an optical illusion of piled-up cubes. One has to concentrate hard to spot the underlying layout: lozenges arranged to form Six-Pointed Stars, whose three colors must be carefully graded by lightness (no. 53); otherwise only surfaces would be discernible – not cubes but Stars, chains of Diamonds, zigzag strips, hexagons, etc. ('Columbia Stars' variation no. 49).

Das Quilting, die Steppornamentik, gehört zu den amischen Quilts genauso wie zu den nichtamischen, und trotz „Bilderverbot" (oder Musterverbot) ist auch bei dem Amischen diese Ornamentik nicht nur abstrakt oder rein geometrisch, sondern auch „naturalistisch": florale Motive wie Blüten, Rosetten, Rosen- oder Tulpenzweige, Weinranken, andere Blattgirlanden, die so genannten Federranken, „princess feathers", Herzen, Körbe, stilisierte Sonnenblumen etc. Dazu kommt eine Vielzahl geometrischer Muster, so z. B. Blütenmotive, die wie Maßwerk aus einander überschneidenden Kreisen konstruiert sind, Sterne, Quadrat- und Rautengitter, die in der englischen Terminologie den schönen Namen „pumpkin seed" (Kürbiskerne) tragen, Schraffuren aus Parallellinien, Zickzack-, X- und Kreuzmuster, Wellenlinien, Zopf- und Flechtbänder, Bogenscharen („clam shell"), Fächer u. a. // Während das Quilting bei den Lancaster-Amischen meist sehr fein und reich ist, wobei die großflächigen Kompositionen wie Diamond in the Square einen idealen Untergrund dafür bieten, ist die Steppornamentik bei den kleinteiligeren Quilts aus dem Mittleren Westen (Lone Star Nr. 34) und Kanada (Tumbling Blocks Nr. 46) weniger aufwändig. // Von der Funktion her betrachtet, sorgt das Quilting zwar für den Zusammenhalt von Unter- und Oberseite und fixiert die dazwischenliegende Füllung, für die reine Funktion wären allerdings so dichte und kunstvolle Steppereien nicht notwendig. Textilien mit Mustern zu versehen, scheint ein schwer unterdrückbares Bedürfnis zu sein. // Obwohl das feine Gespinst der Steppstiche sich dem „pieced design" unterordnet, indem es der Felderung und – meist – auch ihrer Farbigkeit folgt, bildet es doch eine eigene ästhetische Aussage mit dem lebhaften Schattenspiel und Relief, das die Stepplinien im weichen Untergrund verursachen. Den Farben und der Geometrie der Flächen fügt somit das Quilting eine weitere Ebene hinzu: die Effekte des Lichts und eine deutliche Dreidimensionalität.

Quilting is an integral part of Amish and non-Amish quilts. Despite the 'iconoclasm' (or prohibition against patterns), even the quilting is not purely abstract or geometric on Amish quilts but may also be 'naturalistic': floral motifs such as flowers, rosettes, rose or tulip sprays, vines, foliate garlands, what are known as feather scrolls, 'Princess Feathers', hearts, baskets, stylised sunflowers, etc. Then there are a great many geometric patterns, including floral motifs constructed like tracery of overlapping circles, stars, grids composed of square and lozenge-shaped elements, which are delightfully designated 'pumpkin seeds', hatching consisting of parallel lines, zigzag, Xs and cross patterns, scallop borders, interlaced bands, 'clam shells' (arcs), fans and many others. // Lancaster Amish quilting is usually very fine and ornate. Large field compositions such as 'Diamond in the Square' make an ideal background for it. The quilting designs used for the more intricately patterned Midwestern ('Lone Star' no. 34) and Canadian ('Tumbling Blocks' no. 46) are less elaborate. // Viewed from the functional standpoint, quilting does ensure that the backing and the top are firmly attached to each other and keeps the padding between them in place. However, again from the purely functional standpoint, such dense and intricate quilting is not at all necessary. Putting patterns on textiles simply seems to be a basic aesthetic need that nothing can suppress. // Although the fine tissue of quilting stitches is subordinate to the 'pieced design' since it follows the boundaries of the fields as well as – usually – the colors, it does make an aesthetic statement in its own right in the lively interplay of shading and relief generated by the lines of quilting on the soft ground. Quilting, therefore, adds another plane to those of color and planar geometry: the effect created by light and a noticeably three-dimensional impression.

In a systematic of Amish 'pieced designs', the monochrome Plain quilt would be at the beginning or, put more precisely, would be their precursor. There are good reasons for assuming that this is the earliest type of Amish quilt. The earliest Amish Plain quilts known to have survived bear the embroidered dates 1840 (or 1849) and 1869. At that time multipiece, indeed extremely intricate 'pieced designs' with the most elaborate patterns imaginable, using patterned fabrics, etc., were fashionable among the neighboring Anglo-Americans. The Amish quite obviously wanted to demarcate themselves deliberately – as they have demonstrated in other aspects of their lifestyle – from an immediate environment

In einer Systematik der amischen „pieced designs" würden die einfarbigen Plain Quilts am Anfang stehen oder, besser gesagt: die Vorläufer bilden. Einiges spricht dafür, dass dies überhaupt der älteste Typus amischer Quilts ist. Die frühesten amischen Plain Quilts tragen die aufgestickten Jahreszahlen 1840 (oder 1849) bzw. 1869; es sind zugleich die ersten erhaltenen amischen Quilts. Zu dieser Zeit waren bei den angelsächsischen Nachbarn vielteilige, ja sogar äußerst kleinteilige „pieced designs" Mode, Quilts mit aufwändigsten Mustern, mit gemusterten Stoffen etc. Ganz offensichtlich wollten sich die Amischen – wie in ihrer sonstigen Lebensweise – auch mit ihren Quilts bewusst von ihrer andersgläubigen Umgebung abheben. Diese Haltung ist in den folgenden Zeiten ein Grundprinzip geblieben. // Die Schauseiten von Plain Quilts bestehen aus zusammengenähten Stoffbahnen einer einzigen Farbe; manchmal ist die umlaufende Stoffborte farblich abgesetzt, sonst gibt es als Zierde nur das Quilting. // In einem nächsten Schritt – könnte man aus der Sicht des Systematikers sagen – wird der Schauseite ein Innenrahmen anderer Farbe eingefügt, der den Umriss der Gesamtfläche gleichsam nachzeichnet: Inside Border-Quilt oder Open Window. Beispiele in der Sammlung Schlumberger sind die Nrn. 69 und 73. Gelegentlich kann der eine Rahmen auch einen zweiten umschließen: Double Inside Border. // Deutlich zeigt sich dabei eine Tendenz zur Zentralisierung, die sogar bei Plain Quilts zum Vorschein kommt, betont doch dort die Steppornamentik das Zentrum. Im Englischen spricht man von „center medallion style", der (mindestens) auf das 18. Jahrhundert zurückgeht und bei den Amischen auftaucht, als er in ihrer Umgebung längst aus der Mode gekommen war. Besonders wird er bei den Amischen in Lancaster County gepflegt, die auf dem quadratischen Format geradezu insistieren. // Center Square ist gewissermaßen die Entsprechung zu Inside Border/Open Window. Anstelle eines inneren Rahmens besitzt der Quilt eine farblich abgesetzte Innenfläche in Quadratform. // Obwohl das Muster Bars mit seinen parallelen Streifen – schmalen, in die Länge gestreckten Rechtecken – eine Richtung besitzt, findet man es auch bei den Lancaster-Amischen. Bezeichnenderweise bilden die Streifen hier das zentrale Quadrat (Nr. 12) und sind damit in ihrer Tendenz gleichsam gebändigt, vor allem dann, wenn ein ausgeklügeltes Rahmenwerk und Eckquadrate für die feste Verbindung des Bars-Feldes mit dem Quadratformat sorgen (Nr. 44 u. a.; im Gegensatz dazu siehe etwa Nr. 3). // Vor allem aber kann dem Innenquadrat ein weiteres, auf die Spitze gestelltes Quadrat eingefügt werden: Diamond in the Square, auch Center Diamond genannt (Nrn. 9, 11 u. a.). Dieser Typus lebt von großen Flächen in wenigen, sehr bewusst gesetzten Farben und ist gleichsam der Inbegriff amischer Quilts: ernst, streng, festlich,

CENTER DIAMOND / **DIAMOND IN THE SQUARE**, ca 1920/25
Amische Quiltmacherin der Familie Lapp / **Amish Quilt-Maker from the Lapp Family**, Lancaster County, Pennsylvania / 73 x 73 cm

that lived by a different faith. This stance has continued to be a basic principle informing their lives. // The tops of Plain quilts consist of bolts of monochrome cloth, all of the same color, sewn together. Sometimes the outer border stands out in a different color but the quilting is the only decoration. // In the next phase – again viewed from the systematic standpoint – is adding an inner border of a different color, which traces, as it were, the outline of the field as a whole: the Inside Border quilt or 'Open Window', as exemplified by nos. 69 and 73 in the Schlumberger Collection. Occasionally there may even be a second inner border: Double-Inside Border. // A clear trend towards centralization shows up, even in Plain quilts, where the quilting decoration emphasizes the center of the quilt. The Anglo-American term for this approach to design is 'center medallion style', which goes back to the 18th century (if not even further back) and surfaces among the Amish long after it had ceased to be fashionable among the neighboring Anglo-Americans. The Lancaster County Amish cultivated it; they might be said to have insisted on the square format. // 'Center Square' is, so to speak, the equivalent of Inside Border/'Open Window'. Instead of an inner border, the 'Center Square' quilt has a square inner field in a different, stand-out color. // Although the 'Bars' pattern with its parallel stripes – narrow elongated rectangles – does, on the other hand, go in a specific direction, it, too, occurs among the Lancaster County Amish. Here the stripes characteristically form the central square (no. 12) and are thus checked in their directional tendency, especially when a sophisticated border system and square corner blocks ensure that the 'Bars' field is firmly anchored to the square format (no. 44, etc.; in contrast, however, see for instance, no. 3). // Most importantly, another square,

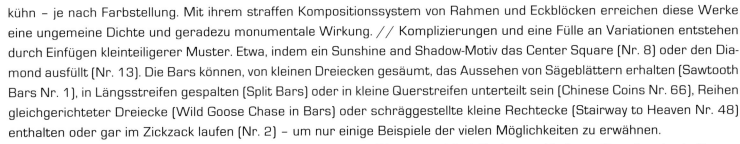

kühn – je nach Farbstellung. Mit ihrem straffen Kompositionssystem von Rahmen und Eckblöcken erreichen diese Werke eine ungemeine Dichte und geradezu monumentale Wirkung. // Komplizierungen und eine Fülle an Variationen entstehen durch Einfügen kleinteiligerer Muster. Etwa, indem ein Sunshine and Shadow-Motiv das Center Square (Nr. 8) oder den Diamond ausfüllt (Nr. 13). Die Bars können, von kleinen Dreiecken gesäumt, das Aussehen von Sägeblättern erhalten (Sawtooth Bars Nr. 1), in Längsstreifen gespalten (Split Bars) oder in kleine Querstreifen unterteilt sein (Chinese Coins Nr. 66), Reihen gleichgerichteter Dreiecke (Wild Goose Chase in Bars) oder schräggestellte kleine Rechtecke (Stairway to Heaven Nr. 48) enthalten oder gar im Zickzack laufen (Nr. 2) – um nur einige Beispiele der vielen Möglichkeiten zu erwähnen.

Zentralisierte Quiltmuster sind auch Sunshine and Shadow (Nrn. 4, 8, 60, 63), dessen Variante Grandmother's Dream (Nrn. 22, 24) und Sunshine Star (Nr. 35), aber auch Lone Star (Nr. 34). Allerdings bestehen diese Quilts nicht mehr aus wenigen großen Flächen und Farben, sondern sind grundsätzlich anders komponiert: kleinteilig und vielfarbig. // Bei Sunshine and Shadow sind es ausschließlich Quadratstückchen gleicher Größe – man könnte auch One Patch-Muster dazu sagen; so bilden sie den Übergang zu Schachbrett- oder Reihenmustern. Im einfachsten Fall – One Patch-Quilts – sind kleine Quadrate ganz unkompliziert aneinandergereiht (S. 13; als sehr ungewöhnliche Variante dieses Musters könnte man Nr. 47 ansehen). Die meisten „Schachbrett"-Muster bestehen jedoch aus größeren quadratischen Blöcken, die in sich wiederum in kleinere Quadrate unterteilt sind, etwa zu Vierer- (Four Patch) oder Neunermotiven (Nine Patch, Nrn. 15, 23). Aus mehreren Neunermotiven lassen sich dann Double Nine Patches bilden (Nrn. 5, 26, 31). Die Lancaster-Amischen betonen natürlich den schachbrettartigen, quadratischen Charakter dieser Muster und integrieren sie in ihr zentralisierendes Kompositionsschema mit breitem Rahmen, Eckquadraten usw.; andere amischen Gemeinschaften hingegen bevorzugen längliche Formate (Nrn. 18, 20). // Die mehrteiligen Elemente müssen, damit das Muster entsteht, mit einfarbigen Quadratblocks alternieren.

one that stands on one of its corners, can be added to the inner square: 'Diamond in the Square', also known as 'Center Diamond' (nos. 9, 11, etc.). This type is based on large surfaces in a few, very consciously chosen colors, and, as it were, exemplifies the Amish quilt: solemn, austere, festive, bold – depending on how the colors are selected and deployed. With their taut composition system of frames and corner blocks, an extraordinary density is achieved in these works and an effect that is nothing if not monumental. // Complications and a host of variations are produced by adding more intricately detailed patterns, for instance, by filling the 'Center Square' (no. 8) or the 'Diamond' (no. 13) with a 'Sunshine and Shadow' motif. 'Bars' can, if lined with minute triangles, be made to look like saw blades ('Sawtooth Bars' no. 1), be split into longitudinal stripes ('Split Bars') or subdivided into small horizontal stripes ('Chinese Coins' no. 66), can incorporate rows of triangles pointing in the same direction ('Wild Goose Chase in Bars'), small rectangles set obliquely ('Stairway to Heaven' no. 48) or even running in a zigzag pattern (no. 2) – just to mention only a few of many possible variations.

Other quilt patterns with a central focus are 'Sunshine and Shadow' (nos. 4, 8, 60, 63), 'Grandmother's Dream' (nos. 22, 24), a variant of it, and 'Sunshine Star' (no. 35) as well as 'Lone Star' (no. 34). However, these quilts no longer consist of a few large surfaces and colors but are composed along essentially different lines: they are intricately detailed and multi-colored. // 'Sunshine and Shadow' is composed solely of little square pieces of identical size – it might also be called a 'One Patch' design – and, therefore, represents a transition to checkerboard or row patterns. In the most unsophisticated example – 'One Patch' – small squares are simply sewn together to form a checkerboard pattern (p. 13; no. 47 might be viewed as a highly unusual variant of that pattern). Most 'checkerboard' patterns, however, are made up of larger square blocks, subdivided in turn into smaller squares to form 'Four Patch' or 'Nine Patch' (nos. 15, 23) designs. 'Double Nine Patches' are formed of several 'Nine Patch' motifs (nos. 5, 26, 31). Lancaster County Amish quilt-makers of course emphasize the checkerboard, square character of such designs and integrate them into their

Wenn die Farben dementsprechend angeordnet wurden, können sich die kleinen Quadratstückchen über die Blöcke hinweg auch zu Ketten verbinden (Double Nine Patch Nr. 19, Nine Patch Blockwork – Irish Chain Nr. 30). Bei den richtigen Ketten – den Irish Chains – dominiert dann das Gitterwerk, das diagonal oder parallel zu den Quilträndern die Fläche überzieht. Nine Patches oder Schachbrettmotive mögen an den Kreuzungen der Ketten noch erkennbar sein (Nrn. 29, 64) oder auch nicht (Nr. 27). // Mit kleinen rechtwinkligen Dreiecken, also diagonal halbierten Quadraten, lassen sich ähnliche Mustervariationen durchspielen: von Broken Dishes (Nr. 50) – gleichsam ein One Patch-Muster, bei dem die Quadrate durch Dreiecke ersetzt wurden – bis zum Gitterwerk aus Dreiecken: den Ocean Waves (Nr. 65). // Das Kompositionsprinzip, Quadratblöcke, die ein Motiv tragen, mit einfarbigen, bis auf das Quilting leeren Diamonds abzuwechseln, gilt für zahlreiche weitere Reihenmuster, wie etwa Birds in Flight (Nr. 74), Variable Stars/Ohio Stars (Nrn. 42, 54), Crown of Thorns (Nr. 68), Bear Paw (Nr. 70), Baskets (Nrn. 61, 71), Shoofly (Nr. 58) – auch an diesen Beispielen zeigt sich die Vielfalt der Sammlung Schlumberger. // Bei anderen Reihenmustern aus Quadratblocks ist es durchaus möglich, auf leere Diamonds zu verzichten, wie Roman Stripes (Nr. 52) oder Bow Ties (Nr. 56) zeigen, Fans (Nrn. 36, 38) oder auch der eigenartige Streak of Lightning/Rail Fence (Nr. 37), der das Raffinement, mit dem aus einfachsten Grundelementen ein äußerst verblüffendes Muster gestaltet werden kann, besonders gut demonstriert. Nur drei rechteckige Stoffstreifen in drei Farben – grau, schwarz und rot – bilden den quadratischen Block, und es gibt vier Positionen, in denen er angeordnet werden kann. Mehr ist für dieses kompliziert und dreidimensional wirkende Muster nicht nötig. // Ähnliches gilt – mutatis mutandis – für die effektvollen Tumbling Blocks; hier sind es allerdings Rauten, aus denen ein allover-pattern aus Hexagrammen oder Hexagonen entsteht, das einzig und allein durch die raffinierte Farbgebung seine Räumlichkeit gewinnt (Nr. 67 u.a.). // Mit Quadratblocks aus schmalen Stoffstreifen in hellen und dunklen Farben wird auch bei den Log Cabin-Quilts gearbeitet. Gewissermaßen in Fortführung des

centralized composition scheme with broad borders, square corner blocks, etc. Quilt-makers from other Amish communities, on the other hand, prefer longitudinal formats (nos. 18, 20). // Design elements composed of several pieces must alternate with monochrome square blocks to create the desired pattern. When the colors are arranged accordingly, the small square pieces can transcend block boundaries to link up and form a chain ('Double Nine Patch' no. 19, 'Nine Patch Blockwork' – 'Irish Chain' no. 30). In real chain patterns – 'Irish Chains' – the grid effect is dominant, covering the entire field in diagonals or paralleling the edges of a quilt. 'Nine Patches' or checkerboard motifs can either be still distinguishable where chains intersect (nos. 29, 64) or no longer show up at all (no. 27). // Similar pattern variations can be created with small right-angled triangles, that is, diagonally bisected squares: ranging from 'Broken Dishes' (no. 50) – a 'One Patch' pattern, as it were, with the squares replaced by triangles – to a grid composed of triangles: 'Ocean Waves' (no. 65). // The principle of composition according to which square blocks composing a motif alternate with monochrome 'Diamonds' that are empty except for the quilting informs numerous other row patterns, such as 'Birds in Flight' (no. 74), 'Variable Stars'/'Ohio Stars' (nos. 42, 54), 'Crown of Thorns' (no. 68), 'Bear Paw' (no. 70), 'Baskets' (nos. 61, 71) and 'Shoofly' (no. 58) – also these examples illustrate the variety of the Schlumberger Collection. // It is, on the other hand, possible to do without empty 'Diamonds' in other row patterns composed of square blocks, as is shown by 'Roman Stripes' (no. 52) and 'Bow Tie' (no. 56), 'Fans' (nos. 36, 38) and even the peculiar 'Streak of Lightning'/'Rail Fence' (no. 37), this last epitomizing the creation of an extraordinarily striking design from the simplest of basic elements. Only three rectangular strips of cloth in three colors – grey, black and red – form the square block and there are four positions in which it can be arranged. Nothing more is needed for this complex and three-dimensional-looking design. // The same is true – with due alteration of details – of the stunning 'Tumbling Blocks'; here, however, lozenges form an overall pattern of hexagrams or hexagons, which creates a spatial effect solely through its sophisticated color scheme (no. 67, etc.). // 'Log Cabin' quilts are also based on square blocks made up of

Kompositionsschemas von Streak of Lightning entstehen, je nachdem, mit welcher Seite die Blocks aneinanderstoßen, die verschiedenen Muster, wie zum Beispiel Straight Furrow (S. 15, Nr. 6), Barn Raising (Nrn. 39, 41), Courthouse Steps (Nr. 40) oder andere.

Von der lapidaren Ausdruckskraft, Monumentalität oder schlichten Eleganz der scheinbar so einfachen, zentralisierten großflächigen Quilts geht der Weg dieser Systematik über die Klarheit, Übersichtlichkeit und unumwundene Direktheit vieler Quadratblock-Reihenmuster bis zu den kompliziert und unruhig gemusterten Quilts am Ende der Systematik.

Ornament – neben Architektur und Bildnerei die dritte Gattung der bildenden Künste – wurde als „Muster auf Grund" definiert (Alois Riegl). „Wesentlich in dieser Gattung ist die Kategorie des Rapports, der Wiederholbarkeit von Formen. Die Reihung des Gleichen, also die Wiederholbarkeit erstellt die Gattung im Unterschied zum Bau und zum Bild."[2] Ornamentgeschichte ist ablesbar am Verhältnis des Musters zum Grund, daran, wie weit sich das Muster von seinem Grund, ein Motiv aus seinem Rapport löst und damit verselbständigt und bildhaft wird, also in eine andere Gattung überwechselt. // Die amischen Quilts sind auch charakterisiert durch das enge Wechselspiel zwischen Muster und Grund, die sich oft nicht voneinander trennen lassen und miteinander identisch sind. Gerade die stärksten Quilts der Amischen gehorchen diesem Prinzip am genauesten. Jedoch, auch wenn in ihnen Muster und Grund nicht isolierbar sind, durch Isolierung des Einzelmotivs aus dem Rapport, Vergrößerung und Monumentalisierung (Diamond in the Square) erlangen sie gleichsam Bildcharakter, Bildhaftigkeit – in unseren an moderner abstrakter Kunst geschulten Augen.

1   Orlofsky Patsy and Myron. Quilts in America. New York 1974. ISBN 0-07-047725-6; Quelle: http://www.geocities.com/hollywood/boulevard/7123/qsource38.htm
2   Bauer Hermann, Kunsthistorik. München 1979, 47f.

narrow strips of cloth in light and dark colors. Depending on which side the blocks are joined, a wide variety of patterns, including 'Straight Furrow' (p. 15, no. 6), 'Barn Raising' (nos. 39, 41), 'Courthouse Steps' (no. 40) and others, is created that build on the composition underlying 'Streak of Lightning'.

From the terse expressive powers, monumentality or simple elegance of center-focused, large-field quilts that seem so simple, systematic analysis proceeds via the clarity, clearly discernible articulation and point-blank directness of many square block row patterns to culminate in quilts of complex and turbulent design.

Ornament – alongside architecture and image the third visual arts genre – was defined in the 19th century as 'pattern on a ground' (Alois Riegl). 'What is essential to this genre is the category of connection, the iterative potential of forms. Paratactic juxtaposition of what is identical, that is, its iterative quality, is the distinguishing feature of this genre, differentiating it from architecture and image.'[2] The history of ornament can be read in the figure-ground relationship, in the extent to which a pattern detaches itself from its ground or a motif from its relationship to the overall pattern to become autonomous and an image in its own right, that is, can be carried over into another genre. // Amish quilts are also characterized by the closeness of the figure-ground relationship. Figure and ground are often indissolubly linked, even identical. The most powerful Amish quilts are those that are most profoundly informed by this principle. However, even though figure cannot be isolated from ground on them, they nonetheless attain image character, become pictures, so to speak – in our eyes, schooled as they are on modern abstract art – when the individual motif is detached from the overall pattern, is magnified and monumentalized ('Diamond in the Square').

1   Orlofsky, Patsy and Myron. Quilts in America. New York 1974. ISBN 0-07-047725-6; source: http://www.geocities.com/hollywood/boulevard/7123/qsource38.htm
2   Bauer, Hermann, Kunsthistorik. Munich 1979, 47f.

ANHANG / APPENDIX

MONOGRAMME / **MONOGRAMS**

BILBLIOGRAPHIE (IN AUSWAHL)
(chronologisch)
BIBLIOGRAPHY, A SELECTION
(in chronological order)

[Kat. Ausst.] Abstract Design in American Quilts. Introduction: Robert M. Doty. Essay: Jonathan Holstein. Whitney Museum of American Art. New York 1971. 16. S. m. 7 Abb.

Die bahnbrechende Ausstellung in einem reinen Kunstmuseum, die von einer kleinen Katalogbroschüre begleitet wurde, zeigte Quilts der Sammlung Gail van der Hoof und Jonathan Holstein. Holstein widmet sie dem ein Jahr zuvor verstorbenen Maler Barnett Newman.

[Exhib. cat.] Abstract Design in American Quilts. Introduction: Robert M. Doty. Essay: Jonathan Holstein. Whitney Museum of American Art. New York 1971. 16 pages, 7 illustrations.

This ground-breaking exhibition in a museum devoted to fine art and accompanied by a small catalog brochure showed quilts from the Gail van der Hoof and Jonathan Holstein Collection. The collector dedicated it to the painter Barnett Newman, who had died the year before.

[Kat. Ausst.] Quilts. Musée des Arts Décoratifs, Paris. Lausanne 1972. 96 S. m. farb. u. s/w-Abb.

Quilts der Sammlung Gail van der Hoof und Jonathan Holstein, darunter einige amische Quilts.

[Exhib. cat.] Quilts. Musée des Arts Décoratifs, Paris. Lausanne 1972. 96 pages, illustrated in color and black and white.

Quilts from the Gail van der Hoof and Jonathan Holstein Collection, including some Amish quilts.

Holstein Jonathan, The Pieced Quilt. An American design tradition. Greenwich/Conn. 1973. 192 S. m. 95 farb. u. 43 s/w-Abb.

Zur Geschichte des amerikanischen "pieced"-Quilt und seiner europäischen Vorläufer.

Holstein, Jonathan, The Pieced Quilt. An American design tradition. Greenwich, Conn. 1973. 192 pages, 95 illustrations in color and 43 in black and white.

On the history of the American 'pieced' quilt and its American precursors.

[Kat. Ausst.] Amish Quilts 1870–1920. Collection Monika Müller, Zurich. Musée d'Art et d'Histoire, Genève; Musée de l'Impression sur Étoffes, Mulhouse. [Genève] 1975. 19 S. m. s/w-Abb.

[Exhib. cat.] Amish Quilts 1870–1920. Collection Monika Müller, Zurich. Musée d'Art et d'Histoire, Geneva; Musée de l'Impression sur Étoffes, Mulhouse. [Geneva] 1975. 19 pages with black and white illustrations.

Bishop Robert u. Elisabeth Safanda, A Gallery of Amish Quilts. Design diversity from a plain people. New York 1976. 96 S. m. 157 meist farb. Abb.

Diese Publikation und der folgende Band von Phyllis Haders waren die ersten Bücher, die sich einzig und allein amischen Quils widmeten.

Bishop, Robert and Safanda, Elisabeth, A Gallery of Amish Quilts. Design diversity from a plain people. New York 1976. 96 pages and 157 illustrations, most of them in color.

The publication and the following book by Phyllis Haders were the first books devoted entirely to Amish quilts.

Haders Phyllis, Sunshine and Shadow: The Amish and their quilts. New York 1976. 87 S. m. farb. u. s/w-Abb. [A new and expanded edition: Pittstown/N.J. 1984]

Haders, Phyllis, Sunshine and Shadow: The Amish and their quilts. New York 1976. 87 pages with illustrations in color and black and white. (A new and expanded edition: Pittstown, N.J. 1984)

Hostetler John A., Amish Society. Baltimore/London 1980 (3. Aufl.). 414 S. m. Abb.

Hostetler, John A., Amish Society. Baltimore/London 1980 (3rd ed.). 414 pages with illustrations.

Pottinger David, Quilts from the Indiana Amish: A regional collection. Photographs by Susan Einstein. Museum of American Folk Art. New York 1983. 88 S., 138 Farbtaf.

Pottinger, David, Quilts from the Indiana Amish: A regional collection. Photographs by Susan Einstein. Museum of American Folk Art. New York 1983. 88 pages, 138 color plates.

Pellman Rachel u. Kenneth, The World of Amish Quilts. Intercourse/Pa. 1984. 178 S. m. farb. Abb.

Pellman, Rachel and Kenneth, The World of Amish Quilts. Intercourse, Pa. 1984. 178 pages with illustrations in color.

[Kat.] The Esprit Quilt Collection. Text: Julie Silber. San Francisco 1985. 40 ungez. S. m. 27 farb. Abb.

[Cat.] The Esprit Quilt Collection. Text: Julie Silber. San Francisco 1985. 40 pages [n. p.] and 27 illustrations in color.

Pellman Rachel u. Kenneth, Amish Crib Quilts. Intercourse/Pa. 1985. 96 S. m. farb. Abb.

Pellman, Rachel and Kenneth, Amish Crib Quilts. Intercourse, Pa. 1985. 96 pages with illustrations in color.

[Kat. Ausst.] Quilts des Amish 1870–1930. Musée des arts décoratifs de la Ville de Lausanne. Lausanne 1988. 29 S. u. 40 farb. Abb.

[Exhib. cat.] Quilts des Amish 1870–1930. Musée des arts décoratifs de la Ville de Lausanne. Lausanne 1988. 29 pages and 40 color illustrations.

Coleman Bill, Amish Odyssey. Toronto/New York 1988 = Das Leben der Amish. Photographie Bill Coleman. Heidelberg 1988. 144 S. m. farb. Abb.

Coleman, Bill, Amish Odyssey. Toronto/New York 1988 [Das Leben der Amish. Photographie Bill Coleman. Heidelberg 1988]. 144 pages with color illustrations.

McCauly Daniel u. Kathryn, Decorative Arts of the Amish of Lancaster County. Intercourse/Pa. 1988, 160 S. m. farb. Abb.

Quilts auf den Seiten 40–73 und 88–89.

McCauly, Daniel and Kathryn, Decorative Arts of the Amish of Lancaster County. Intercourse, Pa. 1988, 160 pages with color illustrations.

Quilts on pp. 40–73 and 88–89.

Granick Eve Wheatcroft, The Amish Quilt. Intercourse/Pa. 1989. 192 S. m. farb. Abb. [Paperback Edition 1994]

Granick, Eve Wheatcroft, The Amish Quilt. Intercourse, Pa. 1989. 192 pages with color illustrations. (Paperback Edition 1994)

Hostetler John A. (Hrsg.), Amish Roots. A treasure of history, wisdom, and lore. Baltimore/London 1989. 319 S. m. Abb.

Hostetler, John A. (ed.), Amish Roots. A Treasure of History, Wisdom, and Lore. Baltimore/London 1989. 319 pages, illustrated.

Kraybill Donald B., The Riddle of Amish Culture. Baltimore/London 1989. 304 S. m. Abb.

Kraybill, Donald B., The Riddle of Amish Culture. Baltimore/London 1989. 304 pages, illustrated.

Hughes Robert u. Julie Silber, Amish. The Art of the Quilt. New York 1990 = Quilts. Die Kunst der Amischen. Schaffhausen u. a. 1990. 207 S. m. 82 Farbtaf. [English Paperback Edition: New York 1993] Hauptwerke der Esprit Collection.

Hughes, Robert and Silber, Julie, Amish. The Art of the Quilt. New York 1990 [Quilts. Die Kunst der Amischen. Schaffhausen et al. 1990]. 207 pages with 82 color plates. (English Paperback Edition: New York 1993)

Masterpieces of the Esprit Collection.

Peck Amelia, American Quilts and Coverlets in the Metropolitan Museum of Art. New York 1990. 262 S. m. 231 Abb, davon 95 farb.

Peck, Amelia, American Quilts and Coverlets in the Metropolitan Museum of Art. New York 1990. 262 pages with 231 illustrations, 95 in color.

Pellman Rachel u. Kenneth, A Treasury of Amish Quilts. Intercourse/Pa. 1990. 128 S. m. farb. Abb.

Pellman, Rachel and Kenneth, A Treasury of Amish Quilts. Intercourse, Pa. 1990. 128 pages, color illustrations.

Holstein Jonathan, Abstract Design in American Quilts: A Biography of an Exhibition. Louisville/Ken. 1991. 230 S. m. farb. Abb.

Zu Entstehung und Wirkungsgeschichte der legendären Ausstellung des Whitney Museum of American Art, 1971.

Holstein Jonathan, Abstract Design in American Quilts: A Biography of an Exhibition. Louisville, Ken. 1991. 230 pages, color illustrations.

Deals with the legendary exhibition mounted at the Whitney Museum of American Art in 1971 and its impact.

Hufnagl Florian, [Kat. Ausst.] Abstraktion und Farbe. Die Kunst der Amischen. Quilts der Sammlung Ziegler. Die Neue Sammlung, Staatliches Museum für angewandte Kunst. München 1991. 59 S. m. farb. Abb.

Hufnagl, Florian, [Exhib. cat.] Abstraktion und Farbe. Die Kunst der Amischen. Quilts der Sammlung Ziegler. Die Neue Sammlung, Staatliches Museum für angewandte Kunst. Munich 1991. 59 pages, color illustrations.

Kraybill Donald B., Patricia T. Herr u. Jonathan Holstein, [Kat. Ausst.] A Quiet Spirit. Amish quilts from the collection of Cindy Tietze and Stuart Hodosh. UCLA Fowler Museum of Cultural History. Los Angeles 1996. 232 S. m. farb. u. s/w-Abb.

Kraybill, Donald B., Herr, Patricia T. and Holstein, Jonathan, [Exhib. cat.] A Quiet Spirit. Amish Quilts from the Collection of Cindy Tietze and Stuart Hodosh. UCLA Fowler Museum of Cultural History. Los Angeles 1996. 232 pages with illustrations in color and black and white.

Gottschling Marion, Der Patchworkquilt. Studien zur kunsthandwerklichen Textilgestaltung insbesondere bei den Amish People in Nordamerika. Diss. Berlin 1997. 330 S. m. Abb.

Gottschling, Marion, Der Patchworkquilt. Studien zur kunsthandwerklichen Textilgestaltung insbesondere bei den Amish People in Nordamerika. Dissertation Berlin 1997. 330 pages with illustrations.

Cunningham Joe u. Eve Wheatcroft Granick, [Kat. Ausst.] Amish Quilts 1880 to 1940 from the Collection of Faith and Stephen Brown. The University of Michigan Museum of Art, Ann Arbor; Smithsonian American Art Museum's Renwick Gallery, Washington D.C. Ann Arbor/Mich. 2000. 80 S. m. farb. Abb.

Cunningham, Joe and Granick, Eve Wheatcroft, [Exhib. cat.] Amish Quilts 1880 to 1940 from the Collection of Faith and Stephen Brown. The University of Michigan Museum of Art, Ann Arbor; Smithsonian American Art Museum's Renwick Gallery, Washington D.C. Ann Arbor, Mich. 2000. 80 pages, color illustrations.

Antique Ohio Amish Quilts. The Darwin D. Bearley Collection. Einführung: Jonathan Holstein. [Akron/Oh.] 2006. 160 S. m. zahlr. Farbtaf. [Deutsche, englische und französische Ausgaben]

Antique Ohio Amish Quilts. The Darwin D. Bearley Collection. Introduction: Jonathan Holstein. [Akron, Oh.] 2006. 160 pages, lavishly illustrated in color (editions in German, English and French).

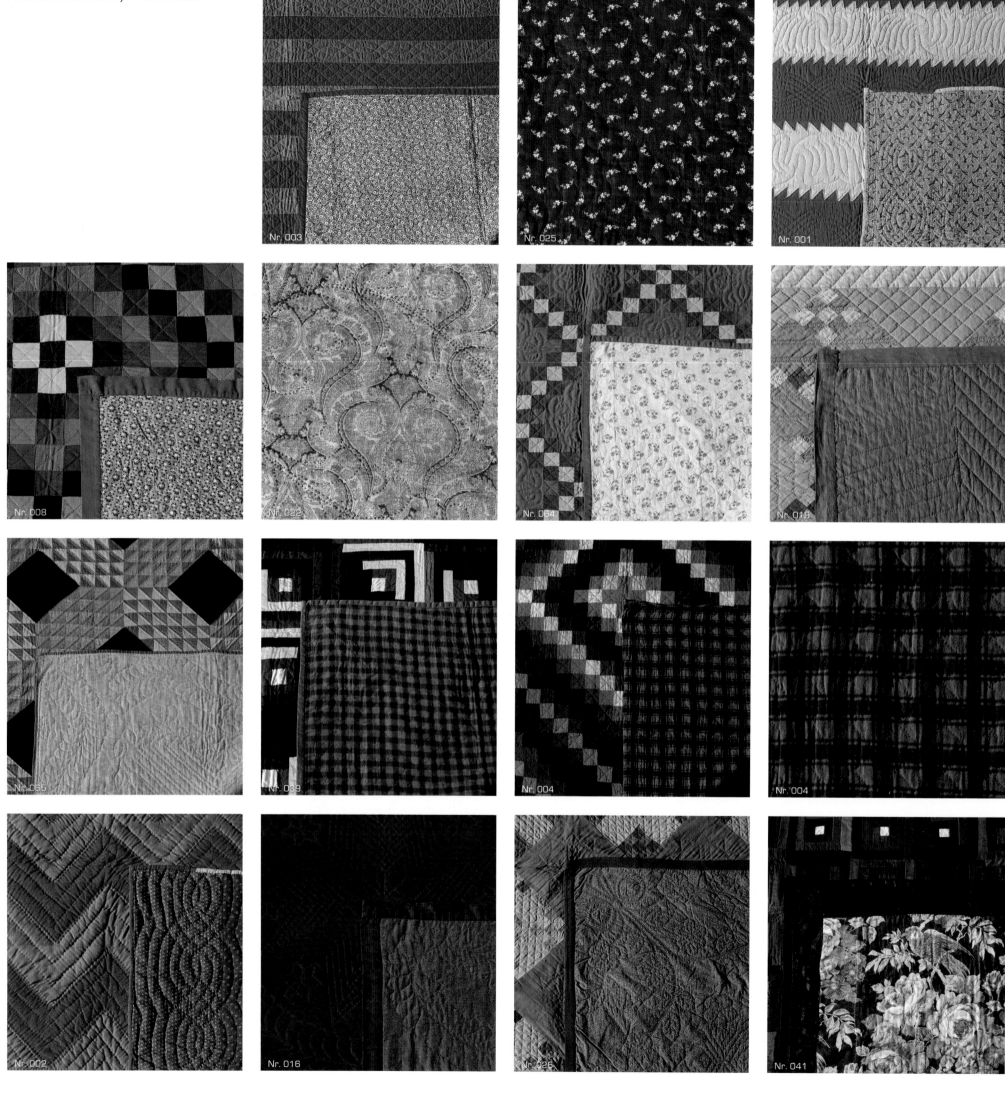

Nr. 003

Nr. 025

Nr. 001

Nr. 008

Nr. 022

Nr. 064

Nr. 019

Nr. 065

Nr. 039

Nr. 004

Nr. 004

Nr. 002

Nr. 016

Nr. 026

Nr. 041

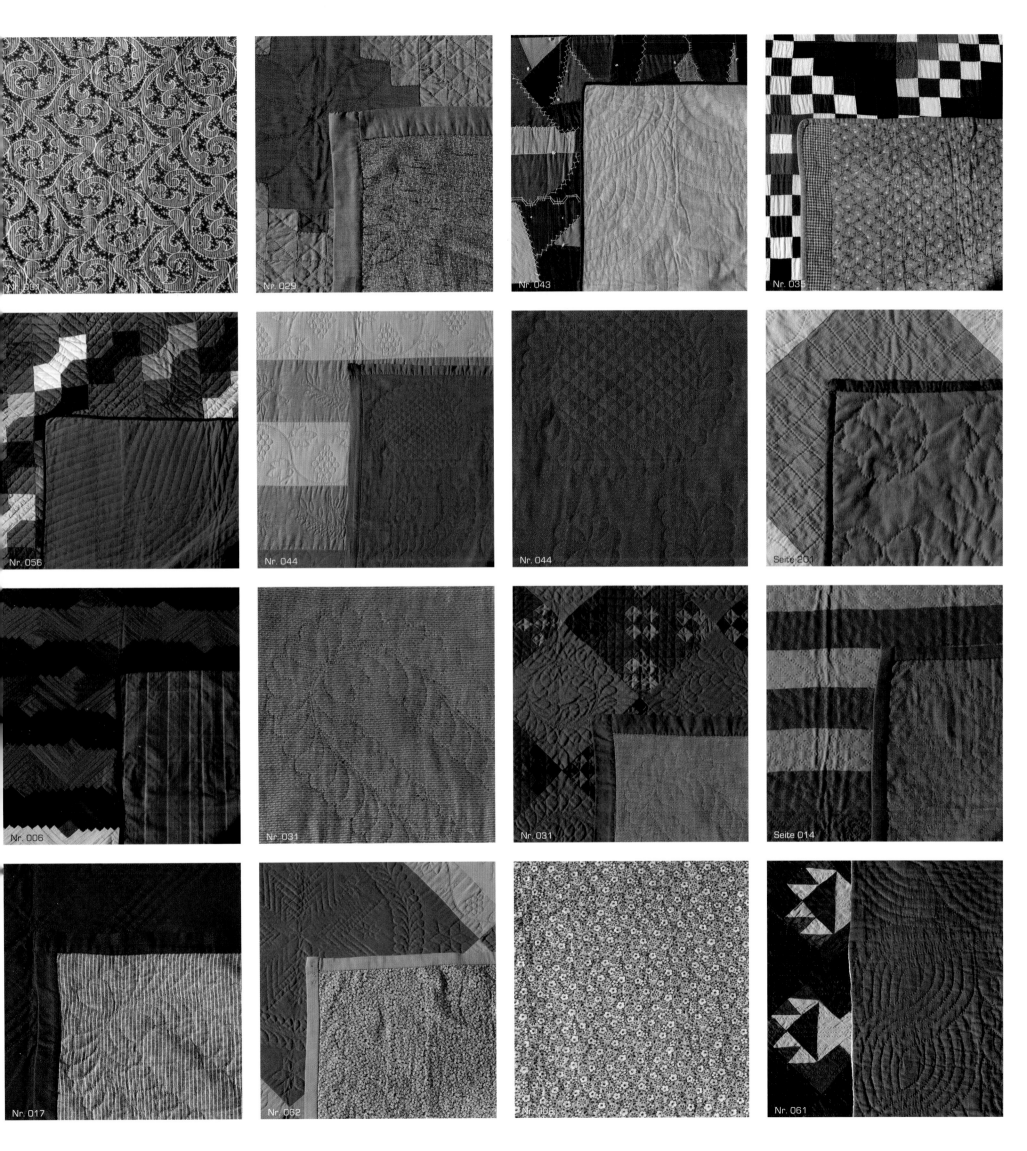

REGISTER / **INDEX**

Das Register schlüsselt Quilt-Typen und Muster auf und enthält darüber hinaus einige Sachbegriffe wie „Quilting" oder „Rückseiten". Die **fett** markierten Zahlen verweisen auf die Katalognummern der jeweiligen Quilts. In Klammern hinter den Katalognummern wird auf jene Seiten außerhalb des Katalogteils verwiesen, auf denen der jeweilige Quilt erwähnt oder in einer weiteren Abbildung dargestellt ist. Danach folgen allgemeine Verweise.

The following index lists quilts by type and design and, moreover, contains references to terminology such as 'quilting' and 'backing'. Numerals in **boldface** refer to the catalog numbers of the respective quilts. Pages outside the catalog section on which a quilt is mentioned or is represented in another illustration are referred to in parentheses following the catalog numbers. General references follow.

> = siehe / **see**
e = **english text**
d = **deutscher Text**

Appliqué quilt 193

Backing / Rückseiten 192 Abb./ill., 195, 197 Abb./ill., 202 Abb./ill., 210–211 Abb./ill.

Barn Raising 17
> Log Cabin

Bars 003 [192 Abb. Rückseite/ill. backing, 201d, 203e, 210 Abb. Rückseite/ill. backing, 211 Abb. Rückseite/ill. backing]; **001** [20e, 21d]; **014** [20e, 21d]; **012** [25e, 26d, 195, 201]; **021** [198]; **044** [195, 198, 201, 202 Abb. Rückseite/ill. backing, 211 Abb. Rückseite/ill. backing]; **066**; 2 Abb./ill., 14 Abb./ill. [211 Abb. Rückseite/ill. backing], 22e, 24d, 25e, 26d, 195, 196, 199, 201
> Chinese Coins, Sawtooth Bars, Split Bars, Stairway to Heaven, Wild Goose Chase in Bars, Zig Zag Bars

Baskets 061 [196, 204, 211 Abb. Rückseite/ill. backing]; **071** [196, 204]

Bear Paw 070 [192 Abb. Rückseite/ill. backing, 196d, 198e, 204, 208 Abb. Monogramm/ill. monogram, 210 Abb. Rückseite/ill. backing]

Birds in Flight / Flying Birds 074 [196, 198, 204]

Bow Ties 056 [20e, 21d, 196d, 198e, 202 Abb. Rückseite/ill. backing, 204, 211 Abb. Rückseite/ill. backing], 212 Abb./ill.]

Broken Dishes 050 [196, 204]

Center Diamond 7, Nr./no. 022, 201d, 203e
> Diamond in the Square

Center medallion style 201

Center Square 17, 25e, 26d, Nr./no. 022, 199, 201, 203

Chinese Coins 066 [18, 196, 203]

Columbia Stars > Tumbling Blocks

Courthouse Steps 17
> Log Cabin

Crazy Quilt 043 [196d, 198e, 211 Abb. Rückseite/ill. backing]

Crown of Thorns 068 [196, 204]; 17

Diamond in the Square 007; **011** [201d, 203e]; **016** [6, 210 Abb. Rückseite/ill. backing]; **017** [198, 211 Abb. Rückseite/ill. backing]; **025** [6, 25e, 26d, 197+210 Abb. Rückseite/ill. backing]; **028** [198, 208 Abb. Monogramm/ill. monogram]; **032** [20e, 21d, 208 Abb. Monogramm/ill. monogram]; **033** [20e, 21d, 198]; **045** [198]; **059**; **062** [208 Abb. Monogramm/ill. monogram, 211 Abb. Rückseite/ill. backing]; 11 Abb./ill., 17, 22e, 24d, 25e, 195, 196, 199, 200, 201d, 201 Abb./ill. [211 Abb. Rückseite/ill. backing], 203e
> Center Diamond, Floating Diamond, Nine Patch Diamond, Sunshine Diamond

Double Inside Border 201

Double Irish Chain 064 [204, 210 Abb. Rückseite/ill. backing]

Double Nine Patch 005 [18, 98, 203, 208 Abb. Monogramm/ill. monogram]; **019** [204, 210 Abb. Rückseite/ill. backing]; **026** [203, 210 Abb. Rückseite/ill. backing]; **031** [203, 211 Abb. Rückseite/ill. backing]

Double Wedding Rings 072 [18, 196d, 198e]

Fans 036 [196, 204]; **038** [20e, 21d, 196d, 198e, 198, 204]

Fence Row 074

Floating Diamond 009 [25e, 26d, 201d, 203e]

Flying Birds > Birds in Flight

Four Patch 203

Garden Path / Old Maid's Puzzle 057 [196d, 198e, 198]

Grandmother's Dream > Sunshine and Shadow

Hands 061

Inside Border Quilt 201
> Open Window

Irish Chain – Nine Patch Blockwork 030 [204]; 204
> Double Irish Chain, Triple Irish Chain

Jacob's Ladder 055 [198, 208 Abb. Monogramm/ill. monogram]

Log Cabin – Barn Raising 039 [20e, 21d, 192 Abb. Rückseite/ill. backing, 195, 197 Abb. Rückseite/ill. backing, 199, 205, 210 Abb. Rückseite/ill. backing]; **041** [195, 199, 205]; 195, 199, 204

Log Cabin – Courthouse Steps 040 [23 Abb./ill., 199, 205]

Log Cabin – Straight Furrow 006 [199, 202f Abb. Rückseite/ill. backing, 205, 211 Abb. Rückseite/ill. backing]; 15 Abb./ill.

Lone Star 034 [16 Abb./ill., 20e, 21d, 200, 203, 208 Abb. Monogramm/ill. monogram]

Love Rings > Garden Path

Monograms / Monogramme 208 Abb./ill.

Nine Patch 015 [203]; **018** [203d, 204e]; **020** [6, 203d, 204e]; **023** [203]; 196, 204
> Double Nine Patch

Nine Patch Blockwork > Irish Chain

Nine Patch Diamond 200 Abb./ill.

Ocean Waves 065 [20e, 21d, 65, 204, 190f Abb./ill., 210 Abb. Rückseite/ill. backing]

Ohio Stars / Variable Stars 042 [20e, 21d, 195, 196, 204]; **054** [196, 204, 208 Abb. Monogramm/ill. monogram]

Old Maid's Puzzle > Garden Path

One Patch 12, 13, 199, 203, 204

One Patch Variation 047 [18, 203]

Open Window / Inside Border Quilt 069 [201, 208 Abb. Monogramm/ill. monogram]; **073** [201]; 199, 201

Pieced quilt Nr./no. 069, Nr./no. 073, 193, 194e, 195d

Plain quilt Nr./no. 069, 193, 200e, 201d, 201e

Quilting 20e, 21d, Nr./no. 019, 199, 200, 201

Rail Fence / Streak of Lightning 037 [196, 204]

Roman Stripes 052

Rückseiten / Backing 192 Abb./ill., 195, 197 Abb./ill., 202 Abb./ill., 210–211 Abb./ill.

Sawtooth Bars 001 [203, 197 Abb. Rückseite/ill. backing, 210 Abb. Rückseite/ill. backing, 211 Abb. Rückseite/ill. backing]

Seven Sisters > Tumbling Blocks – Variation

Shoofly 058 [196, 198, 204]; 17, 215 Abb./ill.

Split Bars 203

Stairway to Heaven 048 [196, 203, 208 Abb. Monogramm/ill. monogram]; 17

Star 26

Star of Bethlehem > Lone Star

Stars > Columbia Stars, Ohio Stars / Variable Stars, Sunshine Diamond, Sunshine Star

Straight Furrow 15, 205
> Log Cabin

Streak of Lightning Nr./no. 002
> Rail Fence

Sunburst Octagon 12 Abb./ill.

Sunshine and Shadow 004 [203, 210 Abb. Rückseite/ill. backing]; **008** [197 Abb. Rückseite/ill. backing, 198, 203, 210 Abb. Rückseite/ill. backing]; **060** [203]; **063** [199, 203]; 7, 17, 25e, 196, 203

Sunshine and Shadow – Grandmother's Dream / Trip around the World 022 [25e, 26d, 195, 199, 203, 208 Abb. Monogramm/ill. monogram, 210 Abb. Rückseite/ill. backing]; **024** [203]; Nr./no. 013

Sunshine Diamond 013 [203, 211 Abb. Rückseite/ill. backing]

Sunshine Star 035 [203]

Trip around the World > Sunshine and Shadow – Grandmother's Dream

Triple Irish Chain 027 [204, 208 Abb. Monogramm/ill. monogram]; **029** [204, 211 Abb. Rückseite/ill. backing]

Tumbling Blocks 046 [6, 193e, 194d, 199, 200, 202 Abb. Rückseite/ill. backing]; **051** [18]; **067** [204]; 7, 196, 199, 204

Tumbling Blocks – Columbia Stars Variation 049 [199]

Tumbling Blocks – Variation of Seven Sisters 053 [198, 199]

Variable Stars > Ohio Stars

Wedding Rings > Double Wedding Rings

Whole cloth quilt 193

Wild Goose Chase in Bars 203

Zig Zag Bars 002 [203, 210 Abb. Rückseite/ill. backing]

IMPRESSUM / IMPRINT

© 2007 ARNOLDSCHE Art Publishers, Stuttgart; Die Neue Sammlung Staatliches Museum für angewandte Kunst – Design in der Pinakothek der Moderne, München / Munich, und die Autoren / and the Authors

HERAUSGEBER / **EDITOR**
Prof. Dr. Florian Hufnagl
Leitender Sammlungsdirektor
Die Neue Sammlung / Staatliches Museum für angewandte Kunst – Design in der Pinakothek der Moderne, München / Munich

AUTOREN / **AUTHORS**
Laura Fisher, Fisher Heritage, New York, NY
Dr. Corinna Rösner, Die Neue Sammlung, München / Munich
Prof. Peter Weibel, ZKM, Karlsruhe

WISSENSCHAFTLICHE BEARBEITUNG DER QUILTS /
SCHOLARLY EXAMINATION
Dr. Corinna Rösner, Die Neue Sammlung, München / Munich

ÜBERSETZUNG / **TRANSLATION**
Joan Clough (Deutsch/Englisch – German/English)
Uta Hasekamp (Englisch/Deutsch – English/German)

VERLAGS-REDAKTION / **EDITORIAL WORK**
Sarah Schwarz
Julia Vogt

GRAFIK / **DESIGN**
Nalbach Typografik, Silke Nalbach

OFFSET-REPRODUKTIONEN / **OFFSET REPRODUCTIONS**
die repro, Ludwigsburg

DRUCK / **PRINTING**
Raff GmbH, Riederich

Bibliographische Information Der Deutschen Bibliothek
Die Deutsche Bibliothek verzeichnet diese Publikation in der Deutschen Nationalbibliographie; detaillierte bibliographische Daten sind im Internet unter http://dnb.ddb.de abrufbar.
Bibliographical information: Die Deutsche Bibliothek
Die Deutsche Bibliothek lists this publication in the Deutsche Nationalbibliografie; detailed bibliographical data are available on the Internet at http://dnb.ddb.de.

ISBN 978-3-89790-262-6

Made in Germany, 2007

FRONTISPIZ / **FRONTISPIECE**
Bars, Puppenquilt / **Doll Quilt**, ca 1935
Amische Quiltmacherin / **Amish Quilt-Maker**, Holmes County, Ohio / 48 x 33 cm

ABBILDUNG SEITE 11 / **ILLUSTRATION PAGE 11**
Center Diamond/Diamond in the Square, ca 1930
Amische Quiltmacherin Barbara Fisher / **Amish Quilt-Maker Barbara Fisher**, Lancaster County, Pennsylvania / 218 x 214 cm

ABBILDUNG SEITE 212 / **ILLUSTRATION PAGE 212**
Bow Ties, ca 1935
Amische Quiltmacherin Lydia Beachy (Bluntschli) /
Amish Quilt-Maker Lydia Beachy (Bluntschli), Mifflin County, Pennsylvania / 200 x 195 cm

ABBILDUNG SEITE 215 / **ILLUSTRATION PAGE 215**
Shoofly, Crib Quilt, ca 1945
Amische Quiltmacherin aus der Familie Dettweiler / **Amish Quilt-Maker from the Dettweiler Family**, Geauga County, Ohio / 107 x 92 cm

BILDNACHWEIS / **PHOTO CREDITS**

Objekt-Fotografie / **Object Photography**: Rainer Viertlböck
Fotoassistenz / **Photographic assistant**: Leonie Felle

Die Objekt-Fotografien für dieses Buch wurden auf dem neuesten Stand der Technik erstellt. Eingesetzt wurde dafür ein 16shot digital back von Sinar mit einer Auflösung von 88 Millionen Pixel. Die fotografische Aufgabe bestand darin, sowohl die Farben der Quilts möglichst originalgetreu wiederzugeben als auch die plastische Struktur des Quiltings und die Stofflichkeit des Materials visuell spürbar werden zu lassen. Die digitale Nachbearbeitung der Bilder erfolgte daher immer im Vergleich mit den Originalen.
The quilt-photographs for this book represent state-of-the-art technology. A Sinar 16-shot digital back with a resolution of 88 million pixels was used. The task confronting the photographer was to reproduce the colors with as close to one hundred per cent accuracy as possible and to render visible the sculptural texture of the quilting as well as the physical properties of the materials. Digital processing of the photographs was always done in direct comparison with the originals.

Die Neue Sammlung dankt für die großzügige Unterstützung durch die Sinar AG, Schweiz. / **Die Neue Sammlung thanks the Sinar AG, Switzerland, for their generous support.**

Seite 19/20 / **Page 19/20**:
© Bill Coleman, www.amishphoto.com

Seite 17 / **Page 17**:
© copyright Photodisc Image, StockTrek.

Die vorliegende Publikation erscheint anläßlich der Ausstellung /
The present publication is published on the occasion of the exhibition
„Diamonds and Bars: Die Kunst der Amischen – Quilts der Sammlung Schlumberger"

Die Neue Sammlung
Staatliches Museum für angewandte Kunst – Design in der Pinakothek der Moderne, München
Die Neue Sammlung
State Museum of Applied Arts – Design in the Pinakothek der Moderne, Munich

ZKM / Zentrum für Kunst und Medientechnologie Karlsruhe – Museum für Neue Kunst
ZKM / Center for Art and Media Karlsruhe – Museum of Contemporary Art

ARNOLDSCHE art books are available internationally at selected bookstores and from the following distribution partners:
USA – ACC/USA, Easthampton, MA, info@antiquecc.com
CANADA – Hushion House Publishing Ltd., Toronto
UK – ACC/GB, Woodbridge, Suffolk, sales@antique-acc.com
FRANCE – Fischbacher International Distribution, Paris, libfisch@wanadoo.fr
BENELUX – Coen Sligting Bookimport, Amsterdam, sligting@xs4all.nl
SWITZERLAND – OLF S.A., Fribourg, Information@olf.ch
JAPAN – UPS United Publishers Services, Tokyo
THAILAND – Paragon Asia Co., Ltd, Bangkok, info@paragonasia.com
AUSTRALIA / NEW ZEALAND – Bookwise International, Wingfield, customer.service@bookwise.com.au

For general questions, please contact ARNOLDSCHE Art Publishers directly at art@arnoldsche.com, or visit our homepage at www.arnoldsche.com for further information.

Besuchen Sie uns im Internet / **please visit our homepages**
www.arnoldsche.com
www.die-neue-sammlung.de

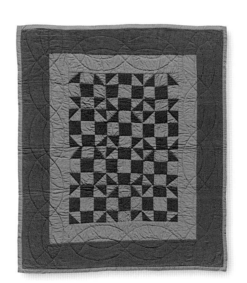